Before
You Do

Before
You Do

Making Great Decisions
That You Won't Regret

T.D. Jakes

SIMON &
SCHUSTER

London · New York · Sydney · Toronto

A CBS COMPANY

First published in Great Britain by Simon & Schuster UK Ltd, 2008
A CBS COMPANY

Originally published in the US in 2008 by Atria Books,
A division of Simon & Schuster, Inc.
1230 Avenue of the Americas
New York, NY 10020

3 5 7 9 10 8 6 4 2

Simon & Schuster UK Ltd
1st Floor
222 Gray's Inn Road
London
WC1X 8HB

www.simonandschuster.co.uk

Simon & Schuster Australia
Sydney

A CIP catalogue record for this book is available
from the British Library.

ISBN: 978-1-84737-380-9
Printed in the UK by CPI Mackays, Chatham ME5 8TD

I dedicate this book to my home church, The Potter's House of Dallas, to my partners in ministry—Bishop's Circle VIP, Bishop's Circle, Aaron's Army—and to all of those who understand that destiny will open its doors based on the integrity of your next few decisions. These are the words of wisdom that I believe will help you with those difficult choices before you do.

Contents

Before
You Do

Introduction:
Before You Decide

"Nothing is more difficult, and therefore more precious, than to be able to decide."

—*Napoleon Bonaparte*

A milestone moment stared me in the face. Like every father, I had anticipated this situation. I knew I would be uncertain of my heart's response, except I knew I would feel a tender pang when I remembered the long ago little girl in pigtails begging me to push her higher and higher on the playground swing. That little girl once ran to me for comforting hugs, a compliment on her newest selection of hairstyle, or an advance in her allowance to purchase the latest CD. Now that little girl had blossomed into a beautiful young woman and she was now standing before me, asking for the largest gift I could possibly bestow—her freedom.

I realized that our meeting for the big ask was a formality. To-day, at a certain age, young people inform you, more than they re-quest. In fact, by all intents and purposes my little girl and her groom-to-be were grown. But you and I know that it takes a life-time to really be grown. Consequently, I thought I would use this sober moment to impart some wisdom that I now share with you.

Faced with the prospect of a new life-season for both of us—her season would change from daughter to wife and my season would change from father to father-in-law, I stood before my daughter with a mixture of emotions that swirled in my heart like paints blended on an artist's palette. The reds and yellows of my joy blended with the blues and violets of the loss of her childhood. All of it was bordered by bridal white.

The room was warm and filled with the sounds of a busy res-taurant. I heard the lethargic sound of a sax played from the stage. It whimsically moved from note to note and provided the room a somber, yet titillating, atmosphere of sensual relaxation. I looked at the soon-to-be newlyweds; they were clearly nervous, especially the groom-to-be, as we began a conversation that I considered one of the most important that we would ever have together. As the waiter brought over a steaming bowl of clam chowder, I started my own piping hot conversation. Clearly, there were many more im-portant issues here than white rice or brown or such ceremonial ones as style of garter belts and flavor of cake icing. This was the greatest step they would ever make, in my opinion, and it was a de-cision that is too often romanticized. My focus was not on the wed-ding or the size of her train.

Grasping for a starting point, I muttered something to my daughter like, "You have grown up over night. It was only yesterday that you were in pigtails and looking for barrettes."

She laughed with some embarrassment as I shared a family

story about her pouting and taking all of her clothes off when her mother and I were in an all-night prayer service. She was three years old and had had enough. It was a hilarious moment that we often laughed about. We have laughed out loud remembering Sarah with the annoyed look on her face and a pile of clothes on the old church's wooden floor. Her thumb was in her mouth and a look of disdain for the full-blazed service that went on and on and on. I told her fiancé, "You have no idea what a pistol you have in my daughter," and we all smiled at the memory.

I was trying to break the ice to some new, unexplored conversation; we had not talked to this extent before.

Being a minister, I have seen far too many blissfully beautiful weddings that ended in horrendously heinous divorces. So my focus wasn't on the wedding plans, but on the far more difficult process of marriage that would follow it. I know that more times than not, Stella may get her groove back only to find out that she has been kicked in the groin by domestic violence or the emotionally painful consequences of not thinking through the next move carefully and holistically!

I did not want my daughter hurt. I wanted her to understand the long-term consequences of her relationship decisions. While the colorful kaleidoscope of emotions turned within me as I envisioned my baby girl all in white walking down the aisle, I welcomed the opportunity to address both of them regarding this pivotal, life-altering, sacred decision.

My wife and I had already reluctantly given our blessing on their engagement and impending nuptials, yet I knew that my real opportunity for penetrating their romantic buzz with the reality of married life now lay before me. Both my daughter and her groom were young: He was twenty-one and she was nineteen. Ideally, we would have liked them to have been older. I believe that marriage is for fully grown people. The groom, of course, was new to me, but I knew that my daughter had always been a precocious child. Now as she stood before me, a young lady, I wanted her to enter into this decision, as the vows say, not unadvisedly but reverently in the fear of God. And maybe with a little fear of *me*! Okay, I admit it, I was acting like a typical father of the bride, but what do you expect? This was my first child to marry, and I was as anxious as a cat in a room full of rocking chairs! I attempted to regain my composure as I continued.

"What do you see when you look at each other?" I asked, smiling innocently enough.

My daughter and her young man giggled and sputtered out something along the lines of "my true love" and "the one I want to spend the rest of my life with."

I nodded and then launched into my thoughts on the outrageous implications of marriage. "I hope you see not only the face of your sweetie pie but the face that you'll wake up next to for the rest of your life. The face that you will watch age alongside your own. This will be the face you run to when life seems cold and pains are unbearable. This is the face of your partner of choice. The one you chose like a warrior chooses a weapon or an artist her medium. He is, she is, your weapon of choice when you fight layoffs, mounting bills, pressure, and unimaginable challenge. It's the face that will be beside you if and when the labor pains race through your body and you birth children together. And it may be the face you look to when you have to bury one or the other of you prematurely.

"It's the face that you will watch convulse with the aches and pains of disease and injury. It's the face that will comfort you and the hand you will squeeze when your mother and I pass from this earth and are lowered into the ground.

"In my thirty-plus years of ministry I have seen couples face really difficult things, from parenting children with Down syndrome to rushing to the hospital to find that their teenagers had been crushed in a car accident. So my perspectives are not romanticized by the commercials and soap operas of today. Life is not always easy for people, you know."

My daughter's calamari had grown cold.

I couldn't help but notice it, but still, I continued. They looked ashen, facing perhaps for the first time the enormous ramifications of the decision before them and the certainty of unpredictable scenarios ahead. They now began to glimpse what many don't learn until they are much older. Both her mother and I knew that life could be brutal and challenging and riddled with unimaginable circumstances.

Blinding Love

Now that I had their attention, I continued on even more soberly, through an entrée and into a dessert. I was almost preaching by this time! "Marriage is taken so lightly that people feel like they're shopping for a new car. They find one they like but know that if it breaks down or they simply grow tired of it, they can trade it in for a newer, shinier model in a few years. Neither of you wants that. You probably cannot even imagine that situation. Yet you must be as deliberate as possible, as logical, objective, and thoughtful in your decision to commit, cohabitate, and commingle your DNA.

"The fresh euphoria of love leaves us intoxicated and blinds us to the realities that await us in any close relationship: bills to be paid, diapers to be changed, cars to be repaired, homes to be moved, jobs to be completed, and on and on, throughout all the seasons of life. This is what you're committing to.

"You're not committing to a lifetime of good chemistry or shared ideals or that tingling feeling inside."

I'll spare you the rest of my minisermon.

I did not wish to dissuade them, dampen their enthusiasm, or disguise the joys that married life can afford. I'm an overprotective father, yes, but my words were not only due to that. I earnestly believe that every relationship decision must be made with an appropriate level of care and deliberation in regard to the impact this choice will have on your life.

And no other choice leaves as many footprints alongside your own on life's journey as the decision to unite yourself with another person, a partner, a spouse. The ripples that detonate in your life's pond when the stone of marriage is dropped can become a rhythmic tide of joyful companionship or a tsunami of tortured tantrums. So much of the climate of the rest of your life comes down to this one decision.

I cannot count how many times I have stood before couples all dressed in white and asked them, "Do you take this woman to be your lawfully wedded wife, to live together after God's ordinance? Do you promise to love her, cherish her? . . . Do you take him for better or for worse, richer or poorer, in sickness and health?" After completing these essential vows, I usually then ask them, "Do you?"

And they say, "I do."

I have also often wanted to say to them, "Before you do, maybe you should know the facts."

REGRETS

Life is too short for regrets. That is why it is so important for you to know who you are, what is important to you, and how you want to exist and proceed in the world. This way, when things happen—and things will happen in life, good and bad: you lose your job, someone gets sick or dies, your child gets in trouble in school, or your best friend asks you to participate in something you don't agree with—you will easily be able to decide what to do in the moment and, later, have no regrets.

Regrets are meant to teach us what to do better next time. Considering what you could have done differently to prevent whatever situation you regret is a good way to keep from repeating the same mistakes again in the future. Learning to make decisions in the moment based on who you truly are, and taking actions based on love, kindness, and forgiveness, always with the highest spirit in mind, is the best way to avoid having regrets later.

Due Diligence

Decisions are like falling dominoes in a line, each one toppling one irreversible consequence against another. Our screenwriters and novelists love to examine the power of one single choice and its effects on those caught in its gravity. Whether it's Jimmy Stewart's character in *It's a Wonderful Life* or Denzel Washington's character in *Déjà Vu*, the power of one individual decision can never be underestimated. Fortunes have been gained and lost, marriages mended and torn, children born or buried, all because of one person's decision, which may have seemed of little importance at the time.

In the soon-to-be-released Screen Gems film based on my book, *Not Easily Broken*, the character Dave and his wife, Clarice, never understood on their wedding day that life has a way of knocking you down. But they soon learn that the wedding is easier than the life that comes after it! And believe it or not, weddings are less expensive than many of the mistakes couples make after it. If you see the movie, you'll be reminded that life brings real challenges, and people often give way to pressure and succumb to the pain, losing sight of the passion that first brought them together. They begin to realize that every decision affects them both along with the quality of their marriage. They often drift apart on the raft of bills into the bleak sea of anger and disappointment.

Of course, we cannot scrutinize, analyze, and fantasize about each and every decision we make, or we will become paralyzed by fear, afraid to get out of bed in the morning and choose between Corn Flakes and Cocoa Puffs. Worrying whether to wear the blue dress or the brown skirt are not important decisions. Those are not the kinds of decisions I am talking about.

The larger, more significant relationship decisions of life—who and when to date, court, and marry, shared lifestyle choices and friendships—demand that we bring everything we have to the table to ensure that we make the best choices and never look back. Most of us have learned, some the hard way, the importance of relationships. But do we move into these decisions in a way that will insure positive results?

This is what I want to explore with you in this book. Your future is as strong as the decisions that precede it.

I have good news for you: We can make relationship decisions with a confidence, faith, and fortitude that allows us the freedom to enjoy a contented, fulfilled life.

It's all in how we approach the decisions. My mother used to say that ignorance is expensive. She was absolutely right. It costs to be uninformed or even under-informed. Recently, I was given a rare and unique opportunity to purchase a highly respected marketing firm. It was and is a thriving business with an impressive list of highly financed companies. I was intrigued. It has an impeccable history, and I was elated to be given the option to proceed into what could have been a very lucrative deal for all concerned. But I seldom allow my elation to override my innate, God-given sensitivity and propensity to caution.

I felt that the terms were conceivable and the profit margins looked plausible. Still I spent much money and time engaging a professional firm to do the due diligence that I feel is a mandatory prerequisite before I do business on that level.

After researching stacks of documents, tax returns, financials, employee backgrounds, and contracts between the entity and its clients, I decided that, although it was a good deal, it was not a good fit for where I am in life right now. It wasn't consistent with the life plan I have in place for myself and my family. So, yes, I walked away from what might have been a great deal, because the timing wasn't right for me.

One of the board members, who I assume might have underestimated my proclivity to get the facts first, said, "You are not just a preacher; you are an astute businessman." I smiled but realized that more than that, I am a person who can't afford to make a bad choice and face a setback. At this season in life I have to make every move count. I do not have the life span at fifty to recover from a massive setback economically, emotionally, or spiritually that could result from a bad decision.

Even my own attorneys and accountants were surprised at the amount of money and time I invested in making this decision. Several said, "You did all of that and still walked away?" The money I spent investigating it might have seemed wasted to them, but not to me.

I know that like the issues I raised to my daughter, you cannot make great decisions if you do not take seriously the consequences of that decision and base your decision on thorough information!

CHANGING YOUR MIND AFTER YOU'VE
MADE A DECISION

One of the pitfalls of decision making is wanting to change your mind after you've made a decision. You've probably heard the term "buyer's remorse." That describes the feeling you have when you make a purchase, usually a large or expensive one like a car, a house, or an expensive luxury vacation, and then regret having spent the money. The excitement and over-the-moon feeling you had when you made the decision to spend the money is quickly replaced by a horrible, nagging feeling that you made a big mistake.

Changing your mind frequently once you've decided to do something could be a sign that you are not taking an adequate amount of time to consider all of your options or the ramifications of your decisions before you make them. Life is too short to live with regrets. If you find yourself second-guessing yourself regarding a decision you've made, remember that feeling of angst and uncertainty the next time you have a decision to make and think twice, weighing all of your options, before proceeding ahead.

Pull the Trigger

So often I hear people use the expression "just pull the trigger," meaning commit to a decision and take action. Let's think through this image for a moment. Some questions must be answered before any of us has any business pulling a trigger on any decision of consequence. *What gun are you using? How was the weapon assembled?* And perhaps, most important of all, *what is the target at which you are shooting?*

You may laugh at me for being so literal-minded here, but I think you understand where I'm going with this metaphor. The

act of pulling the trigger takes only a couple of seconds. But selecting the weapon, understanding how to operate it, and making sure
that it's aimed in precisely the right direction, are equally important as pulling the trigger, yet often overlooked. All of these preparations must be made before you pull the trigger or else you can
find yourself shooting a water pistol at a burning house. Or, in
other words, making choices when you are unprepared, un-
equipped, and uncomfortable.

Toward this goal of choosing and using the correct weapon for
making bull's-eye relationship decisions, I ask that you make an
important decision affecting your future right now. I challenge
you to share some of your precious time with me between the covers of this book in order to come away with a better, clearer, stronger idea of how to make life-changing, regret-free decisions about
whom you relate to.

You'll see that I believe relationship decisions come down to
five crucial components:

Research: gathering information and collecting data

Roadwork: removing obstacles and clearing the path

Rewards: listing choices and imagining their consequences

Revelation: narrowing your options and making your
selection

Rearview: looking back and adjusting as necessary to stay on
course

Romantic relationships and the selection of a spouse are the
core of the book; however, the skills and information I wish to

share are not exclusively for seeking companionship. What you learn about decision making can be applied to any area of your life. I will share some ways in which you can protect yourself from the highly expensive and emotionally devastating consequences of making impulsive decisions. And I can help you prevent losing time in procrastination, which is often caused by the fear of making the wrong decision. All major decisions require due diligence and dilatory deliberation, whether you're choosing a husband, selecting a major in college, acquiring property, deciding on a new career, buying a company, or determining where you will live.

My goal is to help you realize, like my then soon-to-be married daughter, that some decisions are so significant that you want to make them with as much certainty as possible. If you do, you'll move confidently into the future with no regrets trailing after you like tissue paper on your shoe. My promise is that if you read this book, you will be equipped, you will know all you need to know about making foolproof relational decisions.

You have probably wished that you could see into the future in order to make a decision now. I can't grant you the power of prophecy, but I can help you know all you need to know to move confidently into the future . . . before you do.

one
Before You Take the First Step—Reflect, Discern

"A journey of a thousand miles begins with the first step."

—*Chinese proverb*

I can trace every success or failure in my life back to something I did or didn't decide effectively. Whether in the course of developing relationships, doing business, selecting investments, or accepting invitations, I've found a direct correlation between my location on life's highway and my decisions to turn, exit, stop, or start. Extenuating circumstances beyond my control were always involved, yet more times than not, I was a victim or victor of my own making, achieving or failing because I did or did not put in place the necessary prerequisites to accomplish my desired goals. Now, to be sure, I am not a self-flagellating individual who uses this premise to blame and belittle myself for past decisions and their consequences. No, I am saying that my decisions set the course of my life.

I have now been married to the same woman, the mother of my children, for over twenty-five years. That relationship decision has set the climate of my life much like a thermostat on a heating system sets the temperature in a room. In keeping with this concept, persons in a room may not know that the temperature is affected by the smallest incremental movement of a drop of mercury in a device at an unnoticed location. In spite of its invisibility to the inhabitants of the room it still affects the comfort level of everyone present. Similarly, my key relationship decision, and many other decisions I have made, affect me and all those around me. Good results are a direct reflection of my ability to think through, discern correctly, and move succinctly from the trajectory of my last decision.

WE ALL HAVE OUR OWN UNIQUE DECISION-MAKING PROCESS

Sometimes we have to make a small decision such as choosing a new hair style or whether to paint the bedroom sky blue or periwinkle. Other times decisions are larger, such as whether or not to move to a new city for a better job, or to keep an old one. We each have our own style and ways to approach the decision-making process. Some of us tend to know exactly what we want. We make up our minds quickly and act immediately. Others prefer to deliberate for a long time, weighing all the angles and options before deciding what to do.

Reflect—Discern—Decide

Good decision making in relationships, business, anything, results from a process of reflection—discernment—decision. This truth recently emerged in a new light for me. I have had the same COO in my for-profit company for nearly ten years. It was interesting to me to note an observation he made about me. Often people who work with you notice things about you that you have not realized about yourself.

He advised some business constituents that it was unwise to approach me with a presentation that was long and laborious. He had noticed what I jokingly refer to as my ADD (Attention Deficit Disorder), that my attention wearied quickly during presentations like those that included the history of a company and who the founder married in 1802. I really would rather be spared the guillotine of losing my head in the details that are largely irrelevant to what I need to decide. In other words, cut to the chase, answer my questions, and leave me to my own thoughts.

He also shared with them that the hardest part of doing business with me was the millions of questions I ask in the name of doing due diligence. I smiled at my COO's remarks and thought they were an accurate depiction of my inward reality. Even my staff members on the not-for-profit side of my organization have learned to come to me expecting multiple questions and to be armed with the answers before setting the meeting.

I do not apologize for this proclivity; I believe that good leaders anticipate tough questions and have at their disposal the answers that predict issues, struggles, and maladies that are inherent in the normal processes of doing business.

Sound decisions are based on great information, so the more significant the question, the more due diligence I require. I believe important decisions demand stewardship. If we are to be good stewards of great opportunities, we must show respect for those opportunities by the level of diligence to which we prepare for the next move.

Relationship decisions are among the most opportune choices in your life, and I remind you that no others leave as many footprints alongside your own on life's journey as those you make to unite yourself with another person emotionally, sexually, spiritually.

Curb Appeal

Several years ago, my wife and I purchased a new home. We did so after selling our previous home and nearly doubling our initial expenditure for it. I searched ardently through the better neighborhoods in our city trying to find a home that would yield a similar return in the future should we decide to sell. I had found a good house in a great neighborhood and began to discuss with my friends and family the possibility of purchasing it. To my surprise, one of my friends advised me against getting the house. He said, "I know you so well that I can hear your uncertainty in how you explained the value of the proposed home. You seem as though you are trying to convince yourself that the deal is a good one. In other words, thou dost protest too loudly."

My friend seemed to know that I wasn't totally happy with the decision to buy that house. It was a great deal, the house would sell easily later, and would no doubt yield a return. The problem was that I didn't really *like* the house. I liked the deal—but not the house!

After this observation, I had to reflect. My goal of getting a house with curb appeal—that was marketable for resale—was not equally important as getting a house that I liked. Ultimately, I decided that my enjoyment of the house was a significant consideration that I had minimized.

Friends, many times we make poor decisions because we have decided what success looks like. Due diligence must include a heart check. Is the goal good looks or good character? Wealth or happiness? Safety or excitement? Is the goal a matter of marrying someone who looks good on paper or looks good in person? Is the goal to find a person who is economically sound or emotionally stable? Yes, you are right. It is possible to have both. But neither is possible if you don't decide that these are the goals. What does success look like to *you*, what comprises a successful relationship to *you*?

After looking at over twenty-eight homes all across the metroplex, I made a choice. By the time I was ready to choose, I had examined the return rate on my investment, the likelihood of foreclosure from my loan, a feasibility study that looked at fair market value (FMV), and comparable properties similar to my investment. The difference this time was that I also factored in the importance of *liking* what I was going to spend a good number of years paying for.

You may not be able to imagine buying a home without this vital consideration. In fact, some people make how they *feel* about their home, how much they *like* their home, their number one criterion for its purchase. They don't consider the kind of neighborhood it's in, its potential resale value, or where the market for homes in their metro area will be in five years. They only know that it has a great view, new appliances, and feels bright and cheery. Maybe you are less inclined to focus on the business of real estate and have little regard to the profitability of a house. Perhaps you gravitate by nature to the cosmetics of the house and your ability to enjoy it and decorate it. I realize that there are many buyers who are more interested in the feng shui of a house, the convenience of a functional kitchen, and the nearness to schools, and who never consider the resale value.

Both sets of factors—your head and your heart—must come into the equation in making this or any significant decision. You must consider both the hard data as well as the intangible internals.

So with both sets of data in mind, I finally bought a beautiful family estate on some extensive farm land! Farm land here is a good buy, and the house was all my rather large family would need as we grow into grandchildren and in-laws. My new property, with its extensive acreage, provides a home for bobcats, coyotes, and a few hungry Angus cows. Every morning when I wake up to the sound of squirrels playing in the tree outside my window and rabbits scurrying across the grounds, I know that the value of my home is not just the appraisal. It also includes the happiness for which there is no price tag. This reminds me of the MasterCard commercial in which the price of numerous items are listed followed by the value of the total experience, "priceless."

SMALL DECISIONS VS. LARGE, FINANCIAL DECISIONS

There is certainly a difference between making small daily decisions such as what to wear or what to order at dinner versus making a larger decision that will have greater consequences in your life. Large decisions, like making a major purchase such as buying a house, can have ramifications for your financial health for years to come. Moving to a new town or community could affect your relationships with your family and friends and could impact your kids, if you have them, for the rest of their lives.

You are also going to have to make decisions about relationships in your life. Considerations such as whether to enter into one, get out of one, or change the status of a relationship are decisions you'll have to make throughout your life. And those choices are not as easy as the prevalent Hollywood romantic movies today would lead you to believe. In the movies, things typically turn out happily ever after.

This is not to say that won't be the case for you. There is nothing more gratifying than a relationship with someone you love and trust, with whom you can share your innermost thoughts and feelings. Having a partner to rely on, to have your back through life's ups and downs, is one of God's greatest gifts. But choosing that person, whether it is in a friendship or a love relationship, is a decision. And because life isn't like it is in the movies, always romantic and easy with a happy ending, you have to make that decision carefully.

Deciding to enter into a committed relationship such as a marriage is a decision that shouldn't be taken lightly. "Til death do us part" is serious. When the tingly, euphoric feelings of new love wear off—and they eventually do—you have to know who you are and who your potential mate is. Knowing things such as what kind of person they are, their character, their life goals, their moral and spiritual beliefs, whether or not they are emotionally stable and available, any health issues they might have, are all important considerations that we don't often see discussed in the movies, that aren't considered very romantic, but that are in fact a very real part of life, and are issues that can wreak havoc on a relationship if not considered.

Spenders marry savers, risk-takers marry conservative investors, and it's often not until after the wedding that people discover their sweetheart is in thousands of dollars of debt. And in many states, once you marry someone, their debt is your debt! Yet, while couples spend countless hours talking about china patterns, whether they should seat Uncle Bob next to Aunt Winnie at the reception, and whose parents they'll spend the holidays with, money is something few couples talk about before they head down the aisle. Yet, the number one reason couples give for divorce? Financial disagreements.

The Cost of Priceless Decisions

Too often we overlook these priceless variables in our decision making. In Luke 14:28, we're told that no one desiring to build a tower will do so without first counting up the cost to see if they have enough to finish it. Counting the cost is very important; however, it is not enough to count the cost solely for the purpose of insuring that you have enough to finish. You must count more than economic costs. While most things that make money cost money, dreams and goals often involve more than monetary expenditures. Many line budget line-items do not add to the bottom line but are priceless considerations in the process of decision making. You will never enjoy the thrill of a priceless experience until the intangible items between the lines are counted in the cost.

If you want to make priceless decisions, be sure you have accounted for the intrinsic value of incalculable expense and return. I cannot tell you what it is worth to watch the squirrels play in my backyard. I know that they will not affect the appraised value of the property, but they definitely contribute to my satisfied smile as I drink my coffee in the morning and watch them dance.

My point is that whether you are a very practical pragmatist, like me, or an emotional idealist, if you do not weigh in on the sum total of what you want, you will never achieve your dreams. Dream deeply. Examine your head and discern what is in your heart. It will help the actual dream to be realized without the nightmare that comes from making a decision that is not well thought out and balanced.

Planned Parenthood

Another example further illustrates the significance of preparation and deliberation like no other: parenting. While we will explore this topic further in chapter 14, consider, for now, the multitude of decisions confronting you when faced with the prospect of parenthood. When you are expecting a child for the first time, you must prepare yourself, your household, and the lives of those around you to be forever changed by the new life you are about to birth into this world.

Foremost, expectant mothers must take responsibility for their own health in order to insure the health of the growing child inside them. They must make sure that they get proper nutrition, including vitamins, protein, and folic acid, all of which have proven vitally important to the proper development of the baby in utero. Mothers-to-be must get proper rest and exercise, refrain from smoking, drinking alcohol, and taking any other substances that would injure or impair the precious cargo within them.

Beyond the mother's health, numerous other considerations must be addressed. Has the household been babyproofed? Locks and safety guards must secure the potentially dangerous contents of drawers, cabinets, and closets. Hard surfaces and sharp edges must be removed from baby's path or padded enough to prevent hard knocks. Gates must contain baby's curiosity as she learns to crawl and toddle from room to room.

You must also consider the daily needs of your new little bundle of joy. Will you use formula or breast-feed or both? Do you have the necessary paraphernalia—changing table, diapers, diaper-rash ointment, bassinet, clothes, booties, blankets, and heaven forbid you forget the power of the pacifier!

Beyond the security and suitability of the environment, there are larger concerns about your child's well-being that must be addressed. How far is the pediatrician's office? The hospital? To what school will you send your child? Many private and now even some public schools have waiting lists that span several years before they have an opening. What about higher education? Have you established a college fund for your child or at least initiated some type of savings plan for his or her future?

Parenthood requires planning. God provides the very first and best example of the ultimate parent, preparing for new arrivals. Our Creator did not make Adam and Eve first and then build the world around them. No, the heavens and the earth, the sky and sea, the animals and plants, and all that we have in our world was created first. Then on the sixth day God created humans in the image of the divine. God had already prepared a place and insured that they would have provisions.

Similarly, in order to be responsible parents, we must prepare our world for the new creation God allows us to bring into this world through the miracle of birth. The demands of parenting are challenging enough. Without adequate planning, preparation, and deliberate changes in anticipation of your baby's arrival, you will be overwhelmed by the process, left to survive by default, providing poorly for your child and neglecting your own needs. Parenthood must be a planned endeavor if it is to produce a healthy and happy child.

Too often we see young ladies who view having children as a means to an end. Children are not bargaining chips played in Vegas to secure a man or his attention. Nor are they the faddish craze that I see in Hollywood where it is now chic and in vogue to have a child without a family to surround it with love. Friends, each life is precious and important, and the statistics show that children need to be reared in a stable environment with loving parents who want them, nurture them, and are ready for the lifelong task of parenting them.

I don't say this to make anyone feel bad who has had a child in less than ideal circumstances. I understand that we are human and anyone can make a mistake. And I know countless people who, against all odds, have made it work in spite of the stats that show it is a perilous choice. But why put yourself knowingly and willingly in an uphill race with a broken tennis shoe just to prove you are able to beat the odds? Especially when a little planning and patience would avoid compromising your life and the well-being of a child, conceived prematurely, left with less-than-ideal advantages, destined to spend his or her life trying to overcome obstacles that were out of his or her control? Life is hard enough when the stage is set and the players are in place!

Life is filled with challenges, but baby momma drama is far worse than you might imagine. It has been the source of many people's pain for years. We must begin to teach our daughters and our sons that actions cause reactions. The consequences of teenage pregnancies and unwed pregnancies at any age can be intense and detrimental to all involved.

When I was growing up, people who made mistakes found themselves in such compromised situations. But today, we see too many young girls listening to the titillating lyrics of songs suggesting that having a man's baby is like buying him a tie. Who would have thought that the time would come that a young girl would walk up to a guy and tell him, "I want to have your baby!" This is ridiculous!

Neither hip-hop nor R and B songs tell you the truth—that babies grow up, ask questions, shed tears, and many times start searching for the missing part of their identity. The family secrets are cumbersome and often lead to bouts of depression and a lifetime battle with low self-esteem.

I am glad to say that such mistakes are not terminal and regret doesn't signal the end of the world. Many people have, in spite of such adversities, become productive contributors to society and have made countless strides for the betterment of all.

However, more times than not, such difficulties require the whole family working to tip the scales and give the innocent child a better chance of success. I confess I have had this situation in my own family and will discuss that in more detail later.

But I earnestly warn you that the stats on prisons, suicides, and drug abuse show that the numbers go up when morals break down and the child comes from a single-parent home! For the sake of all the grandparents who are on fixed incomes and walkers and who are trying to keep up with grandbabies on Big Wheels. For the sake of grandmothers who are trying to find a ride to the school for a conference instead of tending to the garden in their backyards, let's stop the madness.

One wrong decision can sentence your whole family to a lifetime of homework and heartbreak. It could all be avoided by just waiting a little while longer to do things right! If you are not ready to lead another life for the next thirty years or so, slow down. Babies who have babies lose a lot of important experiences and often are faced with the too-much-too-fast syndromes that leave our communities on life support and our marriages on respirators!

WE ALL HAVE REGRETS

We all have regrets. It's a part of life's learning process. But as we get older and progress through life, hopefully, we learn to stop and recognize situations that feel familiar, where if we go on, we might regret our actions or something we've said. Then, when presented with a similar situation we choose to behave differently. You've heard the saying "The definition of lunacy is doing the same thing over and over and expecting a different outcome." The same holds true for regrets.

Each of us can think back over our life and point to a few regrets. Perhaps there was a phone call you should have made to apologize to a friend whose feelings you hurt. But by not doing so, the friendship ended and now you regret it. Or maybe you lied to your last partner about something you did, they found out, and left you saying they could never trust you again. You realize you hurt them badly and now you wish you had done things differently.

It is important to make peace with our regrets by taking ownership of what we did, apologize where necessary, and then work to put an end to repeating the same mistakes again. Dr. Maya Angelou said something very profound about looking back over our mistakes: "When you know better, you do better."

We All Have Needs

God included companionship in human creation. It is as vital a need as food and water. It is more than a want and is for many people such an absolute need that they often make rash and irrational decisions. They are more horrified with being alone than they are with being unhappy.

It is impossible to make good decisions when the decision is rooted in the fear of being alone or the fear of being rejected. Worse, still, is the embarrassment that many of us feel that stops us from admitting our need to have someone share our lives with us. Lately our society has lost its compassion for those who express that need. It seems far more fashionable to act as if we don't need anyone. But while this may get you a good amen at the water cooler in the office, in reality, it doesn't reflect real facts.

We were created with a need for socialization. There is absolutely nothing wrong with feeling that need. The problem begins when the need has you. Many people today are compulsive when it comes to attracting attention to themselves in order to fulfill their needs, often by someone who doesn't really fit who they are or where they are going. When you ignore warnings and compromise your principles, it leaves scars that may not ever fully disappear.

Society's latest craze of detachment and denial of any need for others is not a good goal. And you and I should avoid the tendency to demoralize people just because they want love and socialization in their lives. Many who do admit to being lonely or wanting to be loved are met with stern words and harsh rebuke and told to change their way of thinking. Loving someone is not weak. We must began accepting ourselves for having that need.

You may then go even further by acknowledging that you are someone who flourishes when you are in social environments. Others need a person to support them and, if they have that person, this is all they require. Many people would like a support group that affirms them and gives them a sense of belonging. Either way, it is not wrong to have the need. Most of us get a degree of gratification when we are contributing to someone else's well-being, and when that effort is appreciated, we feel warm and affirmed. It is not wrong to need either one. It is important to know thyself!

Hard Evidence

The first step in making life-changing decisions, even the most personal and emotional ones, without regret is research. Research fuels your decisions by yielding the information on which you can base a sound decision. This is similar to a court case in which the lawyer's job is to present the evidence on which the jury will reach a verdict and the judge will hand down a decision. The case is no stronger than the evidence that is gathered. The strategy for the trial is formulated on the evidence.

In choosing relationships, make yourself a hard jury, one that is not easily convinced and that requires concrete information before reaching a verdict. The decision rendered by your verdict may alter the quality of your life. It is better to lengthen the deliberation process and insure that the decision is appropriate than to reach a hasty conclusion that traumatizes all those involved.

To those of us who often procrastinate on the decision because we feel intimidated by lack of education or any area of weakness, I would relieve you with this statement: It is not how much you know that arms you with the tools of great decision making, but rather how much you *ask*. Ask questions. The most intellectual people I've ever met were people who asked questions of science, art, religion—questions that most others took for granted. You can never know more than you are willing to ask.

A friend of mine who is a college professor tells me that usually his brightest students ask the most questions. In fact, he tells his pupils on the first day of class that there are no stupid questions in his classroom. He works hard to create a safe environment for inquiry, due diligence, reflection, and problem solving. The smart ones ask question after question and end up challenging and educating the teacher. What we often characterize as the "terrible twos" when a toddler runs behind a mother asking, "Why, why, why?" is nothing more than the child's active mind accelerating at a remarkable rate, accumulating and categorizing the received data based on the questions that she dares to ask.

PASSIVE DECISIONS

Knowing who you are and what you want is vital to participating in a successful relationship. While it seems counterintuitive to focus on who you are versus on who the two of you are as a couple, the whole is only as strong as the parts. This is especially true for women. Women have made tremendous gains in our society. After all, it's not uncommon for a women to be a CEO, a race car driver, or even a presidential candidate. Yet our society, advertising, TV shows, and popular books and magazines still suggest that a woman who is accommodating and demure is far more acceptable and desirable than one who speaks her mind and asks for what she wants.

Truly successful and mutually beneficial relationships are based on each party being truthful and up front about their real wants, desires, and feelings. While certainly as a couple you must make decisions together, decisions about who you are as a person and what you want your life to be are yours alone to make. Allowing someone else—a relationship partner, a friend, a parent, or anyone else—to make decisions for you is a mistake. When you let someone else decide who you are and what you want, you give away the power that God gave to you.

And doing nothing is not making a decision. Sitting back and pretending not to see a situation for what it is or procrastinating about what to do until something happens where you have no choice but to go one way or another is just as bad as letting others make decisions for you. It's passive and in the end won't likely serve you very well. Sometimes circumstances are what they are, but you always have the choice to decide who you want to be within them.

We must never attempt to silence that toddler within each of us that continues to question our adult surroundings and selections. That inquisitive process often leads me to consider factors I had never before considered. With my real estate purchase, I had taken a crash course in real estate—asking questions about those twenty-odd houses. I came to understand the laws of zoning and planning in our city. I knew a little more about architectural design. Terms like "finish out" were now part of my vocabulary. "Fair market value" and "comparables" were now in my vocabulary because I kept asking, "Why?" before I made a decision to buy a home that would leave me with a note for the next twenty years.

If you are to make decisions that you will never regret, then you must be willing to think through all the criteria—professional and personal, scientific and subjective, data driven and self-satisfying. Much of the anxiety and later regret that come from the weight of your decisions can be alleviated or avoided altogether if you assemble all your information—that which is clearly consequential as well as that which may seem inconsequential—before you do.

two
Before You Blame—
Accept Responsibility

"Let us not seek to fix the blame for the past. Let us accept our own responsibility for the future."
—*John F. Kennedy*

One day when I asked my children, "Who left the pot roast out?" each of them pointed to the other, even as the smell of onions and carrots reeked from their own breath.

Each one said, "Not me!" and pointed to another sibling.

I can say as a loving parent that my children often play this blame game, and I must admit that maybe they learned this response watching something I did or didn't take responsibility for. What I do know for certain is that I live in a world of people who blame others.

Blame and making good relational decisions are related because so many predicaments are resolvable if someone would own the issue and at least take responsibility for its resolve, if not for its origin. As with so many problems in our lives, maybe we didn't cause it, but it has fallen our lot to fix it, rather than place blame.

WHAT WOULD YOU DO TO TAKE RESPONSIBILITY?

The way to make any kind of change in your life is to begin with a vision. Considering how you want to feel and how you want your life to look is key to making lasting changes. Once you have a vision you can set out to make a plan. Identify the first change you would make if you were to start taking responsibility for your life right now, today. When doing so, don't bring your old thoughts to the process. This is the new you making the list, the one who is not afraid of the future or ashamed of your past. Consider what's kept you from making these changes so far and consider things you can do to deal with these challenges when they come up in the future, because they will.

There are many well-meaning self-help books out there that claim if you follow steps 1, 2, and 3 your life will change in an instant. While many of these books offer excellent advice for people looking to make changes in their lives, the truth is, it just isn't that easy. What these books neglect to tell you is that change is hard. You can't expect to go from doing something one way for years and then one day waking up and doing it differently, just like that.

You are going to have setbacks and challenges. Some days you are going to forget your new vow to take responsibility for your decisions and your life and you are going to fall back into habitual, destructive patterns and maybe even think that change is impossible. The key is, when you have a day like this, you have to get back up, dust yourself off, and start again. Life is a marathon not a sprint. Stay the course.

Every day renew your enthusiasm to take responsibility for your life by sitting down and reviewing your list, praying—ask God to give you the strength to be the best person you can be—and asking for forgiveness on the days you slip back. Soon you will begin to see your life unfold in ways you never imagined.

Decide to Accept Responsibility, *Not* Blame Yourself

When I counsel parents whose children have disappointed them, they often blame themselves. They say, "If only I had paid more attention or not allowed them to watch those movies or not to hang out with their friends or sent them to a better school or . . ." On and on the laundry list goes of things that these parents believe they should or shouldn't have done to avoid the current crisis.

My response to these parents is, "So then you were the *only* voice your child heard? You had total control over this person who is your child—over their environment, what they watched on TV, their peers, their involvement with movies and music and community? DNA plays no part? No one other than you left a mark on their minds and emotions? You and you alone have influenced them to be all they are? Wow!"

I ask them these rhetorical questions to move them away from being a God-player. They are not the substratum of every issue and action that occurs in their child's world. Rather, I want to lead them to a healthier understanding, which is that they are a participatory part of the process but not the only contributing factor in the current dilemma.

It's tempting to think that these self-blaming people are better parents than the ones who are negligent, absent, and unwilling to take any responsibility for their children. I have counseled many of the latter as well. But both extremes—those parents who self-blame as well as those who take no responsibility—are focusing only on themselves, not the children. Good relationship decisions can come from either end of the spectrum.

And it's not only parents who respond in these extremes. Most people gravitate toward one polarity or the other when faced with the hard decisions of life. On one hand, we have the person who assumes responsibility for world peace, global warming, and the extinction of the blue-bellied whale. The other extreme are those who assume no responsibility for anything, perpetually victimized Pollyannas, always pointing their finger at someone else. Their usual excuses are: "It's my parents' fault." "The devil made me do it." "It's the whites' fault." "It's because of the blacks." These people shovel off responsibility rather than raking in the tough reality that we *do* play some part in the state that we now find ourselves in.

It's true that no one got here by themselves. It's also true that you must cooperate with your own dreams and objectives. You can decide to blame others, outside factors, unfair conditions, circumstances, any number of valid reasons for your relationship issues. You can even blame yourself. But the truth is you can decide to do something. And before you do, you must let go of all the blame.

BLAMING OTHERS

Blaming others for what's not going right in our lives is often more common than looking in the mirror and taking responsibility for what we have done to contribute or not contribute to our circumstances. If you ever watch the *Dr. Phil* show on TV you know that he is always telling his guests that they create their own experience. If things are not going right for you and you find yourself pointing the finger at others, turn that finger back at yourself, because that's where you need to begin to make changes in your life. You and only you have the power to take charge of your circumstances and create the life you want. It may be true that your boss is a racist or a sexist, your husband or wife might be a liar and a cheater, your mother may have been a drug addict or an alcoholic, but, in light of those circumstances, you have to decide to assume your right to live the life that God intended for you.

Hereditary Disease

It's easy to succumb to the blame that we see the first parents embrace in Genesis. As God questions Adam and Eve about why they disobeyed him, they make a choice that continues to echo in our lives today. "The man said, 'The woman you put here with me—she gave me some fruit from the tree, and I ate it.' Then the LORD God said to the woman, 'What is this you have done?' The woman said, 'The serpent deceived me, and I ate' " (Genesis 3:12–13, NIV).

Faced with the foul odor of a poor decision, Adam tries to deodorize the obnoxious smell of sin by blaming his wife, who then blames the serpent. The first family would later see their son Cain kill Abel because he blamed his brother for his poor success at sacrificial offerings. He learned this from his blaming parents, whose greatest sin was their inability to accept responsibility for their own actions. The sins of the father (and Mommie Dearest) pass on to the son. They quickly develop a family pathology of blaming that is the inheritance of all people after them. It is amazing how we continue to turn the blame game into an insidious hereditary disorder. Blame is generational and destructive.

How then do we learn how to break this perpetual destructive habit that is, for the most part, a learned behavior?

I have never seen a family that didn't have enough blame to go around. Under close scrutiny, most times, you find that all of the family has contributed in some way to the destructive behavior. To be sure, there are victims in family crises, but many times when investigated properly, you discover that perpetrators were enabled by someone else's silence or cooperation.

So who is to blame—the one who set the fire or the one who saw them set it and said nothing? And what of the person who never checked the smoke detector or the pedestrian who walked by and smelled smoke, but was too busy chatting to investigate it before the flames erupted. Like fire, blame spreads far and reaches wide.

Make the choice to move beyond diving in the Dumpster of past mistakes. Develop a strategy that focuses on where you are going, what you would like to see happen, rather than having your face attached to the rearview mirror, always looking back at what was done and who did it. We want to bring about healing by admitting that we have *all* contributed in some way to where the family is now. Some of us are guilty because of what we said or did; and others contributed by silently standing by and enabling the destructive behavior to occur.

The positive changes come when we move into the future and begin to get the family to discuss what success looks like. Let's devise ways to begin to focus on what a functional family situation would look like for the family. Instead of spending our energy on dividing the blame, let's assign each family person some task that focuses on where we want to see the family go.

When you move toward goals, rather than spending too much energy affixed to the sour pathology of the past relationship or former family interactions, you empower all involved. Let's get the power back. How do you do that? You do it by developing a strategy that is based on destiny and not history.

1. Declare a time-out on blaming each other.
2. Define what success would look like. Specify what you desire to see happen in the relationship, family.
3. Delegate who will do what to make that happen and give rewards of some sort when anyone involved furthers the relationship toward a brighter future.
4. Deliverable goals are those goals that are attainable. Relationships in trouble desperately need to have good news. Develop some attainable goals that give everyone something to celebrate. It doesn't have to be the ultimate goals that win the war, but small successes that indicate you are winning some battles.

What I love about this plan is that it gives the power back to the individuals who want to see progress. It distracts you from blame and gives you some guidelines for what is productive. It takes the power away from the past, where none of us have the ability to go to undo what was done, no matter who was to blame. It is constructive effort as opposed to destructive effort.

TAKING RESPONSIBILITY FOR WHAT ISN'T YOURS

Taking responsibility for yourself, your actions, and your thoughts is a very important part of being a contributing member of a relationship. But sometimes we can take responsibility too far—taking unhealthy responsibility for others. And often, we use that alleged responsibility for others as an excuse to not take responsibility for ourselves and our own circumstances.

We all know a martyr—a friend, family member, or maybe even us. The martyr is the one who is always quick to say, "Oh poor me . . ."

And fill in the blank. "If only I hadn't gotten pregnant so young I could have finished college." Translation: If I wasn't responsible for you kids I could have had a different life. "If only my mother hadn't been sick, I would have had the career I wanted." In other words: Because I was responsible for my mother there was no way I could go to school to train for the job I wanted. "If only I hadn't stayed married to your father, I would have been happier, but because my parents were divorced and it was so hard for me, I wanted you kids to have a mother and a father." That means: I allowed myself to be unhappy and I am blaming you rather than the person really responsible, me.

While the circumstances these kinds of people love to replay as the reason they are unhappy in life may in fact be true, martyrs focus so much on other people and take responsibility for other people's lives that they never take the time to look for solutions to rise above their own situation.

This passive approach keeps them stuck in their circumstances, and—repeating the story over and over to anyone who will listen, often for year upon year—keeps them attached to their fictional drama. Eventually their life becomes the story, and the woe and hard times become their identity.

This approach to life can have a terribly detrimental effect on the family members who have to endure hearing the story again and again. They learn that life is hard, which is true, but they also learn that they have no control over their circumstances and that the needs of others should come before their own. Often, these tales of sorrow are simply excuses, made-up versions of the truth to hide the fact that martyrs have decided to blame everyone else for their circumstances so that they don't have to take responsibility for their own lives.

We all make choices in life to stay or go, to confront or ignore, to complain or look for a solution. Taking on responsibility for the problems of others as your own. Whether it is your spouse, your kids, or your best friend, it is never a good idea to take responsibility if you are doing it to avoid deciding what you need to do for yourself.

Even in the case of children, your job as a parent is not to provide every single thing your children need. It is to teach them, by example, how to take responsibility for their own circumstances, so they can be active, contributing members of society.

The Blame Commandment

Here's a commandment at the foundation of making regret-free decisions: *We are the people we have been waiting for and no one else is coming.* If we're willing to own the responsibility for our lives, we discover that no matter what others do or don't do to us or for us, we're still accountable to ourselves. We decide how we respond. We decide to continue to move toward our dreams.

Prince Charming isn't waiting for you around the corner. Neither is Miss America. (Unless she and Prince Charming are together and, if so, then they're not looking for anyone else!) Your ship isn't coming in. The tide isn't about to turn. The odds are against winning the lottery in this lifetime. The Publishers Clearinghouse Sweepstakes spokesman is not knocking on your door.

I know this is hard to hear, but it still deserves to be said. In fact, let me say it in a different way: *Blame unto others only as you would first blame yourself.*

The most tragic by-product of alleviating yourself of responsibility is the subtle idolatry of allowing someone else to be the warden that imprisons your future and incarcerates your dreams. It is far healthier to train our children to believe that we have the power to right the wrongs, correct the mistakes, and move forward in spite of the maladies and mishaps of the past. It is empowering to teach those around us that they can overcome insurmountable odds. But it must be far more than a motivational speech. True motivation is evidenced by example. If one person overcame the obstacle you face, their victory is proof positive that you can do it also.

We who have been victimized by someone else's decision can sit like lepers and die at the gate of blame and complaint or we can emerge with a strategy that enables us to say, "I am too valuable to die, too tenacious to wait on anyone's mercy, and too creative to accept your neglect as my destiny." Blaming yourself is not positive, but refusing to blame others and deciding to take responsibility for yourself, for your situation, empowers you. It places the thermostat within your reach and control. Instead of freezing to death or sweating in discomfort, you can set the temperature for your life.

The systems of this world have not been fair, and God knows that's true. Systemic injustice and incompetence have led our nation down the rocky terrain of misguided mayhem. We cannot rest until we demand justice from a system that promises more justice than it delivers or administers. We have shot the deer and destroyed the antelope; the purple mountain's majesty is now obscured by smog. While it is undeniable that we are still a long way off from being the land of the free and the home of the brave, we must own where we are at present.

Personal responsibility has a role at least to walk beside if not in front of social justice. Each of us has a choice to make. We can stand with angry fists raised and perpetually and pathologically blame a system of dysfunction for a legacy of abnormalities and misappropriation of justice, or we can assume responsibility for expediting a cure to a crisis that we did not create but refuse to remain a victim of.

How can we demonstrate our lack of prejudice by excluding

our African-American neighbors from membership in the local country club? How can we demand affirmative action without requiring little Johnny to go to school? How can we require the hiring of all ages if the aged aren't going to continue to be productive? How can we suggest that stereotypical ideas about lateness are racist if we habitually show up late for work? Can you wear an inappropriately low-cut blouse to work and still be shocked when your boss comments on your appearance?

Think about who or what *you* usually blame when something goes wrong—your parents, your spouse, your boss, your kids, God. Take a few moments and make a list of the usual recipients of your own hereditary tendencies to shift the responsibility for your destiny to someone other than yourself. Affirm that no one is to blame. Decide that you can make responsible decisions to change what is in your power to change.

I understand that some have blamed themselves into a state of depression. Blame can be a heavy cross to bear if it does not have a strategy that serves as a Paraclete to lift it to responsibility and even beyond to a relentless reactive strategic plan. It certainly isn't healthy to take the blame for things you didn't do, but it is quite healthy to assume the responsibility for the things that you can change.

Recently I witnessed a stunning example of someone facing enormous loss who chose to step into it and take responsibility for moving on with his life. In the wake of natural disasters such as hurricanes, tornados, floods, and fires, so many people lose all they have. And our government does not respond as well as we, or some of our leaders, would like it to respond.

The combination of a lethargic federal, state, and municipal government combined with an infectious poverty for which our nation seems to have turned a blind eye, created a perfect storm that left the victims of Hurricane Katrina in a precarious state, for which some still wait resolution. Five months after the storm leveled the Gulf Coast area, more than thirty-two hundred residents were still unaccounted for by local, state, and federal agencies.

In the midst of this atrocity that has disgraced our nation globally, I found the silver lining while rummaging through the Ninth Ward in an attempt to help restore New Orleans to new glory. There I met an eighty-year-old man carrying two-by-fours in his feeble hands. As we became acquainted, he shared that he was collecting salvaged wood to rebuild his house nearby. He told me that this was the second time a major storm had destroyed most of his home, but that he never considered living elsewhere or waiting on someone else to rebuild it for him. "My parents left me this house, and it's where I raised my children. My wife died in this house. It's my home. I'm going to rebuild it and pass it on to my children."

Unlike many others who had relocated afterward, or others still in trailers waiting indefinitely on government assistance, this gentleman decided to take responsibility for his future. He gathered the resources he had, old lumber and used wood, to rebuild slowly but surely, the home he had once known. He didn't place blame. He recognized that he was the person he was waiting for.

I learned a great lesson listening to him speak and watching him rebuild his life. I learned not to empower others nor flatter them with the admission that their sins of commission or omission had left me so traumatized that they and they alone could end my suffering. I learned to tenaciously gather the sticks within my reach and to rebuild my own life no matter how battered I might feel by the storms of loss.

It was so amazing standing in the cold and rain, talking to this man while he went about the business of rebuilding his home. I realized that he could still be sleeping under the bridge waiting on a check for too little that would arrive too late. Or he could make the choice he made, to arise from the ashes of this debilitating circumstance and move on with his life. He knew that if he did not, he could only blame himself.

Please do not hear me saying that we should not ask for help when we need it or that those who wait for assistance are passive weaklings. No, what I am saying is that you have the power to lift yourself beyond any dismal realities that you may face.

BLAMING PARENTS

Parents in our society often get a bad rap. Whenever the kids get in trouble, the first people everyone blames are the parents. Events like the Columbine or Virginia Tech school shootings happen, and the first thing asked is, "Where were the parents?" It's true, parents make mistakes. And it may very well be that the parents of children who decided to take up arms and gun down innocent classmates and teachers made huge mistakes in raising their children. The truth is all parents make mistakes, but their children don't become murderers.

We blame parents much too much for failings that are our own individual responsibility.

There is no handbook to being a parent, no test you have to take. Although sometimes it seems like there should be. All it takes to be a mother or a father is a man and a woman—or sometimes today a test tube—and . . . well, you know how it works.

Parents, like everyone, are, much as their children are, figuring out who they are as they go along. When we have the urge to blame our parents for everything that's wrong in our lives, it might be a better idea to stop and consider that they love us, want the best for us, and did the best they could. While I know that every parent wasn't like Bill and Clair on *The Cosby Show*—no parents were like that—most parents want their children to have a better life than they had. When we can look back and consider our parents' circumstances, and perhaps some of the challenges they had to face while raising us, we'll be able to see them and the mistakes they made toward us with a little more compassion. They are human beings just as we are and make mistakes just as we do. None of us is perfect.

If you have a tendency to blame your parents for what is wrong in your life, considering them in this light is the way to release yourself from a painful and disappointing past and allow space to focus on the future.

Having compassion for our parents' journey means it's more likely we'll have a little more compassion for ourselves and the mistakes we will inevitably make in our own lives and those of our children. When you focus less on blame and more on compassion, you can see the gift that exists in good and bad circumstances.

Focusing only on what was wrong in your childhood will only leave you frustrated and stuck in the past. You often hear people say, "I don't want to be like my mother or my father." But then you see them doing exactly that! When you stay focused on the past, on blame and what was wrong, you continue to repeat many of the same mistakes.

Look forward in your life. Acknowledge what didn't work in the past that you'd like to do differently. Forgive your parents and know they did the best they knew how. Then look to your future with the understanding that you can accept all of who you are, good and bad, and move ahead.

Decide to Change, Not Blame

You cannot change the past by blaming yourself, your ancestors, or anyone else. But you can change the future if you decide to use today to affect tomorrow. Construct a way of escape that enables you to move beyond the perpetuation of pathological habits that result from pointing the finger at others.

It is important to know that we were created to be leaders, innately and instinctively. Humans are leaders, exceeding any other living being. Birds still use their original mode of transportation, animals still walk on all fours, snakes still crawl, only man consistently improves the world, moving from the horse and buggy to the three-hundred-horsepower engine. We are the only species that continues to work on ourselves. We fly because we decided we were too busy to walk. We have telephones because we decided we were tired of screaming across the street. We have iPods because we decided that CDs were too fragile, cassettes too destructible, eight-tracks too cumbersome. We keep changing our world because we decide we can make it better. You have the power to evolve, transform, develop, relocate, rebuild, reinvent, or do whatever else is necessary to achieve your goals. But nothing will happen or change in your situation until you decide you want it to.

It is my intent as we travel on this journey to share ways in which you can transport yourself beyond the dismal into the blissful by making the choices and the decisions you will never regret. Decisions that are appropriate for what you want to be and where you want to go. Just as you would gather wood to build a fire, I challenge you to begin the arduous process of collecting the information you need to make the decisions for the future you want. And if you do, you are one step closer to accomplishing what you want, to reaching a milestone in your life.

Now I have more to share with you, and you have many decisions to make, but before you do, first stop and ask yourself if you're willing to own the responsibility for where you are and where you're going, blaming no one, not even yourself. If you're willing to recognize the vast power you hold in the choices you make, then your life will truly never be the same.

But before you do, there's more you need to know.

EMOTIONS BEHIND TAKING RESPONSIBILITY

To take responsibility for the quality of your life and your decisions, especially if you're used to blaming others, won't necessarily be easy at first. You may experience a wide range of emotions.

You might experience anger, thinking that life is unfair and that this isn't what you wanted for yourself. You always envisioned a husband or a wife to be there to take care of you; you didn't ever expect to have to take responsibility for your life on your own.

You may feel fearful, afraid that you won't be able to do it, and that if you fail, you'll only have yourself to blame. Maybe you'll feel annoyed that you have to consider your life in a different light, from a different perspective. You may even feel sad over the way you've blamed others in the past, knowing deep down inside that your life wasn't proceeding the way you wanted because of your choices and decisions.

You might even feel ashamed of your past mistakes and unsure if you really can take responsibility and move forward.

Whatever emotion comes up for you, know that it is normal when making change—especially drastic ones such as trying to adjust a lifelong way of thinking—to experience a wide range of feelings, good and bad. However you feel, don't judge yourself. Acknowledge what you are feeling, ask yourself if your thoughts are rational or whether they are just fear talking, and then stay fast to your commitment to yourself to stop blaming others and take responsibility for your life.

three
Before You Leave Junk in Your Trunk—Clean Up Emotionally

"Success is to be measured not so much by the position one has reached in life as by the obstacles which he has overcome while trying to succeed."
—*Booker T. Washington*

A recent speaking engagement took me back East and converged with the opportunity to visit with an old friend. He's someone I've known since my boyhood in West Virginia, the kind of friend who feels like family. So when he offered to pick me up at the airport, I agreed and looked forward to catching up.

After exchanging greetings curbside, my friend grabbed my bags and rushed to deposit them in his trunk. This proved to be a more daunting task than either of us had anticipated. The trunk was full, and he began unpacking a myriad of lost-and-found items belonging to every member of his family, including the dog! Out came a set of old golf clubs, a wheel from his daughter's tricycle, a soccer ball, an emergency tool kit, an old moth-eaten blanket, two pairs of running shoes, Fido's chew toy, a leather briefcase with a broken handle, and a fourth-grade math book. All of it was enveloped in something—various bags, empty cups, and wrappers from the mall food court.

My friend stuttered and stammered, and then both of us burst out laughing until tears rolled from the corners of our eyes. Catching his breath, my friend said, "Look's like I've got some junk in my trunk!"

I truly had to struggle to suppress my laughter when he said that, because I wasn't laughing at the car or my now-squashed suitcase. I was laughing at what my children would have understood the phrase "junk in the trunk" to mean. Today the kids use this term as a compliment to a woman whose curvaceous body includes an ample, extremely attractive rear. They might use this term to describe a beauty like Beyoncé whose fabulous figure exemplifies junk in the trunk. I don't know how this term originated, and even though I am a minister, I would be lying if I said I didn't know what it means.

Looking at my friend who was bent over the messy trunk trying to arrange utter garbage and hearing him characterize it as junk in the trunk almost made me howl. His backside jiggling and his trunk lid rocking was enough to take me into total, unabridged hysteria. This definitely was not a Beyoncé moment! I knew for sure that his wasn't the kind of junk in the trunk that anyone appreciated.

As we drove away, my bags somehow wedged in the backseat,

I assured my friend that I knew his current life stage well and had been there and done that. Instead of telling him why my shoulders had been shaking like I had Parkinson's disease, I knew I needed to help my friend feel less self-conscious about his junk. So I reassured him that I knew what it was like to practically live in your car, rushing from home to work to the gym to church and playing chauffeur to your kids in the midst of it all. With so much rushing, commuting, snacking, drinking, and chauffeuring, our cars can sometimes become like miniature landfills, microcosms of our present season with all its demands, designations, and demarcations.

But my friend had so much junk in his trunk that when he wanted to *use* his trunk for storing something he wished to transport, there simply wasn't room. Can you relate to this? None of us deliberately sets out to use our cars as Dumpsters. We don't intentionally scatter clothes, the kids' toys, and Burger King wrappers in the trunks of our hard-earned SUVs or discard Hefty bags in the backseat of whatever is our current mode of transportation. The junk just accumulates as we live our lives until we realize that there's not enough room for the items we *do* wish to take with us.

The amazing thing about my friend's trunk was the contrast with the outside of his beautiful Volvo. It was washed and waxed in a way that anyone would have been proud to ride in it. However, the outside doesn't show you what is inside. It reminds me of what Jesus said about the Pharisees. He said that outside they were clean but inside they were full of dead men's bones (Matthew 23:27-29). You see, nothing about the outside of his car prepared me for the mess inside.

I know some *people* who look far better on the outside than on the inside. Alas, they have junk in the trunk, the kind that smells in a relationship and undermines what could have been, because they refuse to discard what used to be, they refuse to discard what was.

Decide to Clean House

When faced with significant opportunities, we often find our vision impaired by emotional and psychological baggage from the past that impedes our view. For some of us this means that we keep getting into relationships with the wrong kind of person. We keep getting caught in a cycle of attractions that trap us in a riptide of daily drama. Our past disappointment, dysfunction, and desperation have created a script where the actors or actresses may change, but the role they play stays the same. Perhaps this is why the divorce rate goes up from 50 percent to 67 percent for second marriages and catapults to 73 percent for third marriages (U.S. Census 2002). The data reveal that instead of learning from their mistakes, more people repeat them. I suspect that each time they start over, they clean the outside, but that that trunk is still carrying past experiences into contemporary relationships.

For others of us, we find ourselves trapped in an unhealthy workplace environment that we're afraid to leave. Because of the junk in our trunk, we can't see beyond the short-term need for a paycheck. Our vision of a broader professional panorama becomes eclipsed by our feelings of inferiority, inadequacy, and incompetency. We postpone decisions about going back to school and finishing our degree, looking into other career fields, or asking our supervisor about a promotion. And even when we do seek a new position, it does no good to change jobs if we retain old attitudes.

If you are going to make great decisions that leave you with no regrets, then you must clean out the junk in your trunk, let go of the past. Doing so will provide you the necessary space to see, breathe, and maneuver. You often won't know what you have, let alone need, in your life until you can clear the mental and emotional room to experience the here and now.

This process reminds me of a cable reality show I caught one night while surfing channels. The program is called *Clean House* and features a dear friend of the family, Niecy Nash. We were excited to engage Niecy in our newly released movie based on my novel, *Not Easily Broken*. Niecy has the ability to leave everyone in stitches, everyone except for some of those homeowners who do not want to remove any of the artifacts that they have gathered and hoarded like a pack rat. She is both comedic and relentless in her efforts to help the homeowner eradicate the many items that need to be discarded or sold in order to reconfigure what could be a lovely home for them.

Niecy and a team of clean-up experts selected a household in dire need of spring cleaning and refurbishing. More times than not the homeowners have grown attached to something that they don't need but lack the courage or resolve to release it. This home in question was piled with furniture, clothes, knickknacks—room after room after room. What was especially interesting to me was the cause of the homeowner's malaise. As the clean team interacted with her, she revealed that she was still grieving the death by divorce of her marriage and had become paralyzed by the thought of changing anything in her home. Her divorce had been so traumatic that she feared making any other changes in her life, even if they threatened her well-being and stifled the lives of her children still in the home.

With the homeowner's permission, the clean team went through the entire house and began the process of creating a new, healthy environment for her and her family. They removed all trash, clutter, and items that were beyond repair. They sorted and saved items which still had value for a major yard sale that would in turn generate resources to fund some new pieces of furniture and the overall renovation.

You know how these shows end—with the dramatic "reveal" moment when we viewers are as stunned as the homeowner to see the beautiful new "after" environment. The situation on this program was no less predictable or dramatic in its revelation of a clean, clutter-free interior. The removal of the avalanche of unneeded items alone revealed the beauty and functionality of many of the lovely features already in the home. From there, the decorators and designers had chosen furniture and other accessories that both complemented these features as well as reflected the style and personalities of the inhabitants.

I guess they don't call them reality shows for nothing. For at the heart of what made this show compelling, the curiosity that kept my finger from twitching and clicking to the next action movie, ball game, or news program, was the human element, to which everyone relates: the desire to change. And there is no greater avenue for change in your life than exercising the very real power you have each and every day to execute different decisions from the ones that got you where you are now.

KINDS OF JUNK:
PHYSICAL AND MENTAL/EMOTIONAL

There are two different kinds of junk—physical and mental/emotional—and both kinds of junk can weigh you down.

Physical junk is the kind we accumulate in the backs of closets, in those junk drawers, where we can never find a pen when we need to quickly write a note or matches when the power goes out, or in our

home office, where we can never find the tax records or the immuni-
zation cards for the school trip; or the garage, where we can never put
our hands on the citronella candles to keep the mosquitoes at bay.

If you are not the kind of person who tends to systematically dis-
pose of items on a regular basis, your home is probably full of physical
junk. Unpaid bills, old newspapers, magazines and other recycling,
gifts you hold on to from friends or old loves you no longer speak to,
broken appliances or garden tools you mean to have fixed but never
get around to, or those projects you just need a rainy day to complete,
the sweater you're going to knit for your infant niece who is now seven,
and so on.

It is hard to function in an environment that isn't neat and orga-
nized. In fact, living with physical junk in your home is chaotic and
spills out into other aspects of your life. Because you can't ever find
the car keys in the morning since they are buried in the clutter of
unopened mail and take-out menus on the kitchen counter, you are
always late for work. Eventually this could cause you to appear unpro-
fessional or, worse, could lead to losing your job.

Maybe your kitchen is disorganized, and you keep buying items
you already have in the fridge because you can't see what's already
there. Not only does this make meal preparation and family time frantic and stressful, but it also leads to wasting food and precious dollars
that could be better spent elsewhere.

Physical junk is not only annoying to step over and try to live around
but it takes away from the quality of your life and that of your family's.
Making purging and organizing a regular activity is time well spent.
Make it a family affair. Assign rooms or zones to family members
and make them responsible for keeping their area neat. It will save
you time and money in the long run and give you and your family
peace of mind and a place to truly come home to.

Mental and emotional junk is the regrets we have about past mistakes, the grudges we hold when we feel we've been done wrong or the hurts we hide under clouds of anger, cynicism, and reclusiveness. Mental and emotional junk, while you can't literally see it, can weigh you down as well. If you are the type to hold grudges or hang on to past mistakes, even your own, then you know the feeling of being weighed down by mental junk.

It is hard for a relationship to survive when either party hasn't processed their mental junk. Like blame, mental junk keeps you stuck in the past. If an old beau has hurt you, and you've never let that hurt go, each time your mate does something similar you will react to them, probably with unwarranted fervor, as if they were the original person who hurt you. The new mate is left feeling upset and confused at your over-the-top reaction to a small infraction that on its own was insignificant.

Like housecleaning to keep our homes free of physical junk, you have to focus on keeping your mental and emotional house clean and in order as well. Praying, journaling, meditation, and exercise are common ways for you to be sure your emotional issues of the past aren't seeping into your current relationships. These activities help you remain on top of and aware of your emotions and feelings, and rather than stuffing them inside, help you process issues as they arise.

When issues do come up, it's best to talk to those you are in relationship with in kindness, truth, and honesty. That old adage "love means never going to bed angry" is a good motto for keeping mental junk where it belongs—out of your trunk and in the trash.

Decide to Discard

Many people I counsel have started having a relationship before letting go of things that should be discarded. I call this condition "spiritual necrophilia." You likely know that necrophilia describes people who have intimate relationships with dead people. Yuck! Who wants to sleep with dead people, you ask? People do it every day—maybe not literally, but they do it figuratively when they hold on to dead issues, past experiences, or unhealthy unforgiveness. How can someone love you when you are in love with the dead? As dank as a corpse, these people are emotionally reeking of the remains of toxic issues that they seem unwilling to release. They keep the drama alive by rehearsing it, reliving it, or doing whatever they can do to keep the fire burning on the dead issues, a relentless funeral pyre that emits a putrid smell whenever someone new tries to come around.

Often on *Clean House*, homeowners have a difficult time relinquishing grandma's pink plaid sofa or the set of dishes they received as a wedding present for their first marriage. The items no longer serve any real purpose other than to hold the husk of a memory that has faded like a dried flower pressed between the pages of a book. Once the homeowners are challenged and confronted with the reality of their sentimental souvenirs, items that only collect emotional dust, they usually let go and allow the item to be sold or given away.

You may need to have your own inner garage sale. I challenge you to look in your emotional closets and see what needs clearing out. I hope that you have no dead relationships lingering, but if you do, then I admonish you to let them go and bury them. You must make room for new life, and sometimes this new space requires removing items, relationships, and obligations that no longer serve the purpose for which they were originally intended.

The last closet to clean is the one between your ears. It gathers more debris than any attic, more soot than an old chimney. Worse, no one but you knows what is there. Clean out old memories that attract unforgiveness. Some people think that unforgiveness punishes the person who hurt you. It does not. What it does do is keep your heart filled with anger, hostility, and bitterness. Forgiveness is not for the benefit of the person who hurt you. Forgiveness is a gift you give yourself. Through it, you unhook yourself from the past and free your soul to escape the dismal and experience the delightful again.

Test your mind for worry. If you find that you are thinking the same thoughts several days in a row, you aren't thinking, you are worrying. Stop that right now and make the decision in your mind to move from rehearsing the same thoughts to resting your mind until something fresh comes. Like the show demonstrates, when people find it hard to sell old memorabilia, it may be painful to part with old emotional habits. Ultimately, however, the release is liberating and allows you to have a new experience.

This is a moment in your life to consent to discard the ills that afflict you. You can only find the power to do that as you become convinced that there is more life in front of you than there is behind you!

WHO CAN HELP YOU WITH YOUR JUNK?

Dealing with junk isn't as easy as it sounds. Ancient Eastern philosophies like feng shui propose that physical things have energy. They can represent old relationships, which could mean old hurts and disappointments. For example, if you are holding on to a photo of an old love who lied to you or jewelry from the man who left you for another woman, each time you look at the physical item, whether you are conscious of it or not, you are reminded of sadness and pain. You may be holding on to other items, given to you by people you love, your parents or siblings for example, out of obligation, even though you don't have room for them or they don't really reflect who you are now in your life.

If you have made the decision to clear away your physical junk, you don't have to do it alone. Ask an impartial party for help. Choose someone who has no emotional attachment to your items such as a professional organizer or even an honest, straightforward friend, and let them help you identify items that no longer serve you and help you let them go. So many organizations and causes in the world need all of the clothes, books, CDs and other items that you may have to give away. It is often helpful to think of purging our physical junk as a way to give to others who are less fortunate. After all, you probably don't really need four black wool sweaters, but a homeless person some-where definitely does.

Mental junk like a divorce, the death of a loved one, serious illness, depression or childhood traumas often leave us feeling angry, hope-less, or weighed down. The only way to release ourselves from the burden of carrying these pains with us in our lives is to make an active decision to do so. And sometimes we need help. Of course the love, listening, and support of a good friend or family member may be all you need. Like the Beatles song says, "I get by with a little help from my friends." But friends, while often well-meaning, often bring their own issues to the table and aren't always the best at giving us uncon-ditional support. So if chatting with your best friend over an afternoon cup of tea doesn't work, and you find that your mental or emotional junk has you feeling out of sorts, consider talking to a member of your clergy, a mental health professional such as a therapist or counselor, or joining a support group.

Talking is often the best way to purge the hold of painful or emo-tional junk. Knowing that there are others who understand your feel-ings and support you unconditionally can be very cathartic and leave you feeling like you've lost the burden of carrying fifty extra pounds!

Rocky Road

Often the accumulation of junk in our trunk feels like a rockslide tumbling down on us, trapping us for the rest of our lives. But we do not have to stay buried by the boulders of past mistakes. In fact, once we begin lifting them off our chest and placing them aside, we discover that many are only pebbles that can be easily swept away if we will only try to see them in a new light. Yet so many of us keep seeing those rocks as insurmountable. A Greek myth tells of a man named Sisyphus who was being punished by the gods. Each day he rolled a large rock up a steep hill, a task he was doomed to repeat endlessly because once he reached the summit at the end of the day, the rock rolled back down to the valley from which he had started.

Breaking these kinds of cycles requires making a decision. It doesn't matter how many mistakes you've made, how traumatic the circumstances from which you have come, or how distant you feel from the childhood dreams that once motivated you. If you want to change, you can. You have to want to move on with your life. It won't happen overnight and it won't be easy, but the insatiable desire for a better life that gnaws at you just before your eyes flicker and you swim into unconsciousness each night will not go away unless you take action. And before you take action, you must decide to do so.

Do not wait for a health crisis, job termination, or loss of a loved one to catalyze your desire for lasting change. Before you can catalyze you must cauterize. Create a vantage point that allows you to look into your past without fear, blame, shame, anger, bitterness, or self-reproach. Become the person God created you to be.

Like a sea captain getting rid of weight that bogs down the cruise, we must cast aside the weights that so easily beset us. We must find a way to clean out the trunk, remove the stench of a dead past, and move ahead, free of all encumbrances that threaten to leave us attached to the dead at the expense of losing the living, who want us to be free.

You must not allow your unwillingness to forgive, your bitterness, or any other deep scar to dictate the direction in which you travel or the velocity at which you progress. It is far too heavy, weighing down your trunk, and slowing down your progress. It will impede your journey and leave you spiritually lethargic and emotionally anemic!

Unpack Your Trunk

Just as the junk in your trunk did not suddenly appear there overnight, removing it requires some time and patience as well. Some items need to be discarded and thrown away. You may have relationships that need to be severed. Others may require some final closure in order for you to move on. The relationship itself may clearly be dearly departed, but you're still waiting on the eulogy.

Don't be surprised in some cases if this closure involves writing a letter or giving a present to the person with whom you are ending the relationship. One man I know had bought a beautiful ring for the woman he loved only to be betrayed by her. He couldn't return the ring and didn't want to poison another relationship by giving it to someone else. So months after he and his betrayer had broken up, he realized he wanted to write her a letter and send her the ring. It wasn't so much that he wanted this woman, who had hurt him so deeply, to have the ring as much as it was his desire to relieve himself of this souvenir of what might have been.

Other junk simply needs to be put back in its proper place. Like my friend's golf clubs, which have their spot in his garage, some

issues aren't going away but can be contained. If you are supporting adult children who have returned home, you must not allow
them to disrupt every area of your life. You and your spouse must
find a way to keep a date night, to spend time alone enjoying each
other's company without intrusion.

If your work consistently spills over into your evenings and
weekends, then it's time to talk frankly with your boss about your
workload. If you are caretaking aging parents, then you may need
to find additional support to ensure your own mental, emotional,
and physical health. Healthy relationship boundaries can be an excellent way to ensure that junk does not accumulate in your trunk,
consuming space reserved for others and other areas of your life.

Finally, some items never belonged in your trunk in the first
place and were dumped there by people looking for someone to
relieve them of their junk. You may need to relinquish guilt over a
past mistake that a loved one continues to use as a lever of manipulation. Counseling a couple in which the husband had a one-
night fling on a business trip, I found both husband and wife
willing to deal with this blemish and work to make their relationship stronger.

The husband sincerely regretted his foolish mistake and desired to make sure it never happened again. He asked his wife's forgiveness, and she said she gave it to him. However, nearly two years
later they visited me again and their marriage was in far worse
shape than when I first saw them. The wife clearly had not forgiven
her husband and in fact relished the power his betrayal gave her.
She now controlled every move he made and had him believing
that he deserved such disrespect and mistreatment. They had
reached a crucial point in their relationship: either return to being
flawed, forgiving partners with equal standing or go their separate
ways.

Whether it's our children manipulating us by playing on our failures and guilt for not being there when they were growing up, or chasing the dream that our father had for us but which was never our own dream, it's time to return their junk to them.

OTHER STEPS TO GETTING RID OF YOUR JUNK

Sometimes your junk is just about procrastination. When you think about the things you want to do, it's just a matter of considering where you would want your life to go and then taking steps to do what you need to do in order to get there. If you want a particular job but aren't qualified, perhaps you need to return to school and get additional training and education. Maybe you've always dreamed of being an entrepreneur and starting your own business, and now you need to find ways to get financial support or want the advice and counsel of a mentor already working in the industry.

Think through what's holding you back. Consider what you need to get rid of, physical or mental, in order to make room for what you need to add in order to reach your destination, and then get busy doing it.

Road Warrior

Once you've eliminated the junk in your trunk, you can begin to reassess your needs and repack only those tools and items that are useful and helpful for your journey. Most drivers like to have a spare tire and the necessary tools for changing a flat. If your trunk is so full of extraneous items, you may not have room for the essentials that will ensure a smooth journey. Seasoned travelers know that they have to be prepared for the road ahead. In their trunk they might also include emergency items in case they're unexpectedly stranded by inclement weather—a blanket, flares, bottled water, and power bars. True road warriors anticipate what they will need in the worst of situations and prepare accordingly.

What we return to our life's trunk should be similarly conducive to furthering our preparation for what lies ahead. It is amazing how much better you feel when you are not afraid for someone to look in your trunk—in your heart—because you have gotten rid of what might have limited you or embarrassed you.

My prayer for you is that the Holy Spirit would do a Niecy Nash in your heart, a makeover for the soul, and allow you to decide to get rid of the things you have accumulated that diminish you as an individual, as an employee, or as a spouse.

Why don't you take a moment and list the things you know you have to let go of. Ask someone close to you to point out things that you may not even be aware of. Then have yourself a cleaning fit until there is no place in your heart that new companions, new friends, or even new employers cannot go. Your bumpers were as fine as they can be. Your windshield was spotless, the grill sparkling and the interior fresh. It was that junk in the trunk that had to be released. Once your mind is straight, you have no junk in your trunk!

four
Before You Lead— Decide on Your Team

"If your actions inspire others to dream more, learn more, do more and become more, you are a leader."
—*John Quincy Adams*

When confronted with important choices, we gather the information that is important to our decision-making process. We assume responsibility for what we are deciding, the life we are constructing. We get rid of the junk in our trunk, the negative thinking, unwillingness to forgive, bitterness, or any other deep emotional issues that weigh us down. Then we must also consider the team we bring to the task of making the decision.

Professional sports teams send out scouts to identify a player's talent, current level of skill, and potential to fit their pro team, years in advance of his or her eligibility. NFL teams send their scouts to colleges to spot not just seniors soon to be eligible for signing, but the freshmen who have just made the team. Major league baseball coaches have been known to send their scouts to Little League games in hopes of identifying their future pitching prodigies.

The best scouts see beyond where the player may be positioned currently and take an eyeball X-ray into that youth's ability to play several positions on the team envisioned for the future. They realize that every player scouted will not make the team, but that the team will not flourish without a vision of who will play key roles into the future. This is the only way to produce a winning team.

To the coach, the team is a collection of athletes, defined by the positions they hold, assembled by league rules within the salary cap and team budget. Some positions are more valuable than others to the well-being of the team. It's hard to imagine a successful football team without a talented running back, or a winning baseball team that didn't invest in its pitchers.

Personnel considerations must be a fundamental priority, no matter what kind of team it is. To the CEO of an industrial giant, his team is determined by the organizational charts he has in place and by the Human Resources department he has established for recruiting, training, and retaining the people he hires. He knows that a strong HR team is the heartbeat of a strong organization. His talented employees will build a strong infrastructure that operates, produces, markets, and sells the company's products. They are the lifeblood of the corporation; the shareholders and investors count on them for a return on their investment.

A mother's team that she uses to run the house will likely be her children. As her children grow, she recognizes their abilities and talents and matches them accordingly with chores and responsibilities around the home. She matches them by the age level, skill set, and individual temperament—one washes dishes while another empties the trash. As they get older, their responsibilities increase— cleaning their rooms, cutting the grass, preparing meals, and taking care of pets. The savvy mother realizes that as her team succeeds, she is keeping the household running smoothly as she teaches her children about responsibility and teamwork.

CEO of Your Life

Begin to think of yourself as a CEO, as a leader, the one who makes decisions about your life. You are the Donald Trump of your own life. (You may not like his methodologies or mannerisms, but no one has ever wondered who's in charge when he's in the boardroom.) Your team members are those whose contributions affect the quality of your life.

Remember, my friends, that God is the owner of your team but gave you authority to run it. Like Adam in the garden, you have power to subdue and have dominion, and you must know that the earth is the Lord's but God has given you the task to run it. I like this understanding of ownership and stewardship. God owns your life, but you care for it. This gives you the power to make the necessary decisions in your life and moves you from victimhood to being a victor. The next great decision is yours to make.

Now you may not feel like you are the CEO of your own life, or if you do, you may wonder why you always feel on the verge of emotional bankruptcy or a hostile takeover by those around you. But you alone have the responsibility to make the choices that will affect your own performance, productivity, profitability. You have stakeholders and shareholders, those who support you and those who compete with you. In the corporate world, at the end of the day, it is the CEO sitting in her corner office who is held responsible for the bottom line. Similarly, you are the one sitting in the executive's chair in your life and if you don't guide your personal corporation, then you will miss the chance to reap the dividends for which you were created.

Understanding that you are the leader of your life, you must move away from being a peacemaker to being a policy maker. Your goal is not to keep peace but to develop policies.

In the process of being a great CEO of your life, you can expect to be controversial, face conflict, commit fully, and exercise character. Each of these four qualities—controversy, conflict, commitment, and character—emerge from your willingness to exercise strength, wisdom, and determination. You must be willing to examine what's inside yourself and to choose the kind of leader you want to be. Without the deliberate choice to lead, the preparation necessary to inform your decisions, and the will to follow through, your team will flounder searching for someone to direct them.

I have never seen leaders who didn't have these four characteristics. Let's briefly examine each of these four:

They tend to be controversial.

Their decisions create conflict.

They are persons of commitment.

They are guided by their character.

IF YOU DON'T CONSIDER YOURSELF A LEADER

If you consider yourself a leader, then you understand that it is rarely an easy job or one that necessarily makes you very popular. If you don't consider yourself a leader, perhaps you are not taking responsibility for the decisions you make in your life and are relying too much on others to lead the way. You can be a leader at home and/or at work. Leadership at home is the mother who encourages her kids to donate their toys to the local shelter when they no longer play with them or the father who teaches his son the value of honesty when he walks with him to tell the next door neighbor that he damaged his tree while riding his new minibike.

Leadership at home is the couple who, rather than engaging in screaming, yelling, and name calling when they disagree, calmly talk to each other, state their perspective, and respectively listen to the other's point of view. So, by their example, they teach their children how to disagree with another person but at the same time let their needs be known.

Leadership does not only apply to people in positions of power such as presidents, pastors, or corporate CEOs. You show leadership in the way you choose to live your life, the way you interact with others no matter what their social status, and the example you set for your family, friends, and others you come into contact with.

Accept Being Controversial

Exercising leadership requires that you accept being controversial. Many people will not accept where you're going until after you get there. They don't understand the mind-set of a leader, because their opinions are based on where they are in life, not where you see your life going. Necessary members of your team may have myopic visions; they are unable or unwilling to see the forest for the trees. They are not the global thinkers you are. Leaders are not limited to one dimension but see the entire panoramic view of the team, their goals, and life itself. The difference in perspective between their myopic views and your panoramic view usually creates controversy, and a good leader has to be strong enough to live with the turmoil that comes from being misunderstood.

The controversies will hit you from many different directions.

Some will be small and inconsequential and should be swatted away like flies at a picnic. Some people on the periphery of a relationship with you—casual acquaintances at church, business associates in other departments—may gossip about and second-guess what they perceive you are up to. Their rumors and concerns should roll off your back unless you see them influencing primary relationships or other parts of your life.

Other controversies will emerge from those closest to you. It may be someone who overtly disagrees with you, which is actually not as bad as it may sound. Far worse, are the controversies hiding like a riptide beneath the calm surface. People who disagree with you or have competing agendas but who pretend to be in agreement with you can be the most dangerous of all. These may be coworkers, family members, your kids, your spouse, your pastor, or your close friends. They want you to do and to be who they want and need, not necessarily who you must become according to your own personal sense of mission. Communication is the best way to confront these controversies, and I would encourage you to keep short accounts and lean into them as soon as you sense their presence.

Accomplish Amid Conflict

Great leaders are generally tolerant of conflict, able to perform in the eye of the storm that may rage around them. If you have to wait until every conflict is resolved in order to proceed, you will never go forward. Instead, great leaders achieve their accomplishments as they venture through the middle of conflict. Their goal is to balance the extremes, for the betterment of all.

In spite of what we see today in the political and business arenas, where our leaders often rise to power by playing on the polarities of our world, scaring people into voting for them or hiring them, great leaders strategize rather than polarize. Talented leaders balance themselves within the conflict, between the polarities, without yielding to either extreme. They know that the truth is usually in the middle.

Many individuals focus on being recognized for their own talents rather than the team or corporate goals. Others want to be "right" and recognized as smarter, quicker, or more savvy than those around them. They tend to pick fights in order to strut their stuff and gain recognition. Real leaders know how to sidestep these ego-driven obstacle builders and maneuver like a sports car along a mountain road. Leaders keep the big picture and the bottom line in view when others attempt to obscure the view with personal agendas and petty conflicts.

Be Committed

Third, a great leader is a person of commitment. If she's the CEO, she's not off at five. If he's the captain, then he's not the first one off the ship. If he's a manager, then he's closing up after others leave the building. A leader must be committed or she will never achieve her goal.

There are simply too many other demands, distractions, and divisions interfering with your perseverance unless your commitment is firmly in place. Life circumstances will often thwart the schedules and methodologies that we set in place to fulfill our goals. Leaders know they must remain flexible, nimble, and adept at spontaneous course changes. They are not surprised when the laptop crashes, the international plant closes, or the deadline gets moved again. They are not deterred when critics go public and gain press coverage for their negativity. They are not diverted from their real goals when new opportunities present themselves—the good ones versus the great ones.

When family members no longer support their dreams, when a spouse doesn't encourage their passion, when their kids require more of them, these leaders forge onward and refuse to enter a spiral of discouragement, depression, or diversion. They keep their goals in the bull's-eye and refuse to allow naysayers, critics, and detractors to poison their determination.

You may need to maintain firm boundaries when these people attempt to derail your dream. Know when to say no. Know that it's okay to walk away alone with your head held high rather than to conform to someone else's standard of who you should be. Know that no one, even those who love you most, can pursue your goals the way you can.

Be of Good Character

But commitment without character leads to chaos. Character sets boundaries; it may not determine what you will do but will always determine what you won't do. Character let's you know how much you're willing to pay to go up the ladder.

Anyone in power who has no character is dangerous. They become ruthless tyrants. These are the leaders who produce gas chambers, devise weapons of mass destruction, enslave hundreds of thousands of people, lynch anyone who does not agree with them, and terrorize the hearts of all within their grasp. Tyranny, totalitarianism, and terrorism never contribute the kind of leadership that enriches lives and enhances the team.

But good character does not have to be in the spotlight, overtly running the show and screaming for recognition. When your character is forged by determination and your ego is strengthened by enduring past defeats, you do not need to resort to shortcuts to get your goals. If you think you can fast-track success by cheating, lying, or sleeping your way to the top, then you're sadly mistaken.

You carry who you are with you everywhere you go. If you do not build a solid character, then you will not be able to survive for long once you're at the top. Real leadership requires integrity, someone who displays the same character in the boardroom and in the bedroom. Someone who plays by the rules and works hard. Someone who gives others credit when it's due. Someone who lives by faith. Someone who trusts their Creator to help them accomplish all that they were made and called to do.

The Bible tells us that the wicked may prosper for a season but they will not endure and most certainly will not ultimately triumph. Treat others the way you want to be treated. Give as much or more than you take. Remember where you came from. Never lose sight of where you're going.

HANDLING CONFLICT

As a leader you will never be far from conflict and controversy. While not everyone will be willing to step up and take responsibility as the leader, you can be sure there will be plenty of people who are more than willing to sit back and critique everything you are doing. At work, you might take on leadership for a task force or assume the lead on a new product launch, for example. As part of the task force, you must assign coworkers certain jobs. You try to choose roles that coincide with everyone's wishes and strengths wherever possible, but of course, not everyone will be completely satisfied. Further, some of your coworkers are jealous and upset that you were offered the position rather than them and, in response, criticize everything you do, saying, "If I were in charge, I would do it differently." You may hear whispering in the break room or notice employees huddling in the hallways as you walk by.

This is one of the unfortunate but expected by-products of leadership. Not everyone will be happy with your decisions or even happy that you are taking the lead. You can't let these people deter you from your success. Certainly you want to treat everyone with the courtesy and respect they deserve, but as long as you make your decisions based on what is best for the project, you can't worry about individuals who wish to focus on petty, negative issues.

This is also true in family relationships. Not everyone is going to be happy with the decisions you make. But if you are a parent, your job is to lead in a way that is best for the overall interests of the family. Not all of the members of the group are always going to be thrilled with your decisions. Sure, it would be more fun to have a big-screen TV or to upgrade to the latest PlayStation or Wii. But if it means deciding between spending the household money on games and entertainment versus necessary expenses like food, utilities, or health care bills, then a true leader makes the right decision, popular or not.

How You Draft Your Team Members

Every successful coach, CEO, and parent knows that the team dynamics change each season. You assemble and attempt to retain the strongest core of talent available, but even in the midst of such stability, team dynamics will still fluctuate. How your team faces adversity differs from how it handles success. How it prepares for the competition in one market varies from how you approach a different consumer in a different sales channel. How you prepare to face the league leader differs from how you gear up for your division rival.

How you draft new team members depends on an accurate assessment of your team's current needs as well as long-term requirements.

STRENGTHS AND WEAKNESSES

Like people, not all leaders are the same. We all have strengths or assets and weaknesses that make us unique as individuals, and leaders are no exception. The key to effective leadership is understanding that few of us make it on our own. To be a success, good leaders surround themselves with others who complement their strengths and their weaknesses.

For example, suppose you are a quantitative thinker and numbers are your thing, but a team project at work for which you are the manager requires a creative vision. The smart leader calls on his creative-thinking team members and assigns them responsibility for creating an exciting new vision for the project. You are still in charge, but you have the most creative people available working on your side to help you succeed.

At home, you love to cook but hate to clean. Your spouse on the other hand, is Mr. Clean but stays far away from the stove. The smart leader employs spouses or kids to take on the cleaning duty after dinner. You work together to create a meal and a family experience, each focusing on your strengths and acknowledging your weaknesses.

If you find that there are areas in your life where you need more support or things that don't fall into the realm of your strengths, call on your team members to use their skills to help you out.

Some people come into your life for a season and others for a lifetime. Our hearts become broken and our vision blurred when we attempt to make seasonal people lifetime participants. Clearly, some people come into our lives for a period of time to accomplish a specific task for which we want an amiable relationship. But we cannot make a permanent investment into a temporary circumstance.

Relationships can be one of the greatest equitable assets of any individual, so how do we learn how to decide who's in and who's out? Like the pro scout, the CEO, or the wise mother, how do you delegate the right person to the right place so that we can decide how to run the team most effectively?

From my experience, both personally and professionally, in both business and in ministry, I find that most people on a team fall into one of three major categories: confidants, constituents, and comrades. If you're going to be effective, you must decide how to best utilize these three positions on your team. If you relegate a player into the wrong position, you frustrate the individual and terminate the effectiveness of your choice because you've misappropriated that player on the team.

Let's scrutinize each person's contribution and limitation to your team.

Confidants

First, confidants are people in your life for the long haul. They are there for a lifetime. They are lovers par excellence, and their love is the love of a lifetime that generally swings on hinges of unconditional acceptance. In the span of your life, do not expect many of these secret keepers. They will help you bear the burden even when you make poor choices and help you live with bitter mistakes. They are in your life for you and no other reason. With no ulterior motives, they will be there because they are drawn to you and want to be there for you.

We see this vividly illustrated in the relationship between David and Jonathan. David was at odds with King Saul, who just happened to be the father of his best friend, Jonathan. David never finds his trust betrayed or his confidence shattered by his most faithful confidant. Jonathan kept David's secrets and consistently protected his very life, even when faced with displeasing his own family. He wasn't seeking to elevate himself, inflate his own self-importance, or orchestrate his own advancement through his relationship to David.

One of hardest things for me is to be the confidant of public figures. When they do or say something that becomes controversial, others want me to comment on their behavior. But once someone comments about you to someone else, they immediately cease to be your confidant. Many are the times that I have been highly criticized for not commenting on a controversial issue. But I have chosen to be a great confidant rather than a regular informant. I've known details about marriages that I could not divulge even though we live in an age of unquenchable thirst by an insatiable public who think they have the right to know. I've bit my tongue and held my lips while others who were not informed about the facts made almost libelous statements against people I knew well. I've held my peace and let the public find out later what I knew earlier. You see, the strength of confidants is in their silence.

We see such depth of commitment in journalists who refuse to identify their sources in the face of dire threats and legal consequences. In 2005, Judith Miller faced jail time and contempt of court fines for refusing to name her source to the government. A *New York Times* investigative reporter, Ms. Miller refused to participate with a federal prosecutor investigating the identity leak of a covert operative for the CIA. At her trial she was quoted as saying, "If journalists cannot be trusted to guarantee confidentiality, then journalists cannot function and there cannot be a free press."

If our confidants cannot guarantee their confidentiality to us, then they automatically disqualify themselves from the pool of individuals on our team in whom we grant absolute trust. We must rest in the security of such relationships in order to express ourselves, gather information, and glean wise counsel. Otherwise, we will reap the consequences of having the wrong people know too much about us. Confidants not only maintain our secrets, but they refuse to haunt us with their privileged knowledge. The people who really care about us will not throw our past mistakes back in our faces. They refuse to utter the words, "I told you so."

WHO IS ON YOUR LEADERSHIP TEAM?

It is often a hard lesson to learn, and often painful to accept, but no matter how good a person you are, not everyone in the world has you or your best interest at heart. Different types of people require different types of relationships. Work to determine to what level you should interact with people. Only certain people, and typically only a few, belong in your inner circle of confidants. Carefully consider the relationships in your life

The Party Line

Our second group, those I call constituents, are often confused with confidants because constituents walk with you. But they walk with you because they're for the same goals that you're for. They agree to principles on which you've based your life policies, personhood, church, and business. And because they have similar goals and aspirations, they will walk closely alongside you.

However, they are not for *you*; they are for the common goals you share, and as long as it serves their purpose, they will contribute to your team. But if it becomes necessary, they will leave and find someone else who is for what they are for. This commonality is what attracted them to you in the first place.

These people can often appear opportunistic because they live their lives like hitchhikers. They travel as part of your team because you're going in the right direction. But they will hitch another ride if they decide they can get there faster or better with another driver.

You will need constituents. Don't lock them out. Their absence will hinder your journey; they often contribute a lot of energy and passion to the cause for which they fight. But don't love constituents or mistake them for confidants because one day they may abandon and even betray you for the cause.

Nowhere is this better illustrated than in the world of politics. In our recent presidential election year, it's been a daily drama to see which groups support which candidate, which have donated their support to whom, and how many special interest groups factor into the electoral equation. Both Democrats and Republicans have numerous constituents who are all committed to the same party principles and platform. Many voters align themselves with the party line, not with any given individual and his or her strengths. I recall growing up and hearing one of my elders joking about an older gentleman who was a lifelong Democrat: "He'd vote for a first grader if the child was running on the party ticket!"

Too often constituents align themselves in the church with certain doctrines, dogma, and denominations. Instead of inspiring unity, it frequently results in factions, divisions, and disputes over issues that need not become the focal point. I'm reminded of an old saying that a woman shared with me years ago, when I was a minister in the rural areas of West Virginia: "What we believe may divide us, but in Whom we believe should unite us."

Yet constituents, from diverse and distinct backgrounds, can unite to produce radical changes. Recently, various groups and denominations within the Baptist Church convened at the New Baptist Covenant celebration and agreed to lay aside the smaller differences that often separated them in the past and instead focus on the larger causes, such as racial equality, on which they can all agree. They took to heart the Scripture, "Do two walk together unless they have agreed to do so?" (Amos 3:3, NIV).

Your constituents may emerge in your office, your church, your school, or civic group. You may come from different departments, denominations, career paths, or social interests, but you share some common values that unite you. You certainly do not want to mistake constituents for confidants, but you also don't want to avoid working with them to accomplish collective goals. Build bridges where you can. Make peace when possible. Connect with others who share your sense of activism.

What has to be managed here are your expectations. You must understand that constituents will make directional moves that may not include you. They want to go the way you are going, but they may arrive with someone else. They are committed to the destination and not the mode of travel. These are people who may change horses in the middle of the stream as long as the new horse helps accomplish their agenda.

They aren't bad people as long as you understand that these people operate much like scaffolding. When a building is under construction, the scaffolding is right there by the builder's side. When the building is completed, the scaffolding is taken down. Just recognize them for who they are and do not assume that they will become close confidants.

One man said it this way, "All that left me couldn't stay and all that stayed couldn't leave." Some people are seasonal blessings loaned to you to perform a purpose, and when the season is up and the purpose completed, they will leave. This is okay. The apostle Paul says it this way: They went out from us, but they were not of us; for if they had been of us, they would no doubt have continued with us: but they went out, that they might be made manifest that they were not all of us (1 John 2:19, KJV).

Sharing Negative Space

On the other end of the spectrum, you will find team members who do not share your values, principles, and goals as much as they share your common enemies. Comrades are not for you nor do they hold dear the issues that you are for. But they're attracted to you because they're against what you're against. Comrades galvanize around common enemies and make for strange bedfellows.

Perhaps there is no better illustration for comrades than people coming together to work against certain political issues, joining forces to combat something they want destroyed. In World War II, the French and British forces, historically bitter rivals for centuries, were forced to forge an alliance of survival against the common enemy of Hitler's Nazi state.

If comrades were part of a portrait, they would be the negative space, providing clarity to identify what is most important to a person and the obstacles that stand in the way. Comrades are not painting the same picture you are painting, however. Like constituents, they are opportunists, which can be worthwhile because a keen sense of timing is always to be appreciated. When it's necessary to align themselves with someone who's different, when a larger force, issue, or antagonist threatens their welfare, comrades will bolster their cause with those battling the same threat.

But when the fight is over, the fuel is gone. When the foe is vanquished, the giant slain, and the crisis averted, comrades will terminate the relationship and continue their own agenda elsewhere—at least until the next enemy rears its head.

Comrades are like soldiers in a war. Their bond with you is the enemy in front of both of you. Their only connection with you is what you both need removed or destroyed. It may help if you can think of them like the Pharisee and Sadducees who rose up against Jesus. It wasn't that they liked each other; the bond was built on the fact that they both wanted Jesus out of the way.

Have you ever noticed how people who don't even like each other will join together to defeat a common enemy? Most soldiers fight together like brothers, but when the fight is over they go back home, often to never see their comrades again. Their common bond was what they were fighting against. This alliance is more about motives than function. Understanding the comrade requires understanding motives and why some people join forces with you.

If you feel vulnerable and wonder, "how in the world will I ever know one from the other?" I have found that more times than not, people tell you what they are there for, if you will just slow down and listen. When they tell you what makes them tick, believe them!

LEADERSHIP STYLE?

Styles of leadership vary as much as there are leaders. Some leaders are detail oriented, they are hands on, like to work from the ground up, and be immersed and informed of every aspect of a project or activity. Others are more big picture and visionary, they leave the details to those who report to them, relying on the expertise of others to help them toward their goals.

It's critical to making great relationship decisions, to identify the people around you as one of these three. As long as you enter into relationships understanding that everyone you meet will fall into one of these three categories, you will avoid making crucial mistakes of judgment regarding whom to trust with what information. If you confide in constituents or comrades, don't be surprised when your trust is broken. In fact, when such a breach occurs, it's not really their fault. It's your fault because you should have known the role they were playing in your life before you confided in them.

Obviously, you want to anchor your life's team with confidants, filling up the picture of your life with these vital individuals who pump the lifeblood of friendship, encouragement, and wise counsel into your endeavors.

Around them, frame the picture with constituents and comrades, recognizing them for who they are and working with them to accomplish the goals that you share and to overcome the common obstacles. Don't be afraid to accept these individuals only for a season, to fill a specific need on your team, and then to move on. Holding on to constituents or comrades as if they were confidants will only produce dead weight that will inhibit your team's efforts to fulfill your life goals.

Before you turn the page, I encourage you to assess the current state of your team. Are there individuals you have mistaken for confidants who are really just hitchhiking in the same direction of a common cause? Are there ways to include comrades in your strategy to reach the next level, by allowing them to slay certain dragons that threaten you both? If you're willing to be ruthlessly honest with yourself about the relationships in your life, then you will be poised to make the very best decisions. However, you must know whom you're dealing with before you do.

five
Before You Join

"Join the company of lions rather than assume the lead among foxes."

—*The Talmud*

When you decide to marry someone, you agree to create a new joint production, a marriage with the two of you as costars. The next chapter, "Before You Decide to Love," features food for thought to help you decide how best to proceed. As a precursor to considering the many dimensions and dynamics that you should consider in your romantic relationship, I'd first like to turn your attention to another kind of marriage, the union that occurs when an individual chooses to affiliate with a group, institution, program, or club. Making the decision to commit ourselves to a group of individuals, whether it's a church in our community, a professional organization of our peers, a country club for those who have arrived, or a group devoted to a shared hobby or passion, requires due diligence similar to any other major decision.

Families and tribes are the oldest anthropological social groups known to exist. God created us to need other people, both intimately through marriage as well as socially through community. Throughout our lives, we are bombarded with opportunities to belong—from joining the basketball team in high school to a sorority in college, from the PTA to the NAACP, from a bridge club to a retirement community. In school most of us faced the usual cliques—the jocks, the brains, the preppies, the rebels, the beautiful people.

Whatever we may have called them or whatever our own children label them now, the groups remain fairly similar in attracting homogeneous members bound by a common social characteristic or cultural initiative. Like tends to attract like, as the group familiarity provides comfort and security, particularly in the face of diversity and multiculturalism.

The problem with groups, whether we're talking high school sports teams or members at the local country club, is that they tend to be exclusive. Even if they are open to anyone—and many groups appear to be and are not—they still elevate group members into a special category that transcends the rest of the group.

Before you join any group, think it through. Do a personal cost-benefit analysis to determine what's to be gained compared to what you will invest. Read on and I'll show you how to calculate the profit and loss of joining any group, before you do.

Sunday School

Perhaps the institution most affected by our affiliation with its membership is our local church or place of worship. And we certainly have more churches in more varieties than ever before in our country's history. Recently the prestigious Pew Forum on Religion & Public Life conducted its U.S. Religious Landscape Survey and found that most Americans identify themselves as belonging to some distinct religious group. Most of these groups can be categorized into about a dozen major traditions, but within each of these are hundreds of denominations and thousands of churches within those denominations. Indeed, there seems to be some kind of place of worship for virtually everyone!

Finding such a place, however, and comfortably belonging is not necessarily easier just because more offerings exist. It's been said that the church is not a museum for perfect people but rather a hospital where injured souls unite to recover. This is a good sentiment, but too often our churches can be just as stringent in whom they welcome through the doors as the most discriminating Ivy League university. Faith communities should escape the feel of homogeneous exclusivity, but tragically, this is not necessarily the case. I've seen many churches whose members enjoyed screening its visitors as if they were the border patrol guarding an international boundary!

It's fine to seek fellowship with like-minded believers, but we should examine our motives and make sure that we aren't merely looking for another business networking opportunity or an elitist symbol of status. Churches should bring people together to worship, to support, to encourage, to assist, to teach, and to unify. Choosing a church must include an awareness of its affinity with where we are in life and with its ability to meet our current needs.

If a particular church operates like a clique, then do we really want to belong to it? Shouldn't Sunday school be more about how to love God and other people rather than how to display wealth and status? When churches operate noninclusively, we do well to avoid them. In essence, they have shirked their role as the unifier of God's people. When a church has become a country club of social networking and showing off the new Mercedes and the latest Dior, then it has lost its true calling.

After my father passed away, I joined a church as a young man needing the intimacy of a spiritual family and the accountability of a like-minded community. A megachurch would not have likely worked for me at that time because of its size and the ability of new members to remain anonymous. I needed a safe and secure place in which to grieve and to discover the next season of my life. For me at that time, I found it in a small rural church.

This is not to say that you can't find it in a large urban church. The family and community dynamic empowers many mega-churches, usually through small groups and common areas of service. At The Potter's House, the choir members are naturally connected with one another; similarly the deacons, and the many small groups made up of a dozen or so individuals. But for me as a young man, I craved the family-style worship and intimate setting that a small church affords.

As I grew older, my needs changed. Entering into young adulthood, I found myself spread thin by the numerous responsibilities of my job, my family, and other commitments. I wasn't capable of giving my time and energies to serving the church by setting up chairs before the service, ushering, leading a Bible study, or serving the youth group. I needed a place where I could be fed spiritually and still feel that I belonged.

We should be able to find sound teaching and to see it backed up in the various ministries of the church. Many parents want their children to attend church so that they can learn the moral values that they hold in high esteem. However, the teaching of values at church does not replace the need to teach our children our convictions and beliefs at home. Church can never be a moral replacement for what is absent in our actions within the home.

Yes, it's important for families to worship together but keep in mind that you can't join just for the sake of the children. You must join a church for your own spiritual needs and not just the requirements of your family. Membership in a church should last longer than childhood.

WHY DID YOU JOIN? WHY DO YOU STAY?

As social beings we like to belong, it's human nature. But often belonging becomes more about social status than giving back or helping. Consider the organizations you currently belong to and how long you've been involved with each of them. The types of organizations you tend to join can reveal a lot about what is important to you. If the reasons you joined in the first place still hold true, then you should probably remain a member and keep doing what you're doing.

But if you find that the organizations no longer serve your present needs or season of life and are costing you a great deal in financial commitment and time and energy, it may be time to reassess your affiliations.

Associate's Degree

When we join a group, we are not only included in its privileges but in its prejudices as well. One of the greatest challenges of my career in ministry has been maintaining a nonpartisan political stance. It has not been difficult for me to sustain personally because I believe that a person's integrity, experience, and intelligence matter more than his or her party affiliations. However, I have repeatedly found myself the target of various factions, political action groups, and special interests who become frustrated that I will not endorse Candidate X or Amendment Y on the ballot. I work hard to build bridges and find ways for all participants involved in an issue to have their side heard and their needs met.

Another reason I have avoided such political affiliation is because of the many assumptions and stereotypes that people would make if I came out and supported a Democratic or Republican candidate or platform. Whether it be a perception that I was looking for a way to protect the wealth of business owners or catering to the special needs of minority constituents, I would forever be misjudged—more than I already am!—because of such an association. Your decision may be different from mine.

So as you consider committing your time, mental energy, financial resources, professional endorsement, or any other contribution to a group, you must be willing to accept their liabilities as your own. Many of them will require you to sign a contract that legally binds you to accept fiscal responsibility and personal liability for the group. You will be bound by their rules even if you disagree with them.

Before you move into that chic, exclusive neighborhood of the stunning homes you've always wanted, read the fine print on the community covenant contract very carefully. You may not be able to park in your own driveway, paint your house, or plant certain shrubbery without having the board of directors' approval. Ask yourself if the prestige and quality of life you will receive in return is worth the price. For many people, the gain is obviously valuable enough that they don't mind submitting to the groupthink. But recognize that you are giving power over certain areas of your life to other people who may or may not have your well-being at the center of their agenda.

CHOOSING A CHURCH

The decision to join a church is an important one. Our spiritual lives are the center of our existence, and belonging to a church can do a great deal to enhance our experience. When choosing a place to worship, you must consider how well a church serves your needs and those of your family. If you want a more intimate experience and to get to know your fellow worshippers, then a smaller community church is probably a better fit for you than a larger urban or mega-church. Conversely, if your needs include many activities and programs for you and your family, community involvement, and/or opportunities to serve on boards and committees, then a larger church is probably exactly where you need to be. Further, sometimes as our lives change and evolve, so do our church needs. Where a larger or smaller church may have served your needs when you were single, a different church might be better for you as a family.

The Inner Ring

Advertisers consistently capitalize on the fact that we want to feel like we belong to the exclusive group of people who are young, attractive, smart, sexy, hip, and in the know about the latest and greatest. Whether it's the latest diet craze and the book, DVD, and salad dressing that goes with it, or the newest model of European sports car with its savvy technology and sensual silhouette, products are presented to us as desirable and capable of providing us with all we yearn for and to be.

But if you've purchased any of these products, you know they cannot give you what you aren't willing to give yourself. You're never going to feel better about yourself simply because of the club to which you belong or the group you join. We must not expect to receive something from our affiliations that they cannot begin to provide for us.

You may fool everyone in the club, at church, in the office, or wherever, but you will be left knowing all of your insecurities. The only way to feel good about yourself and to grow in confidence is to know who you are and love yourself. This is certainly easier said than done and requires a lifetime of self-education and personal exploration.

The British writer and thinker C. S. Lewis once delivered an address titled "The Inner Ring," which describes this very human desire to belong, to be an insider, to be above those around us for all the right reasons. While it's an urge with which we all must wrestle, Lewis cautions us to face what's at the core of this desire: our fear of being an outsider who must bear the pain of being rejected and alone. He explains, "As long as you are governed by that desire you will never get what you want. You are trying to peel an onion: if you succeed there will be nothing left. Until you conquer the fear of being an outsider, an outsider you will remain."

Until you have peeled back your real motives in your own onion of desire, you will likely set yourself up for disappointment with any group. As long as you go into a group knowing that at best it can only complement or facilitate your goals, then you stand a greater chance of fulfillment. Know who you are apart from being a member of the PTA, president of the Ladies Auxiliary, chairman of the board of directors, and director of the choir. Then you can receive whatever the organization has to offer you without defining yourself by it.

Feeding Time

Over the years, so many boards, philanthropies, and charitable organizations have asked me to be a member that I've had to be very deliberate about where I commit to serving. The challenge has not been in discerning if they are good or worthy causes because virtually all of them are. No, the difficulty lies in discerning where I can affect the most positive change through my contribution. I have also had to ask myself what I receive from such involvement.

As selfish as it may sound, the most important question you can ask before you join any group is "how will this feed me?" Yes, you must be careful not to expect too much from your affiliation with the group, but you must also have solid expectations about what it will deliver. Will it help your career? If so, how? Who else belongs to this organization that you would like to meet? Why do you want to meet them? What perks do members enjoy? How will this church feed you spiritually? What do you gain from joining the Toastmasters? Did you really enjoy those weekend practices with the work softball team?

If you aren't being fed, then you will end up being a nominal member with yet another obligation on your plate. None of us needs another commitment that becomes a weight around our necks. We must be able to point to a tangible benefit, an intangible satisfaction, or a future return if joining the group is to be worthwhile.

The other question you must ask yourself before you join is "what can I uniquely contribute?" Many organizations and institutions want your time, money, and talents. But I venture to say that only a few need what you have to offer that no one else can contribute. It may be your dollars but chances are it's your passion for the cause, your talent for the topic, or your ability to enable that makes you irreplaceable on the team.

Many people can donate time and money. Many can set up the chairs for the meeting or make cookies for the reception. And while all of us may have to serve in very humble ways at times, we should know that what we give cannot be mistaken for the contribution of anyone else. Don't join if you cannot add something new to the group.

Make a list of all your affiliations, clubs, organizations, and committees to which you belong. Be as comprehensive as possible in making your list—include everything from professional organizations to sororities and fraternities, committees at church or school, the choir or deacon board, the local homeowners' board in your neighborhood, the aerobics squad at the gym, or the election committee for your county representative. Next to each write out your level of commitment to that group—high, moderate, low, none.

After assessing the level of your involvement, next to each one write how you feel about belonging at this time in your life: great, okay, necessary, frustrated, bad, etc. Identify the associations that can be severed and take immediate steps to terminate your membership and responsibilities. You will feel lighter and less encumbered and now able to turn your attention to other affiliations that will feed your present needs more effectively.

My final piece of advice is to have clear boundaries and limitations concerning your role in the group. If you committed to chairing the fund-raiser, then don't let someone coerce you into keeping the books for the entire organization. If you promised to mail flyers, don't also agree to speak at the conference—unless you really want to. Determine what exactly will be expected by your participation.

Similarly, set a time limit on your season of involvement and agree to reassess at the end of that time. My wife and I used to joke on our wedding anniversaries that we had talked it over and agreed to renew our contract for another year. While this is not a valid approach to the lifetime commitment of marriage, it is indeed viable for most of our other memberships.

As your needs change, don't be afraid to cut ties to former organizations that may have served you well in the past but which no longer meet your current needs. Don't keep attending the same church simply because it's familiar. Ask yourself if it still serves your needs and those of your family. Does the club you joined back when you were single still provide you with the kinds of relationships that are appropriate for a married man? Many mothers continue to serve on the PTA long after their kids have graduated, more out of mindless repetition than passionate participation.

We are created to be social beings, and belonging to groups with shared goals or similar pursuits is essential to our well-being. However, like any other major decision in your life, you must take a good, long look at the dynamics of your involvement before you join. If you're willing to examine your motives for joining a group, including what you will gain and what you alone can contribute, then you are much more likely to enjoy your affiliation.

Making good decisions regarding your affiliations becomes the key for making great decisions regarding individual relationships. The eternal question that I encounter from many young people, usually in a half-joking manner, is "Should I marry for love or for money?" My grandmother answered it in a way that reflects such wisdom. Her response was, "Hang out with a group of rich folk that you like and then marry for love."

No parents deliberately send their children out to play with bullies, drug dealers, or gang members. We want our children to surround themselves with responsible, well-behaved, Christian young people from good families in nice neighborhoods. While this is a good impulse, we might be better served tending to our own affiliations before worrying about our children.

Think about the person you want to become and whom you need to associate with to become that person, before you join . . .

six
Before You Decide
to Love

"Why love if losing hurts so much? We love to know that we are not alone."

—*C. S. Lewis*

The decision to love is the hardest and easiest decision you'll ever make. It's easy because when you love someone, the joy you experience in being around them is effortless. You know the feelings—the way your entire life seems more vivid and worthwhile because this person is in your life. Yet the cost of loving someone is never cheap. You can't buy love but you must pay the price of maintaining the relationship. You must choose to commit, to remain faithful, to forgive, to serve, to love through the good times and the bad, through sickness and in health, for richer and for poorer.

Deciding to love gets harder as you get older. It's more and more difficult to fall in love because your "faller" gets broken. You've lived long enough to have been disappointed, heartbroken, and jaded. Perhaps you've even become cynical about trusting other people and about the prospect of finding someone to share your life with. It becomes more and more challenging to risk and so much safer and more comfortable to resign yourself to loneliness. I realize that many singles are more than contented with their lives and have no desire to marry or raise a family. This is their prerogative, which I respect, but at the same time I also know many are lonely.

Yet as we get older and have more roles and responsibilities draped around us or smothering us like a mummy's bandages, it is likely that we will crave a meaningful, passionate relationship more than ever. We want someone to love us for who we are and not what we do or what we provide financially or materially. We long for someone to give us permission to let go of all we cling to so fiercely in the daylight hours of our public persona. Like the sensation of swimming in deep water, we desperately need someone to help us end our thrashing around and fighting against the current. Only then can we float and discover how to accelerate our momentum with the tide.

RISKING LOVE AFTER HURT

We've all had relationships that didn't work out for one reason or another. Perhaps we made mistakes that drove our fiancé away or maybe our spouse treated us wrongly. The loss of a relationship can be a traumatic experience and can affect us in our lives for weeks, months, and sometimes years. The key to moving on from the end of a relationship is not to focus on what went wrong or to blame our partners for what we perceive to be their mistakes or shortcomings.

Rather, when a relationship ends, our task is to determine what lessons we can learn from the experience.

You need to understand what role you played in the relationship's demise, and work to come to peace with your partner's behavior as well as your own. This is the only way to truly move forward. Carrying around old hurts and left-over resentments keeps you from being open to prospective interactions and prevents you from being fully vulnerable in future relationships. In a recent interview on the Sundance Channel program *Iconoclasts*, Dr. Maya Angelou said it best: "It takes courage to love somebody, you have to risk everything." No matter what has happened to you, the only hope of a healthy future relationship is to let go of the past.

Real Intimacy

I've counseled many couples who were married, separated or divorced for a while, and now find themselves trying to reconcile and give the relationship a second chance. Often I see a gulf between them that counseling cannot bridge. They're moving in different directions. One partner wants to recapture the intensity of their past intimacy, as if they could somehow get inside a time machine and return to the season prior to their separation.

The other partner has moved on to a new focal point, usually their career or the children. He or she has realized that they cannot depend on the other person to fulfill all their needs or direct the course of their life. As they look into the future, the only relationship they want is one that they feel they can control. Can you relate? In the absence of love, many of us fall for work or sex or money or some substance that makes us feel good temporarily.

Today we have more technology, more counselors, more Viagra, more sexy lingerie, and more marriage seminars than ever before, and yet our divorce rate continues to cross the 50 percent mark. What is it that we're looking for that more sexual education and opportunities cannot provide? Could it be something as basic as the intimacy that comes from sharing daily life and personal realities together? I'm often amazed at hearing divorced men tell me that the things they miss most about their wives are the way they cooked meatloaf, the silence they shared at the end of the day after tucking the kids into bed, and the clutter of her perfume bottles on the vanity in their bathroom. Too often we overlook the small details that contribute to the connection we feel with other people.

During a recent *Dr. Phil* show in which I was participating, we counseled a woman who struggled with sexual addiction and was compelled to have sex with strangers. A guest expert on the show noted the bitter irony that sex addicts are running away from intimacy by acting out sexually. Even though they are engaging in the most intimate of acts, they are disengaging and blunting their emotions to avoid the pain of connecting in a healthy relationship. True intimacy requires transparency and vulnerability, honesty and acceptance, and trust. True intimacy requires deciding to love.

Emotional Condoms

Even if we aren't sex addicts, we are finding ways to divert ourselves from the hard work and frightening pursuit of real intimacy. Back in the day when I still went to clubs, I would see all the clinging couples gyrating on the dance floor. But there among them would always be a group of ladies, clearly friends enjoying a girls' night out, who had no one but each other with whom to dance. My fear is that the number of ladies dancing with themselves has only increased.

More and more, women who are successful in every area of their lives find that they are still alone, no matter how desperately they may long for a husband. A national average puts at 27 percent the number of women of marrying age who have never been married, and the number is 40 percent for African Americans. Add in the number who have divorced or been widowed and we're looking at *over half* the female population. Certainly, this epidemic of loneliness and longing is not exclusive to any one group. However, minority women certainly seem to face the reality of singleness with greater odds against finding a mate.

Many women who can finally afford a beautiful home walk through the door at the end of a long day to the sound of silence. There's no one there. The rooms are tastefully decorated and the beds display beautiful comforters and fine Egyptian cotton sheets. Only, there's no one there to comfort her as she walks from room to room looking for a distraction from her emptiness.

Many ladies can now afford to enjoy a gourmet meal in an exquisite restaurant, only to stare across the table at an empty place setting. It's a table for two, but there's only one there. They can take fantasy vacations to exotic locales or embark on relaxing cruises that they likely won for their outstanding performance at work, but there's no one to enjoy traveling with them. Instead of the men in their lives, these ladies are taking their sisters, their mothers, and their girlfriends.

The old punch line about all the good men being taken, gay, or incarcerated has taken on the ring of bitter truth. Compounding the problem, the socioeconomic gap between women and men continues to grow. To fill the void in their private lives, women have focused on their education, their careers, and their portfolio. Many men have not caught up to the successful corporate level of their female peers. Some had to drop out of school to support their siblings or children they fathered. Some prefer blue-collar jobs that don't require the education or social skills of the boardroom. Consequently, they often feel uncomfortable, even threatened by, the successful women they encounter.

More and more men and women are wearing emotional condoms and focusing more on protecting themselves from heartache than risking vulnerability for the hope of love. There are some dates, some on-line hookups, some internet chats, but there's no real intimacy. As Christians, we rightly tell our single women to wait until they are married to have sex, but then the painful reality is their waiting later and later in life to marry, and forfeiting the choice to bear children.

At a recent ceremony at our church, I was privileged to witness our youth pastor conduct an exchange of vows between young women and young men, ages twelve and higher, who were committing to remaining abstinent until marriage. Their parents and grandparents were present and shared the commitment to help their children remain pure. Each young woman or young man was given a purity ring which represented their promise before God to save the unique gift of their sexuality for their future spouse. They committed to not remove their promise ring until their wedding night when they would give it to their new groom or bride. It was a very moving service and brought tears to many who had seen their own lives shattered by premarital sex and its consequences.

But I wondered, how long would these young people have to wait for a loving, intimate relationship with a committed spouse? According to some experts on human physiology and sexuality, it's usually unhealthy for the human adult body not to engage in sexual stimulation. There seems to be biblical continuity here as the Apostle Paul said it was better to marry than to burn. But before you go out to celebrate the sexologists' conclusion, let me caution you that healthy physical stimulation can be overshadowed by unhealthy emotional involvement. If it's only sex, then it's not real intimacy. The intimacy that satisfies the soul is far deeper than the cravings of lust that satisfy the body.

I wholeheartedly agree that single men and women should wait. However, we—their friends and family—must question what has happened to romance and chivalry, intimacy and committed love. While many wait faithfully, love seems to be hiding from them and sex alone is no substitute. Is it any wonder so many people, even within our churches, do not keep their vow of purity to wait for sexual expression until they find true intimacy?

Also, sex in our culture is more and more objectified. Our reality TV shows that focus on millionaires and bachelors, dating games, and partner comparisons only reinforce a consumer mentality about sex and love. It's a headline in the latest political scandal, a punch line for a sitcom laugh track, an online act that frequently resembles a business transaction more than an outpouring of human passion and caring.

Equal Opportunity Lover

Instead of shopping for an ideal that doesn't exist, be willing to discover what it means to love another human being, flaws and all. Many women (and men) in our country would like to be in a healthy marriage. More and more men struggle to find women with whom they would like to share their lives. My fear is that both are missing each other, looking past each other at the next person coming through the door, rather than the person right in front of them. While women should never settle for someone, I often encourage the single ladies who ask me for advice to consider looking for men who *complement* their strengths rather than share them.

Ladies, you don't have to marry a man who's your equal in every way. The reality is that no one is totally anyone else's true equal. That's the beauty of relationships. If you have a lock but no key, then you can't enter into the shared space of intimacy.

Ladies, you must be willing to reconsider men that you may have dismissed because you saw them as beneath your level of success. It's okay if you're a doctor and he's a plumber. Remind yourself that you are not better than him just because you have more degrees. He's no better because he has more Allen wrenches than you! You are both needed to make a partnership work and run a healthy home. You can do the academic thing while he keeps the car running smoothly and the yard looking beautiful. He can cook and you can take care of the finances. You must allow yourself to meet at your points of need and strengths.

Gentlemen, you must be willing to accept the fact that she may make more money than you. She may be more educated, sophisticated, and refined. But that doesn't mean she's trying to turn you into her male clone. You should not be ashamed or feel threatened by her strengths because they will only make your own strengths sharper and stronger. Strong women are rarely attracted to weak men. They want a man who is confident enough in his own strength and masculine confidence to love her as a woman and respect her as an equal.

Telling Time

We must stop picking out people like we're shopping for a watch. I've counseled numerous professional athletes and celebrities who found themselves struggling in their marriages after their time on the playing field or movie screen had ended. When they were needing a beautiful partner on their arm along the sidelines or on the red carpet, their spouse fit the bill. But now that the limelight has faded and their relationship is about more than the next charity event and the designer clothes they'll wear, they find that there's nothing to hold them together.

There's no substance to the relationship. They had merely auditioned different men and women for the role of spouse and then cast the best-looking, most impressive applicant. If you're shopping for a watch and want to focus on how it looks and not how it keeps time, that's your choice. But if you go about looking for a life partner this way, you will always be disappointed. In moments of crisis, when sickness gnaws at you or your family, when hard times descend like a shroud over the finances, you need a watch that can tell time. You need someone you can count on. Love is more than a seasonal occupation.

Your friends and family, your peers and coworkers, may only reinforce selecting someone they think fits your life rather than someone you love and want to be with. I experienced this in my own field, in which it was assumed that a pastor would marry a musically gifted wife, one who could lead the choir, sing, play an instrument (usually the piano), or select the hymns and special music.

My wife did not match up to any of these. She loves music and has a beautiful voice but does not like to perform, does not play an instrument, and has no desire to organize or lead the choir. I even had some friends in the ministry who encouraged me to think twice before marrying her since they couldn't see what value she would add to my ministry.

At this point I had to ask myself, do I want to marry someone who fits my profession or my personhood? Does it make any difference how talented the woman is if I don't love her and want to share my life with her? I could marry someone who sings like

Aretha, plays piano like my grandmother, and writes songs like CeCe Winans, but if we couldn't share our private lives, our internal worlds, then it wouldn't matter what we shared on the platform. What works for us in public may not work at all in private.

I recently met a multicultural couple who had to overcome numerous obstacles to be together. He's an Indian who was raised Hindu, though a Christian now, while she's a Caribbean woman raised Pentecostal. Their family, food, religion, and culture are all different, but they grew to love each other and decided that this was the person with whom they wanted to share their life. Such differences cannot be ignored, but neither should they inhibit or limit you from being together. The other people in your life will always have something to say about anyone who varies from their preconceived notion of who is acceptable.

In Scripture, we're told that Moses faced a similar problem. "Then Miriam and Aaron spoke against Moses because of the Ethiopian woman whom he had married; for he had married an Ethiopian woman" (Numbers 12:1, NKJV). Even thousands of years ago, the pressure to marry the right person from a socially acceptable culture was great. Miriam becomes so outspoken of her sister-in-law that God struck her with leprosy. Moses' wife did not fit what Miriam thought the person married to her brother should be like.

It's striking to me that this is the first recorded instance of leprosy in the Bible. Since it's a disease that dismembers the body, was she afflicted with it because she was trying to dismember what God had joined together? People will frequently try to annul a union that works for you but doesn't work for them. For Moses, it was cultural but for us today it may be racial, financial, social, educational, or religious.

The Tenth Coin

A single person who longs for a heart's companion is like the woman described in the Bible who had ten coins and lost one. "Does she not light a lamp, sweep the house and search carefully until she finds it?" (Luke 15:8, NIV). In spite of the nine coins she still possessed, the woman did not stop until she swept her house and found her missing coin. You may have nine coins clearly and cleverly in your possession. You have the title, the job, the education, the home, the car, the clothes. You're at the top of your game professionally, but personally you do not have the coin for which you so desperately long.

In such a situation, it's tempting to think, "When I have these other areas going for me, why get hung up on a man? I have my nine coins, why look for a tenth?" It's because you know in your heart that the tenth makes your set complete. In other words, it can be tempting to try and compensate for what you don't have, but long for. I recommend that you be honest with yourself and don't try to pretend that you haven't lost a coin when you sense something is missing.

Many spend years sweeping their lives for the coin of lost love. And so often, as with most lost objects, it's right there—in church, at work, in the neighborhood, at the gym, or on the tennis court.

Be honest with yourself about wanting a relationship. No matter how successful, how large the house, how lucrative the business, whom will you come home to? What will you do when you retire and want to travel? Have you noticed those older couples holding hands and walking around the indoor perimeter of the shopping malls? Who will you walk beside when your hair is silver and your gait is slower?

It's a statistical fact that married people live longer. Numerous sources including annual university studies, U.S. Census findings, and institutions such as the American Association for Marriage and Family Therapy and the National Center for Health Statistics verify that married people are healthier, happier, and live longer than their single or widowed counterparts.

If you're missing your tenth coin and want it, don't ignore it or allow others to talk you out of it. Women who always travel in their girlfriends' gangs or who refuse to go out at all often miss opportunities to connect.

You can have a great apple seed, but if it's hidden on the shelf and not placed in the soil, then it will never grow and develop fruit. When you know what you want, are you in the right environment to find the kind of man you'd like to know? You don't fish for bass in salt water or go deep sea fishing in a pond. Take the risk to look around you and see where you need to be to find what, and whom, you are looking for. Again, we must remember to make the right affiliations if we want to facilitate the kinds of relationships we want to establish.

If you're already married or in a relationship, then your tenth coin may be creating the intimacy that's missing or enjoying the love that you once knew. Obviously, the more history you have with your spouse, the more joy as well as the more pain you've experienced. Whether it's conflict resolution or how to integrate the presence of children into your marriage, all relationships have growth areas that need pruning and fertilizing.

Dealing early with issues that often lead to divorce is essential if you are to make informed relationship decisions. I've devoted an entire chapter in this book to thinking through several crucial areas before you file the separation papers and sever the bond. My hope is that, like the woman who finds her tenth coin, you will be able to secure what's missing relationally in your life and make the necessary decisions to love boldly and passionately. "And when she finds it, she calls her friends and neighbors together and says, 'Rejoice with me; I have found my lost coin' " (Luke 15:9, NIV). If you go into a relationship knowing what you want, then you're much more likely to build a successful union before you decide to love.

seven
Before You Place
Your Love Order

"Love is like the measles. The older you get it, the worse the attack."

—*Rainer Maria Rilke*

Long before eBay, Overstock.com, Amazon, or Yahoo!, or any other search engine, shopping outlet, or online retailer, there was only one basic way to place your order. I'm talking about the good old days prior to HSN, QVC, or any of the multimedia options that emulate the mall shopping experience from the comfort of your home. Back in the day, the only malls were the mail orders we placed from the JCPenney and Spiegel catalogs.

My grandmother and yours lived with bated breath and deep anticipation as they waited for those colorful catalog pages to come to life as delivered by their neighborhood postman. It didn't matter whether you lived in the inner cities or on some back road with only a P.O. box at the country store, you still depended on your mail order catalogs. Such commerce was a huge convenience to those who lived in the most rural areas, but even urban dwellers in their cities relied on them to get what they needed. In our high-tech age of point and click shopping, identity theft, and spam, it's difficult to appreciate the days of the catalog ordering system. Yet for many decades, it was our primary way of finding what we wanted in the size we needed without leaving our homes.

Through this method, our families chose everything from wedding gowns to cookware, from saws to underwear. During the first half of the twentieth century, Sears and other retailers even offered mail order kits for houses! In our age of multitudinous offerings from which a consumer can select personalized options, we should remember the limited options from which we came. Prior generations had to select the details of their orders by looking at flat, one-dimensional pictures. Consequently, it was always a matter of faith when ordering from a catalog. To be sure, the pictures were inviting and the print descriptions as detailed as possible. Still, sometimes you received what you ordered but not what you wanted.

Male Order Catalogs

In the same way a picture doesn't tell you how a fabric feels or wears, how rich or muted a color can be, or whose size twelve we're talking about, dating doesn't always tell you what it will be like to be married. A résumé doesn't tell you what an employee's work ethic is like. A Facebook profile doesn't tell you how someone really looks, let alone how they will treat you after the first date is over. A real estate website won't show you the leaky pipes and the cracks in the ceiling in a home. Some details simply cannot be ascertained until you experience the fullness of the situation.

He may look perfect from his profile online. She might seem like your soul mate because of the incredible compatibility determined by your twenty-nine personality-trait tests. Online dating sites and community chat rooms have given a whole new dimension to male order! However, there is no substitute for the real thing. In fact, I have found that many people are excellent daters. They are so extremely proficient at dating that they are almost professionals. They know how to impress you really well for a night, a concert, or a weekend trip. But that doesn't mean that what you saw in the catalog is what you'll get in the mail!

HOW TO CHOOSE SOMEONE TO DATE

If you are currently dating, discerning whom you'd like to go out with should be an active choice. While physical attraction and appearance is likely the first thing we notice, looks soon fade. You want to choose someone who has other, less obvious attributes that go much further toward potentially contributing to a strong, lasting relationship. When you first meet someone, consider their manners, how they treat the restaurant waitstaff, what types of interests they have, if they share your spiritual beliefs, if they show interest in what you have to say. This will all go a long way in determining what kind of person they really are. I always note how people treat those they are not trying to impress.

Once the newness of initial attraction wears off, there must be something more to sustain a bond or the relationship is doomed. Also, make sure you are the chooser and not the chosen. Think about what you really want.

It is a common mistake, especially among some women, to compare the new beau to the last one and never really consider the person in his own light or in light of your wants. In other words, you may find John to be considerate where Joe was selfish and rude. So you make the mistake of thinking that John is better and he's the one. But then John is lazy and unfocused. So you break off with John and meet Al. Al is considerate and ambitious so you think, ah, nirvana, Al's the one. The mistake here is comparing John to Joe and Al to John, rather than comparing them to the vision you have for what you want from a relationship partner. Focus on the bigger picture and you will have a better chance of meeting someone who is more fully like what you want in a partner.

I can remember counseling a gentleman and his wife. He was deeply frustrated by his attempt to get her to be who she was when they were dating. In reality, he dated her when he was still involved with someone else. Okay, I will just say it: he started seeing her as the other woman while he was still married. They only had a few stolen hours, which they spent devouring each other emotionally, sexually, and intellectually. Their affair exhilarated their senses, and it was heightened by the ecstasy of tasting the sweet nectar of the forbidden fruit. She was his love goddess and he was her stud muffin. They were sure they knew all that there was to know about each other—at first.

They kept on going until his marriage totally dissipated and he had his satiny smooth seductress all to himself. That moment was the last he saw of a teddy, a negligee, or a garter belt. Instead he was inundated with flannel pajamas, wet stockings in the shower, and a barrage of bills he knew nothing about. Gone were the hot baths, the scented towels, and the chilled wine glasses. Instead, he was waking up to a coupon for buy-one-get-one-free Sausage McMuffin at McDonald's that he could snatch on the way to work. When they were dating she had reserved time for him, only showed herself with her hair done, put business on hold to be with him. But now that they were married, he had to try and fit her life into his and it felt like Cinderella's stepsister cramming her foot into the glass slipper. Not what he ordered in the catalog, was it?

You see, sometimes you get whom you wanted but you don't get it how you wanted it. He told me angrily, "I've been hoodwinked. She betrayed me. There's no real passion here, no sense of mystique and intrigue. She's not creative or romantic at all. She reminds me of my old wife."

He didn't know he had fallen in love with the *feeling of an affair,* but he had bought into a *marriage.* The two are not the same, and they will never be.

SATISFACTION WITH CURRENT RELATIONSHIP

In a committed relationship there are always seasons of change. You are closer at certain times than others as the circumstances of life ebb and flow. Yet, if you did your due diligence at the onset, were clear about what you wanted in a partner, and honestly assessed who that person is, what will keep your union strong going forward is recalling what brought the two of you together in the first place. What you enjoyed and admired about this person initially probably hasn't changed.

For a relationship to continue to evolve you must work to grow closer. If you feel your relationship is not what it once was, it could just be that it is evolving into something different. Or, it could be that you must renew your commitment to keeping it fresh and moving ahead. The fundamentals of your mate, if they were truly there in the beginning, aren't likely to change. The basis of your relationship is what's important, and focusing on that makes it much easier to go with the flow of the inevitable ups and downs of daily living.

More Than Skin Deep

Often this sexy society we live in trains us to represent our best seductive self for an evening or two. It shows us what colognes are hot, how to get perfect abs in four weeks, how to lose weight for the summer, and what vacation spots are filled with atmosphere and sensuality. We spend much money marketing sex and none marketing marriage.

And what we have given our attention to is what we are succeeding at becoming. We show men how to appear romantic, look interested, and be great conversationalists. We condition women to eradicate wrinkles, tighten the sags, and look like a model for the latest designer. We advertise face lifts and tummy tucks, Botox and Viagra, all to make us appear younger, more virile, and more attractive.

We don't teach the inevitable practicality of life. We are not on a date. Living is not a staged event. This is our life and who we share it with will see us as we really are. Not as we appear to be. She may be sixty and look like thirty, but when you're married to her, you will still be married to a sixty-year-old woman who thinks like, aches like, and socially processes like the woman she is, not the one she projects.

Consider how different dating is from marriage. Dating may show you how he holds a fork or what she likes to drink. But it doesn't tell you how they pay their bills or how they move in a crisis. Like gifted actors in their favorite roles, many people are better at dating than they are at marriage. They can even live with you and you still don't get the real impact of what it is like when they are locked down to the commitment of marriage and the various nuances of becoming a family unit.

They know what to do to make you have a stunning evening: which restaurant, what Broadway shows, and how to be a great conversationalist for a few hours. But when one gets down to the business of marriage—who balances the checkbook; who comes first, his mother or you; what matters most to her, the career or the children—dating doesn't always show you what you get when you marry. I cannot tell you how many women and men I've counseled who married people who were professional daters but not marriage material!

At first, all some people want is a person who can rattle the headboard, but eventually you will need someone who can pay for the bed! Since baby boomers are living longer, the dating game isn't just for kids anymore. Just For Men hair color has taken away the gray, chiropractors have adjusted the back, Cialis has adjusted the libido, and now he is back in the game. She has her porcelain teeth implants, her breasts lifted, her tummy tucked, her hips inflated, and her lips done. We all look great. We are all out there again, back in the game armed with condoms and living in condos. The jet-setters are from every age and every stage.

Yet no matter how many accessories, treatments, or accoutrements we use, it's not enough. We are dating again but we are no longer intimate. We are having sex but losing love. Both old and young are shopping for love but settling for lust. They place their orders for the custom-made combination package, but when it arrives it doesn't satisfy them.

If you can remember what you really wanted, if you still long for substance more than style, I want to share a few considerations for getting what you order and liking what life delivers.

The Art of Listening

We tell couples they need to talk, but we forget to instruct them on how to listen. And not just how to listen to each other, but how to listen to self. Somewhere in the fine print of meeting, dating, and interacting with someone, they warned you ever so slightly that they were going to be a certain way. The red flags were always there, even if they started out in a lovely shade of pink. You saw how he went into a rage on the highway. You knew she was always late when you came to pick her up for dinner. He went into a panic checking every line item on the bill from the restaurant. She flirted with the waiter and anyone else who looked her way.

All of this was forgotten in the soft embrace and moist kiss of that special someone. You noticed but didn't listen to the voice inside. And as Maya Angelou says, when someone tells you who they are, believe them. Most people don't listen before, during, or after the marriage. Believe me, before you order something the fine print is what you must read to know if you can afford the payments.

The fine print was readable at his family reunion when you saw his environment and how his family interacts with each other, or doesn't. It was in the way his eyes lingered on every woman walking down Fifth Avenue. It was in every phone call she takes outside. Was that some woman screaming at him outside the mall as you approached him for your meeting? Didn't she look like she was pregnant? When you asked who that was, he dismissed her as an acquaintance from work. You knew better, but you weren't listening, were you?

One of my young parishioners told me that she should have noticed what was going on when he started telling her what to wear on every date. And in a couple of months, he was telling her what to wear to school. All of this was a precursor to him snatching her at the high school football game. Distracted by his jersey and car, the young woman made excuses for his controlling ways and escalating temper. He was warning her he was a controller and apt to be an abuser, but she wasn't listening. He didn't do it overtly enough to expose the real product she would be purchasing, but it was there in the fine print. In retrospect she said, "Pastor, I can see it now. I wasn't looking for what didn't work. I was looking for what did work. His birthday was on the tenth, and, guess what, mine was too. His mother's middle name was Helen, and my grandmother's first name was Helen. His favorite band was already on my iPod. We had so much in common, or did we?"

Isn't it funny how people often major on the minor and then minor on the major? They seem blinded to the warning signs that could have circumvented a bad choice. Those who have turned a deaf ear to the warning, miss the glaring issue that eventually leads to the demise of the deeper more fulfilling relationship we desperately want and need. The glaring issue will vary with the person and the relationship, but it is often an issue of possessiveness, jealousy, conflict management, or communication that becomes insurmountable.

This young woman was standing there with bruised ribs and a black eye, telling me that she ended up with more than the envy of her senior class. He was a prize athlete and a real looker. He had a car and he could dance like Emmitt Smith. She won out over all the other girls. She got what she wanted, the dream item in her catalog. But she didn't read the small print, and until the inferno raged around her, she failed to listen to the warning signs going off like a smoke alarm. You say she did it because she was young. I say it happens to women her mother's age and her grandmother's age.

And men, too. She did it because she was deaf to the warming signs and blind to the fine print. There is no age limit on regret. It can happen to anyone who doesn't think before doing.

The Sound of Hope

Some women ignore the signs not because she's deaf to them but because she thinks she can change her partner. Her maternal instincts misfire and she thinks he needs babying in order to become a grown man. Not going to happen, dear. If he had an issue before you met him, you cannot assume the role of savior and try to be his redemption. Nor do you want to try out for the role of his mother. If you succeed, your love life will be incestuous. If he marries you because you're like his mother, then he'll cheat on you with his girlfriend because men never want to be married to their mothers.

I have seen women take men on as a project. She wants to fix him, thinks she understands him, and anyone who tries to tell her otherwise is wrong. They just don't understand him the way she does. A man will change when he has the right woman, won't he? Not likely, my dear.

This ideology of changing after marriage is a fallacy. It comes from an unknowing God complex wherein we start wanting to be someone's redeemer. But we are not, nor can we ever be, God to someone else.

"Oh, no, that's not me, Bishop. I would never try to be God in his life."

I hear you and I want you to understand where your desire to change him comes from. When you have a "need-to-be-needed" complex, you allow that need to influence your choice. Often the more people try to warn you, the less you listen to them. All they succeed in doing is to create a perfect storm. Their criticism just makes it perfect for you to feel that they really don't understand your choice, and it creates a perfect environment for the "us against the world" dynamic. How romantic is that? It's absolutely perfect. It's the stuff of cable TV movies and Harlequin romances. Forbidden love coupled with a few "he-needs-me"s and there you have it—total deafness!

This process happens without your even knowing that you have allowed the need-to-be-needed impulse to take over your decision-making process. Once you're in the throes of the storm's aftermath, you have to figure out, "how did someone like me end up with someone like him?" You had a hope of changing him into what you wanted. The hope was fed by testimonials from people who have experienced massive change through their marriages. But the difference is that the power to change must come from *within* the person, not from you.

If others saw a change in their spouse, it wasn't coming from their influence on their spouse. It came from within the person who changed; that person desired to change. When you try to change your spouse, it doesn't work, and eventually even the hope for change makes you sick. "Hope deferred maketh the heart sick: but when the desire cometh, it is a tree of life" (Proverbs 13:12, KJV).

Hope makes you ill when you keep waiting to see something change and it doesn't happen. You end up sick of waiting for something that isn't happening, sick of envisioning something that never materializes, sick of making lame excuses for what is not working even as it becomes increasingly obvious to those around you. It's not that your intuition isn't working properly. It's not that the warning signs weren't there. Your spouse did not change overnight from Dr. Jekyll to Mr. Hyde. It's that we turn a deaf ear to the obvious, because we want to believe that we can change our order into what we thought we were getting and not what we got.

Sound relationship decisions are not based on hope.

Now add in the fact that people of faith often try to spiritualize every issue. In the name of faith, we often dumb down our instincts and ignore our senses. That is not having faith in God. Faith in God should be just that, faith in God. We must not place our faith in men and women. They will fail us. God gives all of us a will and doesn't force us to change. God gives us the grace to change if we so choose. Change must come from within each of us as we accept the grace God repeatedly extends to each of us.

Leave the salvation of people to God. It will help you so much if you do not pervert the romantic into the redemptive. If the sanctified wife sanctifies the husband, she does it by her life and not her words. ". . . If any of them do not believe the word, they may be won over without words by the behavior of their wives, when they see the purity and reverence of your lives" (1 Peter 3:1–2, NIV). Real hope sounds like actions speaking louder than words.

You aren't looking for a son, a cause, or a charitable situation. You want a man who is a man, flawed but still a man. You want a lady who's a woman, imperfect but a lady just the same. When you place your order you must read the fine print and pay attention to the product description.

Before you commit to keeping an order that is not the right fit for you, not what you thought it was, you must make sure that you're processing all the data and listening to your gut. You must not mistake yourself for God in someone else's life. You must allow the Almighty to work in yours, and to work in the other person's. When you really listen and think things through, you're much more likely to know what you're getting and to enjoy keeping your order, before you do.

eight
Before You Commit— Research

"Gravitation is not responsible for people falling in love."

—*Albert Einstein*

Whenever I happen to be in some of the large retail juggernauts known as box stores, I'm always amazed at the plethora of products that line the shelves. It seems that the options, variations, and offerings only continue to multiply for consumers. When I see the forty-eight varieties of mustard or the latest flat-screen, Blu-ray, Super HDTV, I always wonder how the companies behind them make the decisions that determine the specifications of their products.

Maybe you've had a similar experience. Perhaps you realized the need for a new product—say a cleaner that you could use on your granite countertops without scratching them—only to find it on your next trip to the store. You're wheeling your shopping cart down the aisle, and the next thing you know there it is: NEW SAFESTONE—CLEANS YOUR GRANITE COUNTERTOPS WITHOUT SCRATCHING! It was almost like someone read your mind!

Have you ever wondered why some of the medication you take for various conditions is so astronomically expensive? Some pills I've taken would cost as much as $100 each if I had to pay out of pocket and did not have coverage from my medical insurance carrier. It's amazing to think that something so tiny could carry such a large price tag!

The reason for both occurrences—the new cleaning product you had been wishing for and the high cost of your medication—stems from what corporate leaders refer to as research and development, or R&D for short. In order to know their target audience, the habits and preferences of their consumers, when and where they shop, what problems to fix with old products and what a customer needs to meet with the new, companies spend vast amounts of money each year conducting research, and then developing new products. Obviously, this cost gets factored in to the price of the product, but R&D is considered fundamental if the company is serious about protecting its core business and anticipating trends that will help the corporation break through to the next level of fiscal success.

Pharmaceutical companies sometimes spend billions of dollars to develop new drugs to treat a given disease, condition, or injury. Sometimes they have to spend years in the lab creating new molecular entities, not to mention testing the rate of success versus failure, then in the federal approval process, and finally on production. The Congressional Budget Office Study in October 2006, "Research and Development in the Pharmaceutical Industry" estimated "the average cost of developing an innovative new drug at more than $800 million." You can see why research and development is crucial in the pharmaceutical industry; lives, and quality of lives, is at stake.

But how much research and development have you put into the decisions you make? Particularly the decisions with lifelong ripples such as your relationships? Have you conducted adequate research into verifying the character of your beloved to make sure that he is who he says he is? Have you spent enough time conducting the little tests of compatibility that are essential if you are to commit and spend a lifetime with this person? How much insight have you developed from your research?

New Product Development

It seems nearly impossible to imagine taking a medication that had never been tested, never been studied, never been approved by reputable scientific scrutiny. It's similarly difficult to imagine launching a new product from your company's warehouse without doing any kind of market research into who this product will appeal. Can you imagine allowing your child to take a little blue pill about which you know nothing? Would you purchase a new sports coupe from an automotive maker you've never heard of? Better yet, would you purchase that car without a test drive? Most of us would never take an untested drug or purchase an unfamiliar vehicle, and yet we often remain embarrassed about asking the questions that will determine whether we should spend our precious time with someone whose goals and objectives may not be harmonious with our own.

Now I know that this isn't first or second date conversation, but as things heat up, you might consider adding new dimensions

to your discussions. As you grapple with the possibility of investing your years with someone whom you know in only one dimension, please allow me to guide you to learn what is below the surface
of your prospective partner. You may not feel able to ask the hard
questions or observe with a critical eye these areas that I will share
here, but it must be done. Consider it new product development
that is necessary to avoid repeating your own past mistakes, as well
as the other person's.

You would not entrust your child into the hands of a baby sit-
ter without first knowing something of the person's background,
reliability, training, and experience. Similarly, you must not entrust
your heart—not to mention your resources of time and money—to
someone without first ascertaining their suitability. Many people
do not ask questions or examine the other person critically because
they are so afraid of offending the person or losing the chance at a
relationship. Such a fear conveys a sense of "you're doing me such
a favor to be interested in me that I must take you on any terms." If
you proceed like this, however, you will have to live off the welfare
of codependency and the food stamps of their affection!

So many fearful, even desperate, people go into the partnership of a lifetime with virtually no important information or objective data. They commit to driving down their life's highway with
the circulation to their brain cut off by the blindfold they wear so
tightly. Blindness is a terrible handicap, and self-imposed sight-
lessness is even worse. If there's one deficiency that Jesus healed
more than any other, according to the Bible, it would be blindness.
Nothing leaves us more vulnerable than not to be able to see. Yet I
witness countless people moving into ultra-important relationships with no real insight into the person to whom they're committing.

By the time they work up their nerve to ask the hard questions, they are already married and often in the midst of some crisis. Often these very sincere and loveworthy people are left with a deep sense of regret. As it is in business, one must always ask the hard questions up front. Once the contract is signed, there's no room for negotiation!

Similarly, it is hard to resolve a personal conflict when you didn't do the hard work of research and development before you committed. Four areas of research are critical in really knowing the person you think you know. (In the next chapter, we'll turn our research into development and focus on how to use the data of a person's past to predict your future relationship in four critical areas.) Put on your lab coat and bring your microscope and let's get started!

EXPECTATION: Buyer Beware

The place to begin your research starts at home. Before you can begin to scrutinize the other person, you must recognize your own limitations and motivations for the relationship. Jesus asks us, "Why do you look at the speck of sawdust in your brother's eye and pay no attention to the plank in your own eye?" (Matthew 7:3, NIV). In other words, we must consider how we see ourselves before we can look closely at the other person in our life.

Self-image has so much to do with effective communication. When you see yourself as valuable enough to deserve love and attention from the other person, then you form a boundary that you will not compromise. If this foundation of self-worth is not in place, then you become so grateful for any kind of love that you ignore the price. When this occurs, it's easy to make yourself a victim because you ignore warnings, overlook concerns, and deny reality. In many ways we end up getting what we deserve in relationships to which we have not applied the old adage, "caveat emptor"—buyer beware.

Oblivious to obvious issues, we often choose to live with blinders on rather than to confront the truth. A little self-esteem goes a long way in garnering the courage to ask and answer questions that reveal who you really are and what you really want. I know you don't want to be seen as arrogant—nor do I—but we are all interested in remaining confident. Open your mouth wide, take a deep breath and start the process. Do not sulk in silence and secretly ponder issues that could be resolved by stepping up to the plate and asking, "why?"

You don't want to be like Carlos, a friend of mine whom I counsel from time to time. Like many men, he is unable to commit and finds it difficult to communicate with women beyond superficial subjects. He lacks the will power and courage to engage in a long-lasting relationship. Rather than determining what he wants, he would rather leave them guessing and then disqualify them because they cannot fulfill an expectation that was never discussed. Carlos tends to disqualify the women he dates without them even knowing why or what he wanted.

Since most of us follow familiar patterns and similar scripts, I was not surprised to see his trail of self-sabotage emerge like billboards along the interstate as he described his past relationships. I pointed out to him that by not having open, serious communication but holding on to inner doubt instead, he had subconsciously set himself up for failure. Carlos would never really get down to the hard work of qualifying his interest by seriously looking into what it took for this relationship to grow from puppy love to a full-grown, healthy commitment. He had been in and out of multiple relationships, falling out with each woman over trivial objections. He thought it was them, thought they were just not up to his high standards, but his pattern of past practice said it was, in fact, something to do with him.

Can you relate to my friend Carlos? Do you have blind spots that tend to obscure the view of your prospective partner, either tarnishing them with your own fears or else painting a glossy veneer on a rough surface? So much depends on the expectations you set based on your own self-awareness. Once you look realistically at who you really are and what you desire in a healthy relationship, then you're ready to let the fun begin with our three other areas of research—interrogation, observation, and investigation.

INTERROGATION: Twenty Questions

Perhaps no aspect of dating is more important than asking the right questions. From how he views his relationship with his family to how she feels about having children, the answers to some questions form the "Constitution" that will determine the strength of your union after the fireworks of marriage have long subsided. These questions are so important that I have devoted an entire chapter to the twenty most important questions you must answer before you marry. These questions should be kept in mind as ones that must be addressed directly—not just in vague, polite, ambiguous terms—if you are going to commit to someone, entrusting your heart, your health, and your happiness to their care. You will find them in chapter ten.

Usually, natural opportunities arise to allow such inquiries, but even if they do not, you must still find a time and place to ask your questions. If necessary, you should create your own opportunity and make a date to cover some of the more difficult questions of a personal nature. Remember, you don't have to do all of this in one evening. Over time, using my guidelines here to assist you, develop your own comprehensive list of questions that you deem most important.

Then meet for a cup of coffee or a casual lunch and tell your date ahead of time that you have some things you want to discuss. It doesn't have to be a heavy time of police grilling, but it should be deliberate on your part in order to ascertain the vital information you need to know before you decide to proceed with dating this person exclusively.

Aside from the answers the other person gives, their approach to the entire process of communicating about personal areas can be very telling. Does their response sound rehearsed? More canned than a campaign speech from a politician? Then they have likely prepared this answer and given it before. Try to get beyond their rehearsed response and listen to their real message. Are they being resistant to your line of inquiry? Defensive? Eager to answer as well as to hear your response as well?

Often in my own conversations, particularly before our discussion has ended, I will say, "Let me tell you what I heard so I can see if that is what you meant." I am shocked at how many times I hear something totally different from what is intended! This interaction alone can open up a richer line of communication between us.

When asking serious questions or broaching important areas of concern, your demeanor should be one of a student wanting to know more about a subject of great interest. It shouldn't feel like an interrogation, a condemnation, or an indictment. It should provide a way to gain some insight into the heart and mind of someone you're seriously pursuing. Aside from gaining facts, you are also learning how to communicate with someone important to you, a critical skill for building a long-standing, happy relationship.

Improving communication also emerges in the art of translation. Basically, you are learning his or her language. We all use the same words but have a different language when it comes to love. What you mean when you say, "I need someone to be there for me" may not be what I mean when I say, "I will be there for you." You want to learn each other's language without prior assumptions and inaccurate projections weighing you down.

Such relational literacy will serve you well for years to come and will prevent your treating her like she is you in a different form or thinking that he is just like your best girlfriend. We all need to love and be loved but use different means of expression to communicate our desires. Don't be afraid to check terms and compare definitions. These exchanges can provide enjoyable bantering and don't have to feel like a tooth extraction!

The process of interrogation, as in all of these areas, is not simply one conversation where you go down your list and check them off one by one. Feeling the freedom to ask your questions and to answer someone else honestly forms a crucial foundation for how you will communicate moving forward. Particularly in the area of conflict resolution, the process of inquiry must be a nondefensive exchange of ideas and emotions to facilitate a shared understanding of what you both desire most.

RESEARCH IN LONG-TERM RELATIONSHIPS

If your present relationship has lasted for a long time, then you likely think you know the person very well. You've had long and heartfelt conversations about their family, their financial and physical health, their likes and dislikes, and their past relationships. But it is a good idea, as you date, to continue to have these discussions on a regular basis as you move forward in your relationship. As your union be-

comes more serious the stakes get higher, and expressing your expectations as well as understanding theirs becomes increasingly
important.

OBSERVATION: X-ray Vision

Earlier I mentioned the dangers of being emotionally blind. If you
are to make an informed decision about committing your life to
someone, you must open your eyes along with all your senses to see
the other person. Justice may be blind but make sure your love has
contacts on! You want to see what he or she is saying beyond their
words. You want to develop X-ray vision so that you can learn to
read their motives through their mannerisms.

As the other person responds to your interrogation, keep in
mind that their answers are formed by more than their words. Ascertaining their real motives and the extent of their intentions requires paying close attention. It doesn't always mean that your
intended is deceitful. Many times we are not good at talking about
our deepest selves. We spend all of our lives having to be guarded.
It isn't always easy to disrobe emotionally or mentally with someone we are trying to impress.

Ladies, you must be deductive as you piece together the clues
that he gives you about who he really is and what he's really after.
Men, you must add up the information she gives you through her
body language and what she leaves unsaid in order to know her
character and not just her beautiful appearance. I recommend that
every conversation be enjoyed and then mentally reviewed again
with an option to revisit areas where you still have some uncertainty. That's right, when in doubt, bring it up again!

This area of scrutiny should not be difficult if you are naturally
fascinated by the other person. Simply pay attention—observe ev-

erything and not just what you want to see or what you want to hear. Observe how he treats people he doesn't need in his life, the casual encounters with waitresses, doormen, cab drivers, and ushers at the concert. Consider how loyal she is to her friends, how cruel she is to her enemies, and how familiar with her former boyfriends. Remember, getting to know a person is a lot more than knowing how they treat you. You may not always be on her A list. How would you be treated if you were demoted? This shows the real character of the person you are interested in knowing better.

How committed is the other person to keeping their word? Do they make promises and then don't follow through? Are they quick to make excuses rather than simply take responsibility for a mistake, misunderstanding, or misperception? Notice the patterns that tend to form the longer we get to know someone. If he can't be trusted to meet you on time consistently, then how can he be trusted to be at home on time later? If she tells you that she purchases items that she can't afford, are you listening to her priorities?

Real observation feeds your intuition, providing you with the data that will naturally be processed and interpreted in light of everything else you know about the person. You must watch and not merely pray about your sweetie. If you're going to mix your genes with this person, sharing the most intimate, vulnerable parts of yourself, both literally and figuratively, then don't you think you should pay attention? Stop. Look. Listen. It's not just the children's mantra about how to cross the street. It's the formula for a wise decision about how to proceed across the heart highway to your next decision about a life partner.

SURPRISES

As your relationship grows you will likely have some surprises. We all put our best foot forward when we begin to date, but as we grow comfortable, we are less defensive and apt to be more of our true selves. Honest, trustworthy people, who are ready for a committed relationship, understand that they have nothing to hide. When asking questions of your dates, pay careful attention to their body language and how they respond. Giving defensive and evasive answers, sitting cross armed and failing to make eye contact are all signs that someone isn't being 100 percent truthful. If you notice this behavior during discussions, take note and proceed with caution.

Transparency between partners while dating saves you from major surprises and upsets after marriage. But, it is important that when doing research on a potential mate, to always consider the source of your information. Of course, if the information appears in a major newspaper, it is likely to be true, but if the information is coming from an angry or vindictive ex, take what you learn with a grain of salt, go back to your partner for verification, and look for signals of truth or fallacy.

INVESTIGATION: Private Eyes

You may feel like a snoop, a spy, or a private detective, but you must do the due diligence to find out all you can about your prospective partner's past, present, and future. Casually ask around to those who know them in different roles. Do some Internet research on the person and don't be afraid to Google them. I recall one woman who told me that she accidentally discovered that her fiancé had been married three times before, without telling her about any of these past unions. She stumbled on the information online and was so grateful for the conversation that emerged when she confronted him. She only wished she had thought to be more deliberate about researching him prior to their engagement.

In our age of nanotechnology, you have access to more information than our grandparents ever dreamed of having. You can know whether she was arrested for shoplifting, declared bankruptcy, or won a scholarship. You can tell if he really competed on his college football team, graduated magna cum laude, or ever finalized his divorce. It's public information, not illegal or immoral or unethical, and the other person is likely doing the same research on you.

If you find information that disturbs you, then ask them about it. Perhaps give them a natural opportunity to inform you themselves. You shouldn't expect to know everything about everyone on the first date. In fact, be wary of those who seem totally transparent from your first conversation. Often they do not have strong boundaries and will tell a total stranger their most intimate secrets. But if you're concerned about a discrepancy between what they've told you and what you've discovered from another source, then you must determine the truth. More times than not, if it looks like a duck and it quacks like a duck then it explains why you're in a pond with your date!

Other forms of investigation require a journalistic standard of information: interviewing informed sources about the subject. While you do not want to interrogate the family, it is important to get to know them. The family, friends, and colleagues have vital information as to how he or she thinks or operates that is very important for you.

Be wary if the person only introduces you to friends that they have only known for a short time. Meet people who have known them throughout different seasons of their lives; this will give you a clearer sense of their character.

Ask to see the places where she grew up, the areas that are her favorites, where she spent her childhood. Try to get a read on his family's culture. Every family has issues; there are no perfect families. But as you get closer, you need to have some idea what kind of family you are marrying into.

Physical health issues may be difficult, but they are oh-so-essential to discuss. What about his health and genetic background? Are there serious issues that will come up if you two decide to have children? Many families have emotional issues and anxieties that may not stop you from committing but will provide you with a greater understanding of what's required to honor your vows.

Fiscal health is an equally essential area of foundational understanding. What's her attitude toward money? More important than how much she has or doesn't have, the issue is her tendency to be frugal, generous, future-oriented or present-minded. What are you willing to go in debt to share? What are you willing to save for? What does the other person's current budget look like?

Investigating your potential spouse may feel uncomfortable but cannot be overlooked. Remember, this isn't a secret agent's agenda or a hired detective digging for dirt. You should let them know, "I'm excited about our affection, but I do want and need to know you better." They will respect you if you avoid being sneaky. Be forthright and honest instead. When you do the research necessary to really know someone prior to marriage, then you become free to enjoy the relationship before you say, "I do."

nine
Before You Commit— Development

"Love is blind, but marriage restores its sight."
—*Georg C. Lichtenberg*

In the prior chapter we explored the process of Research and Development, that virtually all companies use to investigate their market and its consumer needs. As we've seen, the research component is essential in providing you with an in-depth look at the person you're considering as a possible life partner. After you've gathered data, gotten answers to your questions, and reached some measure of understanding of who the other person really is, then you are ready to implement the next phase of your relationship assessment—the development of what it will take for you as a couple to make it for the long haul.

It's not enough to know the other person, you must anticipate areas of compatibility that will determine your satisfaction for the remaining years of your life. You must develop the relationship dynamics into anchor points for building a house that can withstand the inevitable storms that life brings. Four crucial areas must be developed—preparation, desperation, stimulation, and celebration.

Depending on your personality, season of life, and relational needs, you may prioritize some areas of development higher than others. All areas need to be included in your process of relational maturation before you commit, and however you prioritize them is fine, as long as you enter into the relationship with your eyes wide open. For example, know that your need for stimulation may also come with a high price tag of daily drama from your mate.

RESEARCH AND DEVELOPMENT
ARE EQUALLY IMPORTANT

Both development and research are important to keep growing and moving forward as a couple.

RESEARCH WHO YOUR PARTNER IS	FOCUS ON AREAS OF DEVELOPMENT
expectation	preparation
interrogation	desperation
observation	stimulation
investigation	celebration

PREPARATION: Proactive Planning

A promise that shows no sign of preparation isn't much of a promise. If you really feel that this relationship is escalating, you should be able to see some preparation in place for what is next. If the person's prep doesn't match up with their plans, you either have someone who isn't much of a planner and tends to be totally spontaneous (which may make for a great date but a horrible marriage) or they lack the ability to be strategic. This is okay as long as you can live with it and know about it going into the relationship.

Most think of economic preparation, but that is only one element. You must ask questions that will reveal the other person's ability to anticipate both issues and solutions before they arise. These kinds of questions show you their preparation levels and will help you know what's important to them: "Where do you see yourself ten years from now?" "If we got married, have you given much thought to where we would live?"

Also, is the person emotionally and psychologically ready to commit? Can they work through issues and conflicts that naturally arise in even the best of relationships? Mental preparation is just as paramount as financial, physical, and emotional groundwork. If families will need to be blended, then the future impact on each family member must be considered. Introductions and conversations will need to happen over time and not in one atomic-bomb revelation. Three-dimensional preparation—understanding the past, maximizing the present, and anticipating the future—is the key to successful, lasting relationships.

PREPARATION

Just as preparation is a key to success in any professional venture, so it is true for personal relationships. It's like taking any trip or journey. Say you and your partner are taking a road trip to the coast. It's a seven hour, three-hundred-fifty-mile drive and you've never been there before. You'll need maps, perhaps snacks, and maybe a packed lunch, water, and your favorite music for the drive. You'll have to make sure the car has enough gas and that you have money for gas along the way, blankets in case you want to picnic. It's a beach trip so you'll need to take sunscreen, your bathing suits, and light-weight, casual clothing for dinner out on the pier. You have to arrange for the cat to be fed while you are away and get permission from your boss to take the time off from work. If you don't consider these issues, you'll arrive at your destination and spend more time and money buying the things you need than you will relaxing and enjoying the sun and the sand. Worse, neglect to bring maps or fill up the gas tank and you may find yourself either lost or out of gas.

At first glance, like a trip to the beach, relationships seem easy and all fun at first. But considering the preparation it takes for just a trip to the beach, and it's clear that relationships meant for the long haul require a great deal of preparation to last.

DESPERATION: Giving and Taking

Desperate times call for desperate measures, as the old adage reminds us. But you don't want to find yourself mired in a quicksand of someone else's desperation. Many times desperate people were desperate before they met you. Their pursuit of you may be influenced by their age or by a need for validation or maybe they want to get their citizenship through marriage! Whatever may influence their motives, you must watch out for desperate people. They do the right thing but for the wrong reason.

Many women or men who discuss marriage on the first or second date come off as desperate. Some say they want to disqualify anyone who isn't headed in a serious direction, which I can appreciate, but bringing up the topic before you barely know the other person waves a red flag, not a white bridal gown. A man wants to find someone who's in love with him, not with the idea of being married!

People are often married to share expenses or to get help with parenting. But what happens when the economics change or the children grow up? Nothing is left to hold them together. You must determine if this person with whom you're considering spending the rest of your life is a whole person already or a fraction looking for someone else to complete them.

One of the real problems here is that we often become involved with a person who is fixed on what they need and have given little to no thought about what they bring. We call them lovers but they are really lusters, takers and not givers. Lust is focused inward, on self-gratification at every level, while love is focused on the other person, on the well-being of your relationship. You cannot be a desperate giver but you can be a desperate taker!

The famous line from the movie *Jerry McGuire*, "You complete me," has always struck me as a little too sentimental and immature. The Almighty created each of us to be complete in the divine image, secure in our identity as God's child. Marriage is not a fifty-fifty deal. It is a one hundred–one hundred deal, requiring both partners to contribute 100 percent of all they bring. Instead of complete-ment, we should focus on someone who complements what we bring, even as we enhance their strengths and compensate for their areas of need. Marriage is creating a union that is stronger than the individuals.

DESPERATION IS A RED FLAG

If you've ever found yourself feeling desperate in a relationship, you probably know now that emotionally you were not at your very best.

Desperation can manifest itself in many forms. You think about your beloved constantly, wondering where they are, what they are doing and when you will see them again. You cease to have an existence of your own, stop calling your friends, dropping everything to run to their side whenever they call. When your partner is happy, you are happy. When your partner is miserable, you are miserable. You have no identity of your own, and your entire existence is wrapped up in your relationship, while nothing else in your life matters.

Having someone want you, who has no interests or life of their own, who calls day and night, and makes you the center of their life 24/7, might seem appealing at first, but it should be a red flag that perhaps they have some holes in their psyche or existence that they are looking to you to fill. Ignoring these situations can become annoying at the very least and at worst can become dangerous.

STIMULATION: Level of Engagement

One of the most overlooked areas to consider in any relationship is stimulation. I'm not talking about the fluttering of the butterflies in your stomach when the other person enters the room. Nor am I talking about their ability to cause a physical reaction in your body or sexual stimulation. The kind of stimulation I have in mind emerges from their ability to engage your mind, excite your emotions, and ignite your imagination on a wide range of life topics.

More marriages die of boredom than any other malady. More partners engage in an affair or become addicted to porn or some other deviant habit because they are bored in their marriages. It's certainly no excuse for such wrongdoing, but boredom works like a low-grade poison that takes its inevitable toll on each of you.

In my travels, I frequently see couples in restaurants totally annoyed with the other's presence. He's buried in his newspaper while she works a crossword puzzle or talks on her cell. They might as well be alone for the way they regard the presence of their significant other. They have become resigned to the boring, predictable routines that now drain the life from them both.

As time passes and the years go by, you will become intimately acquainted with each other's ways to the point of predictability. However, the secret to any relationship is finding ways to keep improving yourself and then bringing that to the table of your relationship. Reading so you can be conversational. Learning something about his or her career field. Caring about the details of their day. When you're engaged by the other person's life, you reinforce their desire to share more about their day and who they are. If you're going to marry an NFL football player, you must know something about sports or you end up being a trophy wife. If your wife works in the music industry, you want to know something about sound equipment or music contracts or something that makes you relevant in her world.

It's also important that you have a life outside of the person you are interested in. Partners who want to grow together know that they must encourage each other to cultivate friendships, interests, and hobbies independently. These people, when brought back together at the end of the day, have so much more to talk about, so much to share. They are stimulating people; they stimulate each other. They must also know how to develop their own lives without ever losing sight of the shared life you have together.

Can you have a disagreement on politics that leaves you both energized and not defeated? Are you willing to read a new novel together and discuss your reaction to the main character's dilemma? Does he encourage you to start that new business you've always dreamed about or does he quench the smoldering ember of hope with his pessimism disguised as realism? Does she encourage you to take that weekend fishing trip with the boys, trusting you to enjoy the great outdoors without her?

Lifelong learning and strident stimulation are the hallmarks of a healthy relationship that can go the distance. Keep in mind that the person you marry will be there longer than you can imagine. Long after the intensity of sexual attraction has worn thin, long after the immediate commonalities of your current life season, long after the kids have moved out and you're left facing each other in the silence of an empty house, you must stimulate each other to grow and enjoy all that life has to offer.

MENTAL STIMULATION

One of the most important components to a successful relationship is communication. The ability to respectfully and honestly discuss issues with your partner is one of the keys to a long-lasting union. Couples who have been married for a long time often remark that one of the things that signaled that something special might unfold between them was their ability to have long stimulating conversations about everything under the sun. Others say that no matter how long they've known each other, they are always learning new things about the other. Staying interested in life and maintaining hobbies and activities that are important to you outside of your relationship make you an interesting person to come home to. Further, sharing interests such as reading, theater, sports, or charitable work can work to bring you closer together and offer other topics for good discussion.

CELEBRATION: Gifts of Comfort

Finally, you must discover your ability to celebrate and be celebrated by the other person in your life. There must be room in your relationship for feeling good and enjoying each other on a daily basis. This is usually easy to do in the early stages of the relationship when the bouquet of roses are delivered to your desk after lunch or when she surprises you with candles and your favorite R and B music back at her place. But over time, as the novelty wears off and the boredom threatens to set in, you need to know how the other person faces the gifts that each day and each season provides.

You must ask yourself what the other person gives to you and how they give it. Are there conditions and expectations with their words of encouragement? What do they want in return for that lovely Cartier watch? If gifts are given conditionally, then you might as well buy them for yourself, because the interest payments will be much more affordable!

Like most people, I want to be where I'm celebrated and not just tolerated. In order to discern the difference, we must pay attention to what the other person celebrates. Do they remember birthdays? What is their attitude regarding the quality of everyday life? Do they notice the sunsets, the smell of spring in the air, or the laughter of a child skipping rope on the sidewalk? Are they more of a pessimist or a realist? And don't think for a moment that pessimists are always the negative, bitter, depressed people. I've seen many cheerful, upbeat, happy-go-lucky-type people who worked hard to mask their anger and pessimism through the façade of a smiling face.

Being celebrated does not mean that life is always a party. Celebration includes comforting and consoling you through the dark days. In fact, the ability to celebrate the joys of life even amid its bitter downturns is a priceless quality that you will find only in a small number of rare, mature individuals. It's easy to celebrate the good times, when it's expected that we'll throw confetti and kiss at midnight, but you need someone to stand by you after the holiday ends and the workday begins.

CELEBRATING EACH OTHER

Recall how you felt as a child on the morning of your birthday. The night before you could barely sleep while you anticipated the party you would have, all of your friends from school who would be there, your aunts, uncles, cousins, and of course your beloved grandparents who always made you feel like the most special person in the room.

While we are older and more mature now, we all want to be celebrated in that way . . . just a little bit, once in a while. Feeling celebrated in a love relationship is essential to its health. It's nice to be the object of the celebration and it's equally important to plan celebrations for your partner. Whether it is for big celebrations like birthdays, anniversaries, and job promotions, or celebrating the smaller things in life that only matter to the two of you, making your loved one feel special and cherished in ways that matter to them helps to create a long-lasting bond between partners.

These areas of development, on the heels of doing your research, are vitally important if you are seriously considering a commitment to another person. You must be willing to interrogate, observe, and investigate them if you are to know who they really are and fine-tune your expectations. You must also examine them through the frames of preparation and desperation, as well as stimulation and celebration. You must make an informed decision about them in each of these categories so you know what you're getting into, before you do.

ten
Before You Get Engaged—Twenty Final Exam Questions You Must Ask

"One who asks a question is a fool for five minutes; one who does not ask a question remains a fool forever."

—*Chinese proverb*

I am always amazed at my children, one in middle school and the rest in college, in their different approaches to the inevitable end-of-semester final exams. My youngest is very diligent and does his homework all along; this makes preparation for his exams quite easy, a quick review. A model student, he stays up-to-date with his studies and accumulates the material sequentially, as his teachers prefer. Needless to say, his mother and I are enormously proud of his study habits and mastery of the subject matter.

My daughters, on the other hand, usually take a different approach. They get their work done throughout the semester, but almost always pull an all-nighter to get the paper written or the project completed. Similarly, their approach to final exams is to wait until the night before and begin cramming fifteen weeks worth of information into a few hours of bite-sized nuggets.

As much as I try to discourage this approach, they usually score high marks and demonstrate that their system works just as well as their more disciplined sibling's. I've learned not to argue with them and to be just as proud of their adrenaline-inspired efforts as I am of their brother's consistency. Whatever works—I'm just grateful that any of them study at all!

Dating for Dummies

One of the study aids that I see my children using in preparation for their final exams is CliffsNotes. As long as they do not use these little booklets as a substitute for reading the primary material, I don't object and can even see the value in having a concisely focused summary of the key points. Another study aid that my daughter showed me is the . . . *for Dummies* series—an overview of a complex topic broken down into bullet points that are accessible to the average student.

If you will imagine your decision to make a lifelong commitment to that special someone as your final exam—the ultimate test as far as relationships go—then I would like to offer you an essential study guide. I hesitate to call it *Dating for Dummies* because there's nothing dumb about wanting to know another person as thoroughly as possible before entrusting all dimensions of your life to them.

And whether you've been studying all along for this major evaluation of your IQ (intimacy quotient) or whether you've failed a few pop quizzes and find yourself cramming for the final, I have some study tips that will ensure your success. Specifically, here are twenty questions that you must ask yourself and your special someone.

Regarding answers to them, there is no one right way to answer, but I've offered some things to think about as you weigh the many possible answers.

1. What do you expect?

Perhaps no other question is so critical to the success of your relationship. While expectations reveal themselves over time, it should also be the focus of direct, candid conversation between you and your beloved. Adjusting expectations will help alleviate disappointments. Too many times our expectations are based on our past experiences, what we do or do not want to see duplicated from our relationship with our parents or others who influenced us.

There is a vast difference between who we are versus how we present ourselves. I often refer to this tension as the friction between our ideal self and our real self. Unfortunately, we do not marry the ideal but the reality. Yet the ideal projections of both you and your partner can create expectations that counter the reality of your relationship once the masks are off. There is nothing more debilitating than overpromising and underdelivering.

The number one killer of relationships is not communication or even finances—it's expectations. Only when we expect our relationships to go a certain way and they veer from our trajectory do we end up offended by the other person. So many people's expectations throughout Scripture almost prevented them from receiving God's blessing. In 2 Kings 5, we see Naaman, an army captain, suffering from leprosy. He's sent to Israel to seek a cure from Elisha, a man of God who lives there. When Naaman arrives at Elisha's home, the prophet sends a messenger to tell the soldier to go wash seven times in the river. Naaman responds by saying, "Well, I thought he would at least come to the door and pray over me and heal me." He *expected* Elisha to greet him at the door. He *expected* Elisha to lay hands on him. It took Naaman's servant to point out that Elisha told him how to be cured, which the leper finally did and was then healed. But his expectations almost killed his deliverance!

When you weigh the answer: It may be wise to minimize your own expectations or at least adjust them to a realistic framework: to expect nothing more than you're willing to give. Someone has said that expectations are nothing more than future resentments. Avoid those resentments by allowing the other person to give freely. You rob the individual of blessing you from their heart when you have unhealthy expectations.

It may require several conversations, but be blunt and ask the other person what they expect from a relationship with you. And tell them, in kind, what you expect. Open up the front door of communication in the house of love you hope to build together.

2. What are your most prized possessions?

This question reveals much more than their pride in the new Mercedes or their appreciation for Aunt Martha's quilts. A person's most valuable possession provides a window into their priorities. Do they value the past more through their love of antiques? Family heritage through the heirlooms that have been handed down? Or are they more focused on present achievements by acquiring status symbols of wealth and power—a certain kind of car, brand of watch, or style of wardrobe?

When you weigh the answer: If you can have an honest conversation about what each of you values most, you will have a good view of future pursuits. Will your individual pursuits converge into shared interests or pull you apart with competing agendas? If you compare the kinds of items that each of you prize, then you can also see how relationships factor into their value system.

3. Where do you stand on faith?

Along with finances and sex, the role of personal faith in the relationship will prove to be a crucial area. Scripture tells us, "Do not be yoked together with unbelievers. For what do righteousness and wickedness have in common? Or what fellowship can light have with darkness?" (2 Corinthians 6:14, NIV). It's not that the two of you must hold identical views and practice your faith in the same ways. But in most cases, you need to share similar views regarding the fundamentals of your faith—how you view God, the role of the church, personal practices. "Do two walk together unless they have agreed to do so?" (Amos 3:3, NIV).

When you weigh the answer: If the two of you are comfortable discussing issues of faith, then your attitude and ability to listen are often more important than specific answers. But think about the role of personal faith, spiritual practices, and church participation before you get too far into the relationship and realize that you're on separate pages in this vital area.

4. What was your last major relationship like? How did it end?

Sometimes it's very obvious who your present love was with prior to being with you. They may talk incessantly about their ex and why the relationship didn't work. They may subtly or overtly compare you to this person who lingers like a ghost in their heart.

Are there exes in his life of whom you're unaware? A man she used to date who still works in the same office next to hers?

It is important to ask how many major relationships the other person has had. You should be willing to grant your partner some privacy regarding this, however, since dredging up the details won't help either of you.

When you weigh the answer: If the volume of exes exceeds the number of years they've been an adult, then you might have a serious problem. Similarly, if you are the first major relationship, then other issues need to be addressed.

5. What are your ideas about sexuality?

You need to discuss your idea of a fulfilling sex life before you marry, not after. I know this may be awkward, but you can make it fun and lighthearted. It doesn't have to be a counseling session or an episode from reality TV. What does great sex look like to you? All great sex is not created equal. What some call blazing saddles might be lukewarm leather to others. Make sure that you have the same sexual rhythm—I use this term to connote frequency and variety.

When you weigh the answer: You cannot build your relationship around your sexual chemistry because only about 10 percent of your time together will be spent in the throes of passion, wrapped in each other's arms. However, you must not ignore the sexual dimension of your relationship either. Having sex does not equate to being intimate, but building intimacy usually results in a mutually satisfying sexual relationship.

6. Do you know your HIV/AIDS status?

If the first question seems too large and abstract, then this one is as practical as it gets. It's about saving your life. After having worked on the Black Clergy Awareness Initiative and listening to the alarming statistics on HIV/AIDS, it is critical that we ask this question.

The Centers for Disease Control and Prevention estimate that more than 1.2 million Americans are HIV-positive with roughly 25 percent unaware of their status. African-Americans comprise the largest population segment, with about four hundred thousand positive individuals, followed by Caucasians, with just a few thousand less. Research continues to show that HIV/AIDS is not a gay disease or a straight disease, nor is it reserved for drug users or the impoverished. This epidemic is no respecter of persons. No matter how beautiful, smart, or smooth-talking the other person may be, you must know their status. And you must get tested yourself.

When you weigh the answer: I'm not saying that if someone is positive that you should not proceed with the relationship, only that you should know what to expect. Years ago blood tests were required of couples acquiring a marriage license, but today not all states require this medical information. As a pastor I know of several couples in my church who knowingly chose to marry despite one of them being HIV positive. This is a life-changing and lifestyle-changing decision, and my concern is that you make it with an awareness of what you are taking on, rather than finding out after you marry.

Don't wait to ask this question. In the heat of the moment when passions flare, neither of you will be inclined to dampen your desire in order to discuss your status. But it must be asked and answered honestly by each of you. And if you haven't been tested recently (within the past three months), then you don't have a right to ask the other person until you know your results. Consider being tested together.

7. What are the secrets that you keep? Will you trust me to keep them too?

No matter who you are or how virtuously you live, everyone has secrets. They may be family secrets dealing with substance, domestic, or emotional abuse. They may be personal secrets dealing with past relationships or present addictions. This is only to be asked or answered where matrimony seems imminent. Never trust a tryst with your secret!

   When you weigh the answer: This question more than any other provides the greatest indicator of whether your marriage will make it over time. You must be willing to listen without judging the other person so that they feel safe enough to answer truthfully. You also want them to accept you and your secrets without criticism or condemnation. If couples are willing to confide in each other, dirty laundry and all, then they can overcome most any circumstance that threatens them.

8. Have you ever been arrested and do you have a criminal record?

Again, this kind of question is never easy to ask. And often it is the most charming, together-looking people who one would never suspect, who indeed have a past record, even numerous offenses. Being direct and frank about such matters can also prevent the keeping of secrets and simmering of shame that might result from a less than perfect past. Instead of hearing the news from someone else, if you ask the person directly, he or she can then contextualize the situation and explain. Perhaps the arrest occurred in their youth before they gave up drugs and straightened up their life. Maybe they were in the wrong place at the wrong time and ended up being trapped by association. Regardless of their rationale, if you are planning on spending the rest of your life with this person, you deserve to know all of them, including the shadows.

When you weigh the answer: You must be willing to believe in the power for someone to change if your partner has a prior record. Like confiding our secrets, revealing criminal activities or court-ordered directives can put a person in the most vulnerable of positions. If you are going to judge the person despite evidence that they have clearly changed since their past offenses, then the relationship will not succeed. You will also need to divulge your own involvement in anything that has crossed the bounds of the law. Reciprocity is key to building and maintaining trust in a healthy, life-sustaining relationship.

9. Do you have children or other children outside of marriage?

I wish that you did not need to ask this question, but frequently a partner will not mention their children for fear that their new honey will lose interest if they discover children are involved. Create an atmosphere of open communication so that the other person will feel comfortable informing you of their offspring. It's not just adults with young children that I'm addressing. Often older singles with grown children won't mention them to their date until after the wedding. Before running the risk of "baby momma drama" showing up on your job, get the facts!

When you weigh the answer: Discovering a son or daughter, regardless of their age, should be a deliberate revelation that begins a conversation about the role that child will play in your new family. This conversation can be highly emotional for many reasons. Many women have had abortions in prior relationships and may feel a sense of sadness, shame, or loss that they need to share, without judgment. You must be willing to accept them, including their past, regardless of whether or not you agree with their past decisions. Some people may have children that they gave up for adoption. Again, building trust and openness is the foundation of any successful relationship.

10. How do you feel about having children?

I'm often surprised at the number of couples who come to me for premarriage counseling who have never discussed having children. In extremes, she may be thinking that her career comes first and they can think about children five years down the road, while he's thinking that starting their family is a priority for their first year. Beyond the initial question of whether each person wants to participate in birthing, raising, and nurturing another human life, you must ask how your partner feels about the role of children in the family.

Will life revolve around the children's school, activities, sports, and music lessons? Will your partner try to relive his high school glory days through bringing a son into the world? Will she be just as content if she never has a daughter?

When you weigh the answer: These issues must be addressed together so that you can craft a vision for your future life, not just as a couple but as a family.

11. How do you feel about disciplining children?

In conjunction with the issue of having children, you must also address how you will discipline the children. Frequently, we tend to parent in a style that's either similar to what we experienced from our own parents or in a way that is a reaction against their methods. Will corporal punishment be involved? Time-outs? Will you reward good behavior? What about giving the child an allowance? How will you discipline your children when they're school age? Teenagers?

When you weigh the answer: Many family civil wars could have been prevented if the parents had simply discussed their differing views on how to maintain order, obedience, and understanding.

12. What are the roles of a husband and a wife for you?

This question gets back to the nature of individual expectations. Do you have traditional roles in mind with a male breadwinner and a female homemaker? A more contemporary view of roles with both spouses working outside the home? A progressive view that includes a stay-at-home dad raising the kids while the mom provides income through her career?

When you weigh the answer: The reality of marriage is that the dance the two of you perform will be unique to your relationship and yours alone. However, the sooner you can start talking about what kind of music and tempo you want for your dance, the smoother and more graceful your steps will be.

13. What role do you see your parents, siblings, and extended family playing in your relationship?

If you come from a close-knit family with big Sunday dinners and gatherings at every holiday and your partner is an only child with parents across the country, problems can obviously emerge regard-ing the role of extended family.

When you weigh the answer: My suggestion is that you get to know each other's family as much as possible prior to the wedding. Attend a family reunion, holiday event, or dinner party and get to know the other people you are marrying because their involvement will affect your relationship, one way or another. You don't have to love the other person's family as your own, but you do need to re-spect and appreciate their role in your beloved's past and future. The last thing you want to do is get stuck between your partner and their family.

14. How do you handle disagreements and disappointments?

Every marriage needs an arbitration clause. This is an agreement of how you will settle disputes before you get into the heat of an argument. Will you allow a cooling off period of twenty-four hours before continuing the conversation? Will you involve your parents, his parents, a marriage counselor, your clergy, or a lawyer? What is your panic button and how will your partner know when it is sounded?

When you weigh the answer: If you're going to learn how to fight fair and overcome the cornerstones of conflict, then you must discuss the rules ahead of time. For instance, you should both agree that arguments are not meant to be had in front of the chil-dren or in a public scene. It's best to discuss the rules and personal tendencies (exploding, withdrawing, etc.) before you need them in the heat of an angry moment or conflict-inducing circumstance. Foremost, you must realize that you will disagree at times, the key is knowing how you will handle it so that both parties feel heard.

This is the key to fair fighting in a relationship, not being right or wrong.

15. What is your vision for this family? Where would you like us to be in ten or twenty years?

No leader operates without a vision for their destination. This question will allow you both to discuss the lifestyle that you desire for your family as well as common goals. Will you homeschool your children? Travel abroad as a family? Live in the suburbs? In the inner city? In a rural area?

When you weigh the answer: One of the beautiful aspects of any marriage is vision-casting the new family that you are beginning through your commitment to each other. As our globe continues to shrink and our multicultural community continues to expand, families now have many more options than they used to have about their lifestyle. Discussing these ahead of time will allow your relationship to grow instead of wither when one of you expects change and the other loathes it.

16. How satisfied are you with your present career?

Most of us fluctuate in our job satisfaction levels on any given day, and this is perfectly normal. However, if your spouse-to-be hates her job and can't leave her worries, fears, and frustrations at the office, then you will bear the brunt of her dissatisfaction. If he is in the process of transitioning out of sales and into elementary education, then this will mean a change in finances as well as lifestyle.

When you weigh the answer: Often you can help each other discover a more fulfilling career in two simple ways: 1) being a sounding board for one another as you examine your relationship with your present employer, and 2) encouraging each other to pursue what you are called to do.

17. What is your debt-to-income ratio?

If you have ever purchased a home, then you know that one of the key numbers in financing your purchase is your debt-to-income ratio. This figure is calculated by dividing your monthly debt payments into your monthly income. Most financial experts will recommend that your ratio be 36 percent or less, and this is, in fact, the cut-off number for many mortgage lenders. A ratio that is higher than 40 percent indicates serious issues about how the other person spends his or her money.

When you weigh the answer: If your special someone has never calculated their debt-to-income ratio, then this information in itself tells you an important clue. When you discuss each other's ratio, you have a natural springboard to discuss such issues as budgeting, impulse purchases, financed purchases, savings. You may want to ask if the person has ever declared bankruptcy, either personally or professionally.

Noticing what he or she spends money on will also illuminate this crucial category of compatibility. Does she have a newly purchased outfit and freshly beauticianed hair on each date? Does he drive a top-of-the line car and have the latest electronic gadgets?

It's not that a cheapskate and a big spender can't fall in love and marry successfully. They simply need to know each other's habits and preferences before that first month's bills roll in.

18. Is there any need or desire for a prenuptial agreement?

You may want to include this question in your discussion of finances; particularly if there is a large disparity between what each of you brings to the marriage in terms of assets, property, and possessions.

When you weigh the answer: I am often asked what I think of such agreements that spell out in great detail who gets what and how much, should the relationship end in divorce. My only response is to remind the prospective bride and groom that their vows make a point of saying, "in sickness and in health" and ". . . as long as you both shall live." Perhaps we should alter our vows to be more honest—"only in health and prosperous times" and ". . . as long as we both feel good"—if we're going to plan the breakup before the marriage gets started.

19. Do you have a will or a living will and can we talk about it?

No one likes to think about issues such as disease, injury, immobilization, or mortality amid the warm fuzzy feelings of being in love. Nothing can kill a romantic moment more than asking your beloved about a living will—timing is everything! But this issue must be addressed so that you both have a clear understanding about how such a significant situation will be handled should it ever arise.

When you weigh the answer: This topic will also facilitate a general discussion of death and how the other person approaches the topic that we all have in common. While it may seem morbid or depressing, a healthy conversation on such topics can illuminate so many other topics—their life attitude, their faith, and other priorities.

20. What annoys you the most about me? What do you enjoy most about being with me?

As much as you and snuggle-bunny love every little detail of each other's behavior presently, the intoxication of infatuation will eventually wear off. You don't want to experience a relational hang-over by discovering how much your beloved hates the way you crunch your vegetables or goes ballistic when you don't balance the checkbook. Being up front and honest with each other about your differences provides a healthy safety valve for future tensions. It also allows you each to address areas where you can improve for the sake of the other person, whether that means leaving the toilet seat down or attending to personal grooming habits.

When you weigh the answer: You will also have a clearer idea of what can change and what's going to be the same on the other side of marriage. Never enter a relationship assuming that the other person will change for you. Instead learn as much about the other person as possible so that you know what you're getting into before he leaves the toothpaste cap off or she hangs her pantyhose all over your bathroom.

ASKING QUESTIONS AND REVEALING SECRETS

Sometimes we avoid asking certain questions of our beloved be-cause we are afraid to hear the answers. Once we hear the truth out loud, it may confirm our worst fears, and then it's harder to move forward together pretending we don't know the truth.

It's not always easy to ask about a person's sexual history or whether or not they have a criminal past, but certainly these are critical con-cerns. Sure, the answers could be embarrassing for you and your partner, but it will be more uncomfortable later if you are keeping secrets that are suddenly revealed in an unpleasant or public way, or if you have to hear the information about your loved one from someone else.

If there are significant issues in your past that you know your partner should know, it's better to reveal them up front than to have them found out later. If you reveal something difficult and your partner walks away, consider yourself lucky to know how they feel up front.

It is important that you understand that there is no right or wrong answer. I often have seen couples who married someone who was HIV positive, and together they built a great life. I have seen those who joined together in spite of the fact that one or both of them had bad credit. It doesn't mean that you can't make it. But I am saying you don't want go into marriage in the dark about these and other important issues. Creating a safe atmosphere for people to be honest requires some effort and sensitivity. No one is going to be open with a sniper. So don't come in to judge but to understand and listen.

If you are not willing to be a safe place for people to be transparent then you aren't ready for a relationship anyway. Even if you make the decision not to pursue a relationship with them, you can still be a good friend to them and at the very least, respect their privacy by not sharing what they shared with you in confidence. Most people ache far more for someone they can trust than they do for someone they only sleep with.

This list is by no means comprehensive, but it will provide you with much of the crucial data you need in order to proceed into a lifelong commitment with another person. If you're willing to do your R&D work and get to know the person beyond and below the surface appearances and romantic emotions, then you will be on your way to mastering the basics of a healthy relationship. Ask these questions now and you will know whether or not they pass your final exam before you embark very far along on the road to saying, "I do."

eleven
Before You Marry

"The goal in marriage is not to think alike, but to think together."

—*Robert C. Dodds*

I have been married more than twenty-five years to the same woman, and it has been quite an adventure. Not every day has been a pleasure cruise. We've encountered many storms where we didn't know if our craft would survive the choppy waters. Yet by God's grace we have endured in spite of the tumultuous winds and inclement weather that we never could have predicted, let alone expected to survive. I do not report this with arrogance but humility as I have seen many good people go down in the sea and drown beneath the tidal waves of what they felt were insurmountable problems.

Not all issues in marriage can be prevented, but many problems can be anticipated and circumvented. While I've learned much from my quarter century of marriage, I may have gained the most insight into marriage by reflecting on the plight of my ancestors— being enslaved. Before you think I'm taking the old joke about our spouse being a ball and chain too seriously or before you think I'm trivializing the suffering of the countless men and women brought to this country in chains, let me explain.

This comparison first occurred to me while I was visiting West Africa along the coast of Ghana. It was such a privilege for me to visit the Spanish castles there where my ancestors in all likelihood were carted away to America for the very first time. My tour guide shared with me some gleanings of history that I had never realized. It had such an impact.

She began to explain that the first enslaved Africans who left those shores were not all one people but were, in fact, an amalgamation of different tribes, often from different countries, who almost always spoke different languages. "Can you imagine," she said, "what it must have been like to be in the hull of a ship tied down like dogs, sick and afraid, frightened and uncertain? You're on a ship for the first time headed for an unknown world, surrounded by people you didn't know."

Wow!—I got it. For the first time, I realized that one of the distinctions of Black Americans, Black Caribbean people, and numerous others of African descent is that we have evolved into, and are still trying to evolve into, being one people. We were not one from the start! All my life I had been taught that we were one people who betrayed each other and sold each other into slavery. Suddenly I began to understand that we were not born one people, but had to become one. I realized why the process of development was, and is, so tough for us. We didn't have the same customs, the same language, the same religion, the same government, or values, or the same anything else. Thrown in the same boat, literally, and chained alongside each other, we had no choice but to become one even amid our tremendous diversities.

The Two Shall Be One

Consider for a moment the plight of enslaved Africans during the middle passage—the weeks spent in the hull of the slave ships—struggling to understand each other while fighting for life. Compare that to the journey of two people struggling to hold a marriage together. In both cases, they're thrown together on the same ship and struggle to become one, while their backgrounds are so different that the unity is difficult and often painful. Like those enslaved Africans, who were given the same name, which suggested they were one people, when, in fact, they were extremely different, married people find it difficult to live up to their shared last name when they are from two different traditions and backgrounds.

Whether you're single, married, widowed, or divorced, it can be challenging to stay in a committed relationship. Two people from unique households, occasionally from different ethnicities, varied educational and emotional backgrounds, come together to become one. Even individuals who grew up together, attended the same church, and ascribe to the same political ideas may find it difficult to understand each other's habits, hang-ups, and heartaches!

Relational expert John Gray captures this notion of different cultures with his metaphor that "men are from Mars and women are from Venus." However, the fault line for me is not merely a matter of gender but also of individual customs, experiences, and values. Most of the couples I encounter do not have a clue about understanding each other or communicating effectively across the language barriers of their distinct perspectives. As if it weren't hard enough for two different genders to understand each other, add to the mix the unique nuances of two different families and you can see how the Brady Bunch ideas we have, end up becoming the Hatfields and the McCoys!

DISAGREEMENTS

In many relationships you'll find yourself paired up with someone who is completely different from you on many levels. *American Idol* judge Paula Abdul in her '80s video and hit song "Opposites Attract" tap danced across the screen with her beloved MC Skat Kat. The two sang, "I'm like a minus, she's like a plus/One going up, one coming down/But we seem to land on common ground."

While we often think we are looking for a female or male version of ourselves, more often than not, we typically end up with someone who is as much like us as water is like vodka. They are both clear and wet, but the similarities end there. What makes life interesting, what makes a conversation stimulating, is people with differing points of view. Those who need others to think and act exactly the way they do are often masking insecurities, and have a deep-seated need to have their views and actions confirmed in the behavior and thoughts of others. Disagreements happen in any relationship where more than one person is involved; it's inevitable. We are all unique individuals, have varying backgrounds and experiences, and are not likely to always agree on everything with friends, coworkers, or especially with love partners.

However, the way we approach these disagreements can determine whether our relationship or marriage makes it to the finish line. Fighting fair, opening yourself to the ideas of others and new ways of doing things can work to expand your consciousness. And who knows, in the end you may even agree to disagree, and that's okay. The important thing is that you are each respectful of your partner's ideas and experiences, and seek to find a way to create an environment where the two of you feel free to express your feelings and be who you really are—without fear of judgment or condemnation. This is what works toward building a strong, lasting bond.

In the marriage ceremony, the officiate declares, "I now pronounce you man and wife." But isn't it funny that something so important could be said so quickly and then take the next twenty years to materialize to its fullest capacity? When the Almighty performed the first union between Adam and Eve, God charged them to be fruitful, to multiply, to replenish the earth and subdue it. In spite of this request for couples to multiply, currently far too many marriages end up dividing instead. In this chapter I'd like to explore the ways in which you can build your "Constitution" for a solid union instead of experiencing a marital civil war.

One Year Honeymoon

"When a man hath taken a new wife, he shall not go out to war, neither shall he be charged with any business: but he shall be free at home one year, and shall cheer up his wife which he hath taken" (Deuteronomy 24:5, KJV). In biblical times, the expectation included exemption from war, from business, and from the stress of life. For one year, the goal was to cheer up each other before transitioning back into the demands of normal life.

Now that is some honeymoon! What impact would it have on our marriages if we were able to obey God's design and give the first year to knowing each other and learning about life together?

Imagine how much stronger your love might be if you had the first year off of work, with no bills, no responsibilities and no demands, just love, life and liberty!

Perhaps this is idealistic but the truth of the matter is that we are moving so fast that we do not have bonding time. Much like planting a sapling, if its roots are given a chance to anchor, then when the storms come they will not break the tree.

Like the ancestral slaves who no doubt spent the first years trying to find a way to understand each other while avoiding the master's whips and the violence associated with our nation's dark past, couples who marry today must fight financial crunches, dual career challenges, and the perils of parenting with only limited time together.

For newlyweds, this latter issue, time together, can be especially daunting. After spending so much time ignoring the clock as they date, flirt, and stare into each other's eyes, they must suddenly find a way to cram their romance into neat half-hour slots on their Microsoft Outlook Calendar! Most couples must work jobs that require them to spend most of their waking hours away from the strange new person they married. They come home through traffic which eats another hour or so and then they spend some time with the child they didn't expect to have so soon. They may end up with two hours a night of waking time to work out the bills, the Parent Teacher Association, the church meetings, the sorority committee meetings, and all the other groups waiting to take a bite out of their calendar. They then need to do all of this, spend quality time talking, get in their workouts, make school lunches, and then make love before enjoying eight hours of sleep. It's not only daunting but practically impossible in our twenty-first-century culture!

The Bible rightly says for a man to dwell with a woman according to knowledge (1 Peter 3:7). What then should we know about each other that helps us dwell and aids us in the fight not to divide? Take time to get to know each other that first year.

Rowing Together

And like growing a sturdy tree amidst the ever-changing seasons, it takes a lifetime to get the rhythm right between two people. This is not a matter of love but of finding "normal." Each of us brings a different idea of normalcy into our relationships. I have seen this over and over again. Both parties tend to think that their ideas are the right ones. They are rowing in the same boat but often in different directions.

We bring baggage into our relationships, whether we are conscious of it or not. Our personal histories, experiences, and personalities carry a combined weight that influences every area of our lives. How do we manage the household? What kind of furniture do we buy? What do we eat and when do we eat together? When do we make love? How often? What does each one of you expect in the bedroom? How do we parent? When should we discipline the children and how will we do it?

We generally have different traditions and conflicting ideas. Because we were not from the same tribe, we inescapably experience a culture shock. The minister says a few magic words and—shazam!—we're in the same boat. The only problem is that we don't know how to row together and often don't understand how to communicate with each other. This has always been the case but now with each partner having equal responsibilities, along with the absence of quality time, we don't have time to learn how to row together!

Of course, some people row together more easily than others. But none of us masters it without a few close calls. Today many married people are like the slaves who jumped off the boat before it landed. Imagine the fear and anxiety that made them choose suicide over slavery. Not good choices either way. Some people feel just that trapped in relationships. They don't know how to work it out and they don't know how to get out. They can't live with their spouse and they can't live without them.

They self-destruct, and while the rest of us eat our dinner, the news blares about husbands murdering wives, suicidal love triangles, and mothers killing their children and themselves. What weight must these souls bear to resort to such horrendous and extreme measures to escape their relationships and its responsibilities? Or what of the damaged homes and hearts of those who live under the harsh whip of domestic violence? Abuse has ravaged so many families, leaving them scarred for life, if not completely destroyed. The impact of a dysfunctional relationship shatters the window through which we look out into the world.

Similarly, but far less lethal, we find those who choose to leap into the aching abyss of divorce or disgrace. The reactions are different but the symptoms are likely similar as the pressure mounts between those who live in cramped emotional spaces like slaves in a ship's cellar. Yes, we share the space with people we love, but many times age, gender, and personality make it difficult to share effectively. The wife may have one primary agenda for the place they call home, while the husband has another. Add children and a couple of pets into the mix and it sounds like the Tower of Babel, each one babbling in a different tongue!

If you are talking about people who jump ship, you need not go back through the middle passage to find them. I see them in my office all the time. Most jump ship because too many things hit them at the same time. They jump because they are afraid that the future holds no newness, no release, no hope of happiness, or no sense of growth. They feel stuck in cramped quarters, afraid of the darkness in their burdened soul, and they want out. They feel left with no solution but to abandon the relationship as it reminds them of yet another area of failure!

Yes, some people continue to jump ship in our contemporary context. But others become like those captives who were pushed off the side because they were too argumentative, rebellious, or unsuitable for enslavement. The slave traders didn't think they were physically healthy enough or emotionally trainable to bring a price at the auctions. In keeping with the metaphor, I must point out that some people don't give up: the other spouse pushes them. Maybe they do it because they feel like the spouse they chose isn't marriage material or can't be domesticated properly.

FORGIVENESS

We all make mistakes. As human beings we are all flawed. Perfection only exists in God our savior. Recall Jesus' words "Father, forgive them; for they know not what they do" (Luke 23:34, KJV). Truer or more significant words have never been spoken, and there are few concepts more important to remember in a long-lasting union. While it is perfectly normal to feel anger and it is a natural human reaction to feeling wronged or disrespected, there is a difference between healthy anger and the caustic emotion of bitterness.

Grudges spread through a marriage or relationship like cancer invades our healthy cells, attacking organs at a rapid speed. Dr. Angelou said on a recent episode of the Sundance Television program *Icono-*

clasts ". . . [bitterness] feeds upon the host. It does nothing to the object of the displeasure." In this case, the host is the marriage, and forgiveness is the medicine and the cure.

You can always rely on God for forgiveness no matter what you've done. When you are tempted to withhold forgiveness, remember a time when you needed to be forgiven and reconsider. Treat your loved one with the love, respect, and the forgiveness and mercy with which you'd like to be treated. It is the Golden Rule: "And as ye would that men should do to you, do ye also to them likewise" (Luke 6:31, KJV). Offering the forgiveness you wish to receive is a good way to work to ensure your marriage remains healthy and free of the disease of bitterness.

Amendments

Our founding fathers knew that the Constitution needed to be a breathing document that allowed for a changing world. It is a wise person who leaves himself room for further light. If you lose your willingness to change, you have lost your willingness to survive. This includes humility and ability to admit our mistakes and ask for forgiveness.

Before you marry, create in yourself an openness to change and an understanding that much correction will be needed for what you will face together. Make this attitude your charter for how you will operate in your new country of togetherness. If you do not create such a flexible constitution, it can be even more challenging to keep the relationship afloat.

Recently, I spoke to a man whom I had once begged not to separate from his wife. Still, he felt it necessary to do so. I had counseled him for a while and knew that he was feeling the typical midlife stress, along with disappointment over a new career pursuit that had not fulfilled his expectations. Updating me on his situation, he explained that he had been living single for the past three years but had recently started talking to his wife again. He said, "I'm afraid to go back home to my wife even though she wants me to return. The grass wasn't so green on the other side, but I don't know if I can go back to the way things were. I guess I'm afraid of regretting it."

I suggested dating her while they rebuilt the relationship and repaired the damage that was done. Basically, I laid out a plan for them to get back in the boat! It was apparent to me that he wasn't happy and that he knew he had made a mistake. But how does one fix what was acceptable at one point but isn't anymore?

Believe it or not, it is easier to jump off the boat than it is to get back on. He thought he was right when he left; he felt he had no choice but to escape his demanding wife. But now he misses the same woman he once abhorred. He needs to amend some things that he said and did, now that he realizes they were wrong and unjust.

Before you divide, separate, or otherwise lose yourself from what you have, be sure to think things through. Many times in a relationship we make a lot of decisions and practice a certain methodology that fits one stage of our lives and not the present. It is in these circumstances that we need to work together as a team to figure out what amendments need to be made in order to accommodate the growth, change, and development of new times and new issues.

You don't have to destroy your entire constitution just because new needs come to light. If you're willing to amend it and grow, it may signal a whole new era! Do not make permanent decisions over temporary circumstances.

Separation isn't as permanent as divorce but the risk is pretty dangerous. Many are the couples who divided up some of the assets, divvied up the goods, and said, "I need more space." You must be careful that in claiming your space you don't fool around and show your spouse how to live without you. Sometimes what we perceive as a need for space is really a need for respect, for direct communication—both asking and receiving, and for change.

We have to respect what we have with each other even when we enter a place of discomfort and pain. Watch out for closing doors on love just because it squeaks a little and has a hole in the screen! I have seen people shut a door that they couldn't reopen. So then what do you do when your season of frustration is over and the other person has moved on because you needed to have your precious space?

Much like the civil rights period whereby the sons and daughters of former slaves fought again, this time not for freedom but respect, some couples must move through one conflict only to face another. Many couples experience a season where they must recalibrate their relationship to insure that the decisions made at one stage of life now fit the growth and maturity of the present.

I told the brother to date his former wife in the hopes that they would talk and amend the rules of their relationship, to build it stronger based on respect and wisdom that they didn't have before.

EXPECTATIONS

We all enter in marriage with certain expectations. We see TV shows with perfect couples, always happy, never having any conflict that doesn't resolve or wrap itself up in a neat and tidy package within the confines of a thirty-minute sitcom, a two-hour Lifetime Television Sunday afternoon drama, or the three hundred pages of a paperback romance. But remember these are forms of entertainment; they are . . . fiction. And what they don't tell us is that while happy endings are possible, they require a tremendous amount of work to achieve.

M. Scott Peck wrote in the first line of his bestselling book *The Road Less Traveled,* often considered one of the preeminent self-help manuals, "Life is hard . . ."

While marriage and partnership can be among life's greatest joys, it can also be challenging and very difficult. Accepting that fact, adding in a willingness to be flexible and releasing the need to be right and to win, will help you go a long way to a more stable, long-lasting relationship.

Mid-Course Corrections

You don't have to be a mean person to become a self-consumed, enthroned egotist who doesn't leave enough elasticity to accommodate past mistakes. Most of us find it easy enough to justify what we want and what we do as a result. In this process, though, we must also create a chance to rebuild the relationship by honest repentance and open confession. Frequently, the stronger personality can arrange the relationship to suit them without understanding how their selfishness disrespects the other person. If this happens in a marriage, a conscious, intentional effort has to take place to bring equity and liberty to the other spouse. I have seldom seen anyone who spent their whole life happy to be oppressed by anyone. Maybe it is a stretch to call it a marital civil rights movement, but let me ask you, have you given each other equal rights or is the marriage unfairly skewed in the direction of one of you at the expense of the other?

Often during midlife crises for men and menopause for the ladies, empty nests from the children's departure, and financial freedom from paid-off mortgages, the couple has the tough task of amending their marital constitution to fit who they have become, not who they were twenty years prior.

If there is one quality that redeems our national history, it is the fact that eventually we tend to correct inequities or attempt to do so. If we didn't make mid-course corrections, we wouldn't survive. Abraham Lincoln knew this about slavery. President Johnson later understood this about civil rights. A growing democracy means that we have to be mature enough to admit when we have it wrong or risk our very existence. Those old battles are fading and new ones are emerging in our nation—global warming, immigration, health care, terrorism, and the economy. But what matters most is that we have the will to survive, the discipline to forge ahead, and the humility to correct our inevitable mistakes along the way. If this is possible with nations, it is also true of our marriages.

We will not last because we were never wrong. We will last because when we were wrong we found the invincible will to correct the wrong and the grace to endure whatever it took to survive it all together, indivisible, with liberty and justice for all those we love. Like our great but flawed nation, our families are never perfect but that doesn't mean that with honest conversation and cultivated respect we cannot find a way to make it across the dark waters and the tumultuous seas onto the stable shores of love and life.

Free your relationship from the shackles of false expectations and limited perspectives. Recognize that you and your beloved come from individual nations that must negotiate new boundaries, new borders, and new policies. Our wedding vows have the power to bring about an incredible emancipation from our loneliness, selfishness, and isolation.

However, the voyage toward ultimate fulfillment occurs every day as you row and row until you find your rhythm together. Before you marry, discuss the diversity of views, cultures, families, and opinions that will combine when you get in the boat together. It can be smooth sailing if you're willing to listen to, liberate, and lavish your partner with the freedom of unconditional love.

twelve

Before You Decide to Take a Risk for Your Marriage

"To live is to choose. But to choose well, you must know who you are and what you stand for, where you want to go and why you want to get there."

—*Kofi Annan*

I was running late that day, as I often do when I am trying to cram in more than twenty-four hours will allow. But no matter how full my schedule, I was not about to miss hearing my son, then eight, speak at the graduation ceremony for our church's Youth Entrepreneurial Camp, an event designed to train children ages six to twelve to be entrepreneurs. I know it sounds a bit early, but in the inner city choices start at a young age, and we thought if we could guide kids toward an empowering vision before the drug dealers or the deviants got a chance, then we might reverse the stats and make a difference.

My son had been practicing his message around the house for days. Because he had grown up watching me speak, he was pretty excited about having this opportunity. It was just a youth event, attended mostly by parents, but to him it was an Olympic arena, so I knew I had to be there. Walking into the auditorium, I saw my wife over in the corner beckoning me toward our son who looked like a big-time wrestler prepping for a bout in the ring.

The moment I saw him I knew he was a little nervous. My wife said he had insisted on practicing alone and had spent most of the morning in the little waiting area. In my best nonchalant voice, I said, "Hi, Dexter. How are you?"

He looked up at me, a slight trace of sweat on his brow, and said, "I'm okay, Dad."

"Great!" I said, pretending not to notice that he looked like he might urinate down his leg and mine. He and I walked out to the waiting area just beyond the hubbub, and I sat quietly, letting him prepare mentally, although I sensed he wanted to ask me something.

Finally, he said, "Dad, when you have to speak do you ever get nervous?"

I smiled and assured him that I did. He looked a little relieved. He hadn't learned yet that the hardest thing about doing something for the first time is learning what's a normal part of the process and what's a warning sign screaming, "You're about to make a *big* fool out of yourself!"

My son said, "So what do you do?"

I said, "Son, I just pray about it and give it my best shot. Armed with all of my preparation and prayers, I just go for it!"

He said, "Well, maybe we should pray." So there in the little cubicle just outside the door of a new experience, he and I prayed. I still get choked up at what a privilege it was to experience that moment with him.

As he did an incredible job speaking, I had more tears in my eyes (yes, I'm a biased, proud father!) than a young girl chopping onions for the very first time. Watching him pace back and forth across the stage, speaking like a pro, I wondered, "Is this the little boy who was about to pee on himself in the cubicle a moment before?" Of course it was, but such is the nature of crossing a fresh threshold into the exhilaration of a new experience.

Much like my son, Dexter, we all face new experiences with some degree of angst. But I say, "Feel the fear and do it anyway." Though it is not an original saying, it works for me. As we talk about some very practical things about relationships and marriage that may seem simple to the pros, I want to encourage those who are rookies at the experience. As you wait in your life's cubicle like Dexter, trying to muster the courage to do something you've never done before, I want to spend a few moments with you behind the stage like I did with Dexter, getting you ready and making you understand that there is a normal anxiety that happens in the final moments before you jump into any new area of your life, the uncomfortable moment I will hereafter refer to as "the edge."

The Edge

For most people, the notion of living on the edge mirrors the feeling I get when I stand on the edge of a roof. High places make me extremely uncomfortable, particularly standing on the edge. I am not opposed to climbing up on the roof as much as I am standing on the edge of it. The journey toward making a decision can often be exciting and fulfilling in its own right. But when you get to that do-or-die moment right before it's time to pull the trigger and fire yourself into a new experience, it's not butterflies swimming in your stomach—it's swimming in a sea with all the sharks of your fears, flaws, and failures.

I've often wondered how many times Dr. King had to go to the restroom before he made his famous speech in Washington. Seriously, I wonder how many times. Often we rob great people of the right to have human feelings, fears, and insecurities, but in so doing we raise them to a status that alienates us from duplicating their work. If we think that they are somehow superhumanly endowed with some specialness, then we are subtly saying that we can never do anything exceptional because of our normalness.

Recently I was asked to attend a meeting with some of the very top officials of NBC and MSNBC. This highly publicized meeting took place over the course of an entire day, and I was astounded at how many of their top executives gave up so much valuable time. They asked us several questions about what it's like to do what we do and why some people might not understand much about the black communities that we work in. They wanted to hear of our experiences and unique nuances and know how their news media could embrace aspects of faith and family, culture and community, more effectively.

The Day of Dialogue, as it was billed, took place with the editorial board of the company and included Brian Williams, the esteemed anchorman who fronts the prestigious network news division, NBC News president Steve Capus, and many other highly influential people. During the meeting, one of the many things we discussed in addition to our programs, initiatives, and community needs was the fact that most black clergy are often asked to weigh in on subjects and perform tasks that their nonblack counterparts do not. It is not uncommon for one of my members to ask me to look over a contract on the closing of a home. I am no legal expert, but because they trust me, I find myself reviewing many subjects that other spiritual leaders might not be asked to know. In most other cultures, single-focus experts are more apt to advise members of their own culture. As we shared this observation with the NBC team, they seemed fascinated to learn that we have classes on everything from debt reduction to entrepreneurial initiative to social etiquette. In my culture, you see, the church is a significant part of the community and is often the catalyst of change. Churches incubated much of black progress, from civil rights to early colored schools prior to integration.

Our clergy duties have included doing a wedding one moment and going to a court trial the next to help a mother get custody of her children. Having a pastor come to a house closing just to give moral support is not unusual for many of us. I have prayed over numerous house closings, reviewed estate planning papers, and discussed living wills, not as an attorney but just as a trusted ally who cares about the parishioner.

From these experiences, I have seen so many people in the nervous moments before a plethora of new challenges. I can tell you about the sweaty palms of a prospective groom waiting with me in the back of the church to recite his vows. I can tell you about a Habitat for Humanity homeowner about to have a reception for her new house or a parent who finished a degree with students half his age while working a full-time job. I have worked with playwrights offstage, with actors about to go onstage. I have worked with athletes before a major game and coaches after a minor setback.

All the preparation in the world doesn't take away the feeling one gets on the edge. This exhilarating and frustrating, nervous and energizing feeling is often a part of facing some new and daunting task. It's the human nervous system's fight-or-flight response rolled into one. I don't care how high up you go in life, some events will always make your stomach clench and your throat dry.

It is not the task that is intimidating as much as it is the newness of the task that makes the pulse go weak. Anytime life calls us away from our comfortable place in the familiar and asks us to do something on the edge of—or beyond—our norm, then we find ourselves alone in a cubicle feeling like an eight-year-old about to make his first speech!

Some of us would even avoid making the change or facing the edge if we could, but God has a way of putting us in a place where we have no choice but to move from the safe center to the uncertain edge of a new experience. In the titillating, terrifying, gut-wrenching, soul-tingling feelings of this vertigo, we learn the value of faith and the fuel of prayer. We don't activate either as adamantly when we are facing the familiar as we do when we face the uncertain.

It is our respect for the gravity of the decision that makes us a little edgy and uncertain, prayerful and careful. It is the anxiety of newlyweds buying their first house, or the worry of a young bride the night before her wedding. I am talking about the fright of a first-time mother who wonders, "Do I have what it takes to bring a child into this world?"

I have sat in the locker room with well-trained athletes who make millions of dollars for playing their game. In the moments just before they go out, the tension in the room is thick and exhilarating! If it is not, they often will not win the game. Respect for the stakes often produces some degree of anxiety all by itself. The only way one can avoid these often unpleasant, nerve-wracking feelings is to always play it safe by sticking to what is easy and familiar. But what a boring, non-progressive life it is to never venture beyond where you start.

I met a man a few weeks ago while in Tobago who told me he was forty-three and had never left the island his entire life. I was speechless as I wondered how one could be content to live on an island twenty-six miles long and six miles wide for forty-plus years and never go beyond its limited borders. But then I know people who live in Fort Worth who have never gone into downtown Dallas even though it's only a few miles away! Can you imagine that there are people who live in New York who have never been to a Broadway play—not because they can't afford it but because they just never consider going beyond their normal routine! I guess I'm just not one of those people who stay put.

Sometimes you have to be pushed over the edge or you will never go beyond where you were born. Relationships do that. Marriage does that. For many of us to stay where we started is to die without growth. However, many of us would never have taken a chance and discovered new dimensions to our identities and interests if circumstances hadn't forced us into action. Our jobs forced us to move. The promotion forced you to learn a new language. Your new assignment taught you to work with people who looked different or dressed different or worshipped different or distinguished themselves from you in some way. You were simply pushed into what became a great and new experience in your life. Every so often, I believe God pushes us into these wonderful possibilities that we would never embrace if the decision were entirely ours. While any committed relationship, especially marriage, has its challenges, one of its blessings is that it brings us to the edge.

All Stirred Up

"Like an eagle that stirs up its nest,
That hovers over its young,

He spread His wings and caught them,
He carried them on His pinions.
"The LORD alone guided him,
And there was no foreign god with him.
"He made him ride on the high places of the earth,
And he ate the produce of the field;
And He made him suck honey from the rock,
And oil from the flinty rock . . .
                              (Deuteronomy 32:11–13, NASB)

The writer in Deuteronomy says that God stirs up our lives like
an eagle stirs her nest. Maybe you've been watching *Animal Planet*
more than I have, but let me share what I've learned about how
mother eagles move their young to maturation. She rearranges her
nest, the safe little haven she's built as a nursery for her brood, so
that it becomes as uncomfortable as possible. Why would a mother
treat her children this way? She doesn't want a nest full of dysfunctional birds who cannot move beyond where they began. She knows
that if her babies stay in the nest, not only do they miss fulfilling their potential, but they also become an easy target for larger
scavengers.

Imagine being a little eaglet who has survived by opening your
mouth whenever you hear the mother eagle coming in with fresh
food. No worries, no unmet needs, nothing to think about, no reason to fly. Perhaps you think your wings might be just for decora-
tion. Then one day your mother begins to pull up the twigs that
she buried in the nest, making it uncomfortable for the eaglets to
rest any longer.

Suddenly your cozy corner has become littered with sharp objects that make it difficult to rest where you once did. Now you are
sitting on sticks, briars, and thorns and realize that you must con-

sider leaving the borders of the familiar and step over the edge into a new experience. This is what it means to "stir the nest"—it means that your butt can't sit around any longer!

Likewise, our God doesn't want us to stay where we started but go beyond to explore and experience all that was created. Marriage can stir the nest. A new job or a new house for a first-time home-owner can be a nest-stirring experience. A child's birth, a move, a career change, downsizing, upsizing, empty nesting—all these con-temporary words we use are just modern-day colloquialisms for a good old nest-stirring moment in your life.

Have you ever had one? I've had many and come to expect that every so often a change occurs and I'm out of the nest and into the air, flapping around on never-before-used wings with the feeling of a full bladder and a much bigger prayer life! In fact, as I look back, every so often I get a stirring just as everything has settled down and gotten comfortable. Suddenly my familiar routine becomes sharp and prickly with that dreaded word, change!

I was privileged to have met Katie Couric as she was stirred from her successful morning program to nighttime news. I met Michael Irvin not too long before he ended his NFL football career and established a life beyond the field. I watched Steve Harvey transfer from stand-up comedy to radio host. Every exciting per-son worth their salt will have something stir them up and move them even when they are a pro at what they did before.

Faith in Action

Like my son Dexter, you may experience fear as a factor between you and what life, especially marriage, will hand you next. But if you can remember that eagles are pushed out of the nest by the discomfort of staying put so that they might fly for the first time, you might go over the edge with a little less fear and a lot more faith.

The eagles learn to fly by being forced to put their faith into action. Many people come to me with a business plan for start-ups that seem very sound, modest, and achievable. I often challenge these entrepreneurs by asking, "Is this all you want? What will you do in three years when you've realized this level of success?" I encourage them to set their goals so high that they cannot achieve them on their own. Set your marriage goals high. Allow God to force you to fly!

"But, Bishop Jakes, what if I fail?" you may be saying. "I've tried flying and fallen to the ground a few times."

If we return to those baby eagles, we'll see that they come mighty close to falling themselves. They flutter and flap and, yes, they fall but the mother is always close enough to catch them up again. The falling is an inherent part of the flying. It is the sensation of falling that teaches them to fly.

Initially you may feel vulnerable and frightened and wish you could go back to where you were before. But hold on, you are not in the air by yourself. The Lord is with you, and even though you are falling in a blur and making mistakes and closing on property for the first time or moving up into a company where you will be swimming with sharks, don't be afraid. This is where your faith grows exponentially. It is in the wind when you are flying and falling that you find God has a way of catching you and then releasing you to try again.

Even if this is your second attempt, don't give up. Even if you feel that your first marriage was a failure, or your first house was foreclosed, or your first business went under, it doesn't mean that you should never try it again.

Scripture tells us to be cast down but not destroyed (2 Corinthians 4:9), which reinforces the truth that we can fall but not fail. Yes, just because you can feel yourself falling does not mean that you failed. There is a second chance and a third that is inherent in the process of teaching eagles to fly.

Chickens don't need these repeat chances to fly because they never rise over six feet above the ground where they were born. But if you are an eagle, you were not made to play it safe. The sky is the limit!

As we go into the last few chapters, I want to share with you some practical tips and pragmatic points that can enhance your life and empower your flight for the next stage of your decision-making life.

Dexter gave his speech that day, and I shed a tear as I watched him take his first flight into what only God and time will tell. I was just happy that I made it to see the plane take off, the eaglet catch the wind, and my son move into his destiny. With his nerves shaking and arms flailing, he found his voice and ended his message to a standing ovation. As we left that day, he said to me what you ought to be saying to your Heavenly Father: "Daddy, what's next?"

It's time to take a risk, and I'm here to help you, before you do!

thirteen
Before You Buy a House

"A house is a home when it shelters the body and comforts the soul."

—*Phillip Moffitt*

The feeling of being in a place where you belong, a satisfying sensation that most of us think of as being at home in our environment, is one of the most compelling reasons to decide to purchase a house. Most of us want more than just a place from which to return after work, eat a meal, and sleep. We want our dwelling to provide more than just basic shelter from the elements—we want comfort, convenience, and a style that says something about who we are. We would like to have a retreat, a safe place, a sanctuary that enables us to recover from the blows of life beyond its doors. We want a place that feels like a home to our family and one that feels welcoming to our friends and guests.

These characteristics come together in many ways—the attitude of the people living there; the sense of style and taste you bring to your décor; and the significant souvenirs, honored heirlooms, and artistic accessories you choose for enhancement. Pride of ownership enables you to paint your dining room red, crank the volume on your sound system, and hang anything you want, wherever you want, on the walls. The truth is that money buys you a house but only love gives you a home.

In fact, one of the greatest experiences that any couple can share together is creating a home. Whether it's a studio apartment or a custom-built mansion, a home that you share has a life of its own. It becomes a shelter, a safe haven from the battering storms of work, worry, and the world. You may have different tastes and needs, assorted kinds of furniture, and various children's toys scattered about, but a home comes together through the love you share within its walls. The choice of a home is an important relationship decision. Often the priority of people beginning new relationships and marriages is buying a house or saving and planning to do so.

Whether married or single, when you're considering the purchase of a house, you must look at the practical aspects of the purchase process. In addition to wanting to find the living space that feels right, we must also be more objective and find a house that is structurally sound, financially within our means, and fiscally sound as an investment.

For the vast majority of us, our homes remain our greatest expenditure and our most valuable asset. Even during a recent downturn in the housing market, putting your money into property remains one of the safest and most lucrative investments. While high-risk stocks and bonds may provide you with a larger, short-term return, home ownership allows you to enjoy your investment even as it accrues value and builds equity.

As I see it, buying a home allows you to enjoy your retirement right now—not at some later date when you retire or when the stock goes up or your bond matures. You build equity year to year, at the same time that you live in a beautiful home that satisfies the needs of you and your family. Then sometime in the future, perhaps when you're empty nesters or want to move to another locale, you have a large asset that provides a large payment at one time. You can then reinvest this profit into another, more valuable property, and continue to grow your assets.

Recently I've heard many people say that since the economy is sluggish and the housing market has declined they can't afford to buy a house. But, with interest rates down and so many homes on the market, buyers can take advantage of some strategic opportunities that are not so prevalent when the real estate market is booming.

HOUSING STARTS

If you have no experience buying real estate, you must start by doing your homework. Most communities offer first-time home-buyer programs and seminars at the local library or community college. Search online for a reputable source of information such as the U.S. Office of Housing and Urban Development (HUD). Here you will learn step by step exactly what you need to do to get started buying your first home.

Ask friends and family members who have purchased homes about their experiences, what mistakes they made and what they've learned so that you can avoid the same fate. Ask them to recommend real estate agents, mortgage brokers, or other professionals who can work with you to secure a mortgage that you can afford.

Buying a house is not the place to try and keep up with the Joneses. The decision to invest in a home must be entered into logically.

However, as I've encouraged you to consider throughout this book, several areas must be evaluated before you do. Let's look at ten items that will help you make the best decisions regarding selection, timing, and financing of a new home.

Motives

Since owning your own home is often considered part of the American dream, most people don't often consider their motives when beginning the process of buying a house. They assume that's what they're supposed to do because that's what their parents and grandparents did, or wanted to do. Often it's the first decision couples make after they decide to engage or soon after they marry. If you're successful and raising a family and upwardly mobile, then of course you should own a house.

In our virtual-office, flex-schedule work world, living near the job is no longer a necessity. Options abound more today than ever before concerning where people live and how they adapt their lifestyle to their environment. You don't have to purchase a house to create a home. Yes, you will need to live somewhere. But depending on the size of your family, your interests, travel schedule for work, and the hobbies you enjoy pursuing, you may find a condo, co-op apartment, town house, or mobile home works best for your needs.

Maybe you want to prove to others how successful you are by owning the big house in the suburbs or downtown or wherever the affluent display their trophy homes. A house would be your way of proclaiming, "I've made it." However, like any status symbol it can never compensate for a healthy sense of self-worth. If you're only buying a house to display your success to others, then you won't be satisfied with the home you purchase. You will forever be looking ahead at a more expensive builder, the next hot new neighborhood, or the latest design trend.

Choose a home for two primary reasons and do not lose sight of them: 1) as a comfortable dwelling place for the needs of you and your family, and 2) as your most significant financial investment. These two must work hand-in-glove in order for it to be a sound purchase that you will not regret. Focus on either one at the exclusion of the other and you risk settling for a property that eventually will be found lacking. When you make good decisions regarding your relationships, it makes it easier to make other sound decisions, such as where to live and how to enjoy the life you build together.

Market

The real estate market, like any product paradigm, is based on the law of supply and demand for whatever the market will bear. In other words, if more properties are available than buyers to purchase them, then it's obviously a buyer's market, with more power for the potential buyer to negotiate with the seller. If desirable properties are scarce, then sellers can command an outrageous sum of money from the numerous buyers eager to purchase their property.

As I mentioned, our country's recent economic climate and the proliferation of properties available in virtually every market have created an exceptional buyer's market. If you have been contemplating a new home purchase, you will find many homes and numerous lenders eager to do business with you, assuming you have a solid credit history.

Do as much research as possible about the specifics of the local market in the area in which you hope to purchase. Do not rely solely on your real estate agent, no matter how friendly they may be or how long you have known them. In many ways, buying a house is like shopping for a doctor when you need an operation. You will need to rely on the Realtor's expertise just as you would a doctor's, but it's still your purchase at stake.

Take ownership of the process long before you sign a mortgage note or a warranty deed. Know your options. Study the comparable properties in your desired area and talk to homeowners and property managers if possible. Try to determine the intangibles, such as the neighborhood attitude—open, clique-ish, friendly, distant, ethnic, racist, elitist—before the moving truck rolls to the curb.

Location

Regardless of the kind of market or the national economy, the fundamental rule of real estate—location, location, location—continues to be true. When evaluating potential properties, you must consider location at both a micro and macro level. Personally, does this home provide convenient access to the other important daily and weekly destinations in your life—your office as well as your spouse's, the kids' school, your church, as well as shops and restaurants?

Once your potential property has passed this test, then you must consider the location in the larger context of your area's overall market. The Office of Federal Housing Enterprise Oversight keeps track of single family home sales and values for the entire country by region and metropolitan area. You can access its website at http://www.ofheo.gov and find the latest report on home values in your area, updated quarterly. The site provides many other educational aids for home buyers, including a mortgage calculator and the latest prime mortgage rate.

Location can make or break a home sale, so think carefully before you settle or compromise just because the price is right. If you can't sit in your yard and enjoy a conversation with your spouse because the traffic noise is so great, that's a problem. Is it close to the airport? Too close? Near the local sewage treatment plant? How far is the nearest park or open space? While neighborhoods, urban or suburban, small town or big city, fluctuate in popularity, some location features will always be favorable selling points. These include access to major thoroughfares and interstates, proximity to natural landmarks such as water or mountains, and the beauty of the site itself, including its views and exposures.

How much direct sunlight does the home receive? How many windows have eastern exposures? What's the angle and pitch of the driveway? Will snow and ice receive enough sunlight to melt in winter? Is the home situated in a valley or downhill so that flooding might be an issue?

While such questions may seem tedious and mundane, you don't want to answer them after the fact, when your car is stuck in the garage because the snow in your driveway won't melt or your basement floods from spring rains.

Financing

The demise of the numerous subprime and predatory lenders doesn't mean that you can relax and take the first seemingly reputable lender who comes along. Know your credit score—a copy is available online from any of the major credit reporting companies such as Equifax—prior to applying for a mortgage. This information is something you check regularly, many experts say monthly or at least quarterly, to ensure accuracy by correcting any misinformation and updating payment history.

Ultimately, your credit score will determine the interest rate for which you are eligible. The higher your score, the better interest rate offered by competing lenders. Obviously you want to do whatever you can to keep your credit rating in good standing. This means making sure that old credit card accounts that you've closed show up as such on your report. You also want to make sure that any factual errors or inconsistencies are cleared up as well.

Even in our technologically advanced, mechanized age, errors still occur, and you don't want to be the victim of a computer glitch that could cost you a percentage point at the closing table.

Once you've verified and cleaned up your credit report, you will want to get preapproved by a mortgage lender. Preapproval is not the same as being prequalified although many people use the two synonymously. Being prequalified typically means that your real estate agent or other expert has calculated an acceptable debt-to-income ratio, which most lenders want to be between 29 and 33 percent.

On the other hand, being preapproved means that an actual lender has carefully examined your credit report, debt-to-income ratio, down payment, and verified how much their institution is willing to lend you for the purchase of a home. After you are preapproved, sellers and their agents will favor you over nonapproved buyers competing against you.

Since financing can become a multifaceted formula, I highly recommend that you seek out an expert you know from a trusted source. Many books on the market are excellent, as well. I have brought in numerous experts, including Suze Orman, to discuss sound financial principles at MegaFest and our conference called BEST (Black Economic Success Training). Books by Suze, Dave

Ramsey, David Bach, and others provide thorough coverage of this complex equation.

Consider how much to spend on improvements or upgrades. If the house requires repairs, new carpet, paint, or new furniture, then you need to factor these expenses into your budget. Neighborhood covenant groups and homeowner organizations may also charge a fee that can add as much as several hundred dollars a month to the price of a home. Bottom line, it's your money and you want to spend it wisely. The extra time, trouble, and tedium of doing your financial homework is often the difference between a satisfied homeowner and buyer's remorse.

Taxation

Home ownership provides one of the best investments because it also allows you to deduct your mortgage interest, the largest component of most house payments, on your annual tax return. Property taxes are also deductible for a primary residence or a vacation home.

If you have lived in your home for at least two of the past five years, then you can profit from selling that home without paying capital gains tax. Individuals may exclude up to two hundred fifty thousand dollars and couples up to five hundred thousand dollars of profit for up to two years. Theoretically, you can sell your home every two years and pocket the profit without taxation. Before calculating your profit margin, be sure to ask a tax professional about your state's laws and limitations as well.

Even if you go over the exclusionary profit margin in the sale of your home, your profit will be considered a capital asset and be given preferential tax treatment. This means your profit will be taxed more favorably than some other kinds of capital assets such as business stock or collectibles such as artwork. Once more, we see the way home ownership can protect your investment more than virtually all other assets.

Selection

Once you've been preapproved and have thought through the kind of loan that best fits your needs, then you're ready for what most people consider to be the best part—actually selecting your home. Most real estate agents will tell you that selecting your home is about trade-offs—choosing your nonnegotiables as well as those items that you can live without. You may decide that a beautiful rural setting on the waterfront is worth the hour commute into your office. Or you may value the convenience of being five minutes from your kids' school more than the size of your yard.

Be realistic about what you and your family really need in a floor plan. If you love watching movies together but rarely have a formal sit-down dinner, then having a home theater may be more desirable than a large dining room. If you don't know a carburetor from a radiator, then you may not need a large garage with the mechanic's workshop. For families with small children, a large, open playroom may be more vital for your sanity than a large master suite.

Whether working with a real estate agent or not, much of your selection process can now be done online. You'll want to view realty websites that offer both agent-listed properties as well as for-sale-by-owner listings. Properties that others might overlook can also provide you with some unique opportunities. Foreclosures and short sales (opportunities to purchase quickly from banks and other lending institutions) require a convergence of timing but can offer amazing deals on worthwhile homes.

Vision

Allow me to offer two pieces of advice that sound contradictory but really work together in allowing you to select your new home. First, try to see beyond the surface appearance of the seller's furniture, style of décor, and taste and imagine how your own design sense could transform the space. Use your imagination to cast the rooms in your favorite colors. Transform rooms, knock down walls, add crown molding, peel away wallpaper. A diamond in the rough can be cut, polished, and set into an exquisite piece of jewelry.

Second, don't ignore your first impression. You may need to question it, but often our "blink" reaction—to quote bestselling author Malcolm Gladwell—to a property is dead-on accurate, without analysis. If you immediately feel ill-at-ease upon stepping into a house, then no amount of new appliances and hardwood floors can overcome it. However, just because you feel good in the home, you shouldn't romanticize the reality of fixer-uppers. A house that needs new plumbing, a roof repair, or an updated kitchen will require more than positive energy to turn it into a sound investment.

Try to find a balance between your vision for what this home can be and the reality of where it is at present. Moving can be such an exhausting process that most people don't want to have to do major remodeling during their first year's residence. However, you may want to make some improvements to make the home your very own. These will likely increase its value as well, so your money will return to you when you decide to sell. Bathroom and kitchen remodels always add considerable value. However, don't choose a home that *must* have improvements made right away unless you walk in with your eyes wide open to this reality.

Timing

Some aspects of timing are out of anyone's control when you are house hunting. You can't control the available inventory or the seller's timetable. But you can be aware of your own timing needs and the places where flexibility is most needed. If you must wait until the school year ends before moving your family cross-country, then don't look at short sales (opportunities to purchase quickly from banks and other lending institutions) unless you have a creative solution for the interval. If you need to downsize immediately because of a financial loss, then you might not have the luxury of waiting for the perfect house.

Sometimes you can work out schedules with your seller that will meet both your needs. Whether they rent the home back from you after closing until they move out, or you rent to own prior to purchase, remaining flexible, communicating needs clearly, and working creatively allow for win-win solutions for both of you. Also, you need to allow time to get the inspection completed—and never purchase a property without one—as well as the official appraisal which your lender will require for verification of the property's collateral value.

Finally, when thinking about how crucial timing can be to finding the right house, I encourage you to avoid what my wife calls "the perfect dress" syndrome. She tells me that she, like a lot of ladies, will go shopping for a special-occasion dress. Sometimes she finds the perfect dress—right color, style, and size—at the first store she visits. Does she buy it? Of course not! She needs to visit a half-dozen other stores and try on several dozen dresses before returning to the first store to buy the perfect dress.

And, ladies, you are not alone—I know several gentlemen who purchase suits, shirts, and shoes the same way. In our consumer-friendly culture, with so many options offered, it's difficult to commit to a purchase even when you find exactly what you want. You fear that a better option, one you couldn't even imagine, may be just around the corner. My experience with houses tells me that the same principle applies. However, I'm not the only one who has lost out on that great home because I waited too long by shopping around. If you find the house you know is right for you, then don't look any longer. Don't wait. Make an offer and enjoy the satisfaction of finding what you wanted.

Closing

Before you're sitting at the table for closing on the purchase of your new home, signing your signature more times than you thought humanly possible on dozens of sets of papers, overwhelmed by how much money you're going to be paying for the next thirty years, you should make sure you have inquired and obtained as many purchase options as possible. Be sure to take the final walk-through of the property to ensure everything remains in working order and good condition. Items such as appliance warranties, roof repairs, purchase credit for new carpeting, and repairs to the sprinkler system should all be ascertained prior to that moment when you sit with the pen poised in your hand.

If you are not clear on such purchase options, or if the terms of your loan have been altered in any way whatsoever, then don't hesitate to take the time needed to review the changes before signing off on them. Do not allow loan officers, real estate agents—including your own—the seller, or even your spouse to pressure you into signing anything that you are not comfortable signing. While it's unreasonable to expect to read every single word in the voluminous stack of documents, you should at least have an idea to what you are agreeing. Again, do not hesitate to seek the counsel of a trusted advisor or recommended expert.

Finally, enjoy the satisfaction that comes from owning your new home. Celebrate your purchase by finalizing your plans for the move and by planning a party in your new dwelling to bless and dedicate the space. Home ownership is one of the most satisfying acquisitions you will every experience. Before you buy a house, allow for ample time for research, education, and completion of the necessary procedures so that you will never regret this incredible investment in the quality of your life and the quantity of future dividends.

Our homes provide a stable base from which we can love, grow, and raise a family. They give us shelter from the storms of life and provide security and comfort. Buying a house is a huge investment. When you plan to buy a house, you're much more likely to make it a home if you first think through your relationships, including your family's physical and emotional needs, before you do.

fourteen
Before You
Have Children

> "Making the decision to have a child is momentous. It is to decide forever to have your heart go walking around outside your body."
>
> —*Elizabeth Stone*

As the preparations for my daughter's wedding accelerate, I recently found myself overwhelmed by another emotion-packed moment. Suddenly, the little girl in pigtails playing dress-up in her mother's closet had stepped into satin pumps that now fit her and a stunning white dress truly fit for a princess. My daughter stood before me as a beautiful bride in her wedding gown.

I had never imagined such a scene when my wife and I anticipated her arrival two decades ago. Nothing proved there was a God to me like watching my wife birth a child, an unbelievably sacred moment of overwhelming joy and divine blessing. To imagine that out of our intimate sexual moment came this person with eyes, lips, fingers, toes, personality, and dimples. Staring into our baby's eyes, holding her in my arms, I was speechless. Here was a living piece of me, with my DNA infinitely infused into her. The birthing of a child gives even the most secular person an eternal life, as you live on through the lives, features, and contributions of your children.

The process of deciding to have children can be a wonderfully exciting time, with parenting books scattered around, conversations with siblings who have birthed your nieces and nephews, and catalogs for baby products.

It's virtually impossible to take into account all of the milestones, miracles, and mishaps that will occur in your relationship with your children. But certain considerations should be addressed long before you're in the doctor's office looking at sonograms or in the delivery room holding a living, breathing bundle of life. If you aren't aware of what you're getting into with the birth of a child, the consequences can be unintentionally painful for you both.

We can see the devastating impact on young lives that experience neglect, abuse, or addiction because their parents are too needy and self-absorbed to care for them. Currently, over one and a half million children and teens are homeless and living on the streets of our country's cities. According to the American Academy of Child and Adolescent Psychiatry, close to one hundred thousand instances of child sexual abuse occur each year, and these are only the reported cases. None of us would choose to have our child become another statistic in these heart-wrenching totals.

While advance emotional, physical, and psychological preparation cannot guarantee perfect families, it can facilitate handling the demands of parenting with greater ease.

PARENTS, BE ENCOURAGED

Few parents try to ignore, neglect, or harm their children. We all do the best we can, knowing that we will fail them, disappoint them, and hurt them despite our best intentions.

No License Required

Before you have children, you must think through the extraordinary demands that will be required of you. The enormity of being responsible for another human being can feel so overwhelming that we might be paralyzed in our tracks—and I don't mean to discourage anyone from experiencing the joyful satisfaction that comes with raising a family. However, you will enjoy the experience much more fully and have a much healthier relationship with your children if you examine the requirements before you do.

No license or training is required to have kids. From riding in a car seat to driving the car, our children are with us for the rest of our lives. Babies grow into toddlers into preschoolers into children into tweens into teens into young adults into full-grown men and women. You must be willing to ride it all the way through. They won't always wear the cute little outfits with the pink booties and the matching knit bunnies. They will not always look as cute as their baby photos. You can't exchange them or return them for a refund. (The current average cost for raising a child until she's eighteen is around a quarter million dollars.) You might want to try, but it ain't happening!

Before you have children, you must understand the life-changing commitment. You can't divorce the child no matter how painful the choices they make or how they turn out. If your child is a prodigal, a jailbird, a crack dealer, a heroin addict, or a stripper, they are still your child. Every day, not just Mother's Day and Father's Day, you will be reminded of this life that you brought into the world. You must consider not just the capacity in your body to grow a baby in your womb, but the capacity in your life for that life to grow into a living, breathing, crying, laughing person. They will leave your body in nine months, but they will never leave your life. Even if, God forbid, they should die before you do, their impact will not subside through their absence.

Before you have children, you must imagine the worst. It's easy to imagine the cute, cuddly Hallmark moments when they leave the hospital, take their first steps, say their first words, and have their first day of school. But think also about how you will respond when they become the neighborhood bully or get arrested for shoplifting while still in elementary school. What will you do when your teen comes home drunk or high, with reefer on his breath? How will you deal with an unplanned teen pregnancy?

You'll be tempted to ask, "Where did we go wrong? How could this have happened to us?" If you can't handle the weight of such a burden, then you need to reconsider why you want to be a parent. Becoming a parent must be a deliberate choice. If you fall into it by accident or if you go into it blindsided by precious moments born of naïveté, then you risk sending another wounded child into the world.

As you have seen from the prior chapters, I believe the relationship you enter into should create an emotional and physical space for your new life together. Whether or not this space will include children is a monumental decision, one not to be taken lightly or left to an unexpected moment of passion.

If you know you want to be a parent someday, then it helps to find someone else who shares your longing. As you make decisions regarding potential parenthood, please keep in mind that so many of these are predicated on the foundation of prior decisions you have made. You may certainly choose to be a single parent, but all the more reason to know what you're getting into before you do.

MOTIVATIONS FOR BECOMING A PARENT

You will often hear Oprah Winfrey remark on her television talk show that "raising a child is the hardest job in the world." She knows this and she's not even a mother! If you are considering having children, it is important to take time to ask yourself if you are emotionally, financially, and spiritually ready to do so.

Examining your reasons for wanting to have children will do one of two things. It will reveal that you are ready, that you understand that the act of nurturing a family will be at once the most rewarding and most difficult and dynamic task you will ever undertake. Or you will realize that perhaps you are not now, or may never be ready to have children. Not everyone is meant to be a parent.

Our motivations to want children vary. Some of us want to have children for the right reasons, because we want to build a family unit and feel the desire to selflessly support another being into a mature, well-rounded adult.

Yet some of us have children for reasons that are less than desirable, ones that are likely to result in heartbreak for you and your innocent child. Reasons such as "I want someone to love me" or "I had children or agreed to have children because my partner wanted them" are immature at best and recipes for disaster at worst.

If you have thoughts like the latter, I recommend some serious soul-searching before proceeding down the road to becoming a parent.

Not Your Own

One of the greatest benefits of having a child is that your life is no longer your own. Your home is no longer your own. For women, even your bodies are no longer your own. As difficult as it can be to make room for a child, both literally and figuratively, in all dimensions of your life, it can help you become less self-centered and more compassionate. When you no longer think of only yourself, you grow in unique ways that do not occur in any other relationship.

The child bridges the practical, everyday aspects of life with the eternal privilege of being God's facilitator for bringing another soul into existence. You must learn to address both of these areas.

Let's think through some of these preparations, starting with the practical. Before you have a child, you must baby-proof the rooms of your home to protect your little one from harm. This includes padding sharp edges of furniture, especially tables, removing glass and other breakable objects, and locking all drawers and cabinets. Better yet, you need to remove all cleaners, soaps, lotions, and anything containing chemicals that could poison your baby.

Such preparations for your baby's arrival are only the tip of the parenting iceberg. From these measures, ladies, you must drill down to a more personal level and consider prenatal care, which may require a level of discipline and self-sacrifice that you've never experienced when considering only your own life. With another heart beating inside your body now, you will need to give up smoking, alcohol, and have your physician review any medications you may be taking for their effect on the embryo growing inside you.

You will need to exercise and to eat nutritious, well-balanced meals. You will need to make sure you get adequate vitamins and minerals, particularly folic acid, which is essential for your baby's neural development. Adequate rest and relaxation is essential during pregnancy, especially when you consider the sleepless nights ahead as your newborn acclimates to a regular schedule.

Preparing a space for baby, or "nesting," will include purchases such as a bed, changing table, and adequate diaper supply. Some baby toys, clothing, and other accoutrements (don't forget pacifiers!) will also be on your list. Many women enjoy these preparatory activities, and they can be shared with your husband or other family members to create a bond of anticipation. However, do not be discouraged if you have no interest in such activities. You don't need to be Martha Stewart or undertake an extreme home makeover to have a baby. It's much more important to work from the inside out and prepare yourself first, then your surroundings.

PARENTING WITHOUT BEING A PARENT

Being a good example to kids in our society is not just a job for parents. We were all children at one point. Think about the impact that having just one adult in your life who cared for you and took an interest in you as a person had on you. And if you didn't have this, think about what effect that had. No matter who you are, or where you go, whether you have children or not, there is some young person who needs your support, guidance, or a kind word of encouragement that could change the direction of their life for the better. If you have kids, remember that whether you are aware of it or not, they are always watching. What you say, how you act, what you do in certain situations is the model for the person they are likely to become. If you don't have kids, consider volunteering for a children's organization, become a Big Brother or Big Sister, give time to an after-school program, a church organization, or reach out to a child in your family, a niece, a nephew, or a young cousin. The world can be a hard, confusing, and lonely place for a child alone. A strong encouraging relationship with an adult can make all the difference in the person they turn out to be.

Daddy Dilemma

While women experience a traumatic upheaval in their bodies, men may experience greater trauma in how a child impacts their marriage. Regardless of how much both parents want a child and prepare for her arrival, she will definitely change the dynamic between the two of you. No matter how much joy a child's arrival brings, daddies, a baby takes another little piece of your spouse. Their attention, their focus, their time shifts from you to this little helpless infant that requires them 24/7.

This shift usually occurs as the mother is naturally preoccupied with her new bundle of joy while the father is left to change diapers and wonder when he can enjoy being sexually intimate again with the woman he married. One minute you're anticipating an evening with candlelight, soft jazz, and sheer lingerie, and the next you're hoping to grab a nap, order a pizza, and wash your wife's nursing gown. You go from having her rub oil into your skin to watching her rub Play-Doh on posterboard! Her hormones are roller-coastering all over the place and your libido only ascends like an escalator. When the kids are school-age, she's exhausted baking cookies for the class bake sale and there's no cookie left for you! Life will never be the same!

You must be patient, men, and realize that she misses you just as much as you miss her. It may require delayed gratification, but if your wife sees how much you love the baby, the product of your love for each other, then she will appreciate you all the more. Once the baby is on a schedule and her body has recovered, she will once again show you her love in the physical forms to which you had become accustomed.

Other than your patience, your encouragement is essential during the transition of having a new family member. Most women lose their pregnancy weight, but many do not. Amid the weight fluctuations, the stretch marks, the lactation, and wrinkles from lack of sleep, your wife may no longer feel beautiful. You must remind her that you love her, stretch marks and all. You made a commitment to love her through richer and poorer, sickness and in health. This includes weight fluctuations, lactation leakages, and bags under her eyes from lack of sleep! Being a parent can bring out the inner beauty of each parent, the love, compassion, and sacrifice that you're both willing to give to this new life you have created together.

Finally, you can show your love for your wife by being as helpful and practical as possible. Offer to give the child a bottle for her 2 AM feeding. Don't wait to be asked to change a diaper. Take charge of preparing the meals or ordering out. Arrange a massage or surprise lunch with girlfriends for your wife while you keep the baby. Showing your wife that you're committed to your partnership in raising the child goes a long way toward finding the new rhythm of your relationship.

Men, don't wait until after she informs you of her condition to discuss your feelings toward parenthood and more important, toward her pregnancy. Voice your fears and concerns. If you're worried about never having sex after the kids are born, then state that and make a plan for the two of you to get away after several months when the baby can be left with Grandma or Aunt Louise. Make your participation as the child's father and your wife's coparent an intentional, flat-out deliberate decision. Both your wife and your children will know this and love you all the more.

PARENTAL BALANCE

The hardest part of being a parent is giving your child enough guidance and support to be the best person they can be and then when the time is right, standing back and letting them go off into the world and make the inevitable mistakes we all make while learning who we are. We want to protect our children from pain and disappointment, but the truth is pain and disappointment are a part of life. Giving your children the tools they need to succeed in the world, a strong foundation of faith, and an education is your job as a parent, as is having the courage to let them go, to spread their wings and find their way, with you there with open arms of support and continued encouragement should they stumble along the journey.

Parental Guidance

The other large consideration that you must think through before having children involves the lifetime commitment to their well-being. Every time one of my children has graduated from high school or when I see my daughter in her wedding dress, I tear up and think, "We've made it." Those moments are milestones that deserve to be celebrated. Somehow that child, their mother, and I all survived the many late nights past curfew, early mornings off to school, and last-minute completion of school assignments. We survived the sirens and frantic phone calls, the constant texting and incessant purchases.

My temptation was to believe that somehow once they had graduated or married they had arrived. Before congratulating myself too much, now I worry about their job and their marriage, their finances, their relationships and the new families they themselves are beginning. Even though your children grow into adults, there will always be something about them that concerns you.

Family never ends. In Genesis 49 we see that Jacob, on his death bed, talked to his children, blessed them. Even in his dying breaths, he was worrying about his children and setting a vision for their futures without him. When Jesus was dying on the cross, his mother was there grieving his agonizing passage. Our responsibilities to our children go beyond the grave. When we bring a new life into this world, we create a tie that death cannot break. But before you tie it, be sure you can stand the tension that the tie will bring.

And I promise you it will be pulled, stretched, and pulled some more. But we can do our part to keep the tie strong and not allow it to break because we're sleeping on the job. I've become a recurring guest on the *Dr. Phil* show, and often we counsel parents who wonder how their child ended up with an unplanned pregnancy or a drug addiction. Now as I've said before, parents can do everything as best they can and still have these situations befall their children. However, sometimes we must make sure that we are doing all we possibly can to protect our children from the media, their peers, and our culture.

On one *Dr. Phil* show, we discovered a middle school where faculty were passing out condoms to thirteen-year-olds without parental consent. On this same program, one mother permitted her thirteen-year-old daughter to have sex in their home. She was clearly more worried about being her daughter's friend than her mother. Now I'm not by any stretch the tooth fairy, and I live in the real world and have a family where this issue has been front and center, but any time we condone and promote sex between children we've sunk into a pit. And before you think I'm just being an uptight preacher, let me assure you that this is about good parenting, not religion.

Before you have a child, you must have dealt with enough of your own issues to have the maturity that will allow your child to be angry at you and at times dislike you.

No matter what we teach them, our kids can fall short, but if we lower our standards, then look how low they will go. If we let twelve-year-olds participate in adult activities, then when will it be ten-year-olds or six-year-olds? How can we fight to protect our kids from predators when we turn down the bed and invite them in?

Someday you will lose the need to be your child's disciplinarian and then you can tell them the inside story and become their friend. But you must earn that right to be their friend by being their mother or father first. They need a boundary-setting parent to protect them more than they need or want a friend.

PART OF THE JOB OF PARENTING

Children face a world that is full of negative influences today, no matter how much we try to protect them, and they are looking to and need you to act as their moral and spiritual compass. In a given day, your kids are bombarded with advertisements and television programs, movies, music, videos, magazines, and websites chock full of images of sex, violence, drug and alcohol abuse, and materialism. Much of it is glamorized and fed to them in such a manner that they begin to feel abnormal if they don't have the latest cell phone by the age of twelve or the latest designer handbag or shoes at fourteen. The MTV program *My Super Sweet 16* depicts sixteen-year-old boys and girls, dressed in designer clothing, looking like rap video hoodlums and honeys rather than teenage kids who are just sophomores and juniors in high school. The characters are typically children of business moguls or celebrities, planning elaborate, sometimes million-dollar parties. Gone are the days of cake and ice cream and a few balloons in the basement. These kids receive Hummers and Maseratis for gifts before they even have their driver's licenses.

It is your job as a parent to counteract this kind of influence by setting an example for your children, teaching them that while most of us enjoy material possessions, we must go out to work and save money for them and that our lives are not meant to revolve around acquiring status symbol possessions.

Let me share candidly here. My own child had a baby out of wedlock, and we supported her and did everything except condone it. This was not how we raised her. This is not what we expected. This was not typical of her behavior or character. But it happened nonetheless. Her mother and I were devastated and experienced the gamut of emotions—anger, sorrow, disappointment, fear, embarrassment. But she is our daughter and we supported her in the midst of making our feelings known to her. Now that she is grown and married, I'm amazed to see how this experience has shaped her life with an unexpected beauty. She displays a maturity and patience that will serve her well with her new husband.

Despite the fact that our ideal was shattered, we faced the reality and now have a beautiful grandson. We never wavered in our love for our daughter nor in upholding the standards by which she was raised. You must maintain the ideals of moral, biblical behavior while extending the grace to deal with the harsh realities that we all encounter sometimes. Our voice is not the only one influencing our child. From MTV to BET, from iTunes to MySpace, there's an entirely different cultural experience out there exerting a thousand different influences on them from every side. Our job as parents is to hold those forces at bay as long as we can, preparing them and strengthening them to lean into those pressures and stand strong.

TO BECOME LIKE YOUR PARENT

Your experience as a child and your views of your mother and father's parenting skills will likely influence how you raise your children. While most of us say at one point or another, "I will never, with my children, make the mistakes my parents made," sooner or later you will find yourself standing in the kitchen, hands on your hips, fingers wagging, repeating, "If you don't stop that I'll . . ." horrified to realize that you have in fact done just what you feared—become your mother!

It is up to you to decide what to take and what to leave behind from your experience in childhood. You can learn from your parents' mistakes and emulate those habits that you feel were good ones. As a parent of your own children, it's up to you to pass on the good and break the cycle of the detrimental habits and ideas that are often unconsciously passed down through the generations.

If you cannot accept parenting as a lifetime commitment, then you should accept this reality and not pretend otherwise. Do not become enchanted by the babies you see in strollers at the mall or in the church nursery. Do not deceive yourself into thinking that you'll just grow into it after the baby arrives. You will be on 24/7 for the rest of your life! A baby is not a cute accessory that can be carted around for display. Your social life will suffer or at least change. Please remember, babies don't remain babies; they do grow up. That process is challenging! If you're single, not every person wants to date someone with children. If you're married, then it will be a little while before date night returns or before you can socialize with other couples or your community group at church. Having a baby is like dropping a beautiful stone into the calm pond of

your life—it will ripple into every relationship and settle far beneath the surface.

Parenting is one of the most amazing and wonderful ways that
we are created in God's image. The ultimate parent loves each of us
as a unique son or daughter. If we are to experience the joy that
comes from being blessed with children, then we must partner
with God to care for them as carefully and comprehensively as possible. This process begins long before we see the little blue line materialize into view on the home pregnancy test. It occurs now.
Before you have children, make sure you're ready for the leap of
faith required to love someone more powerfully than ever before.
You owe it to them and you owe it to yourself. "Children's children
are a crown to the aged, and parents are the pride of their children"
(Proverbs 17:6, NIV). The decision to pursue parenthood is one of
the most life-changing of all decisions. Approach it with prayer,
with consideration, with deliberation, and most of all, with a sense
of humor, before you do!

fifteen
Before You Divorce

"A divorce is like an amputation: you survive it, but there's less of you."

—*Margaret Atwood*

If you know me, then you know I value the institution of marriage. The vast majority of this book is about how to divorce-proof your marriage by making great decisions, whether about whom you date, what groups you belong to, or where you live. However, with divorce as prevalent as ever in our culture, I would do you a disservice if we did not take an honest look at the realities of divorce and what you must consider before you sever the bond that was once a lifeline to your heart.

Divorce has become as commonplace in our culture as fast food and as ubiquitous as a radio jingle reminding us that you can have it your way. These days we're not shocked when someone is on their third, fourth, or even fifth marriage before they hit thirty.

We're not surprised any longer when a marriage lasts only a few months or even weeks. And it's not just the actors, celebrities, and professional athletes that we read about in the tabloids. It's our coworkers in the office, our friends at church, and our family members in the neighborhood.

Many couples still come to me for counseling, but it's clear from what I've seen that many of them have already made up their minds. They want to come to my office for a drive-by attempt to justify what they have already decided. Others seem intent on using the counseling session as a dress rehearsal for divorce court. From their attitudes and actions, it's clear that they view their marriage like a suit of clothes to be tried on, altered and adjusted, worn for one season, and then discarded for the next dress on the runway.

I cannot approach the topic of marriage and the dark eclipse of divorce without first letting you know where I'm coming from. My maternal grandparents birthed fifteen children (yes, fifteen!) together and remained married for over fifty years. Their union ended only when my grandfather went to his grave. My paternal grandmother married three times, each marriage ending with the death of her husband.

While my own parents divorced late in their marriage, I grew up as a child with two parents in my home, both of whom instilled in me a belief that marriage is sacred. I have now been married to the same woman, the mother of my children, for over twenty-five years. While we've had our ups and downs, the d-word has never come up. We tend to treat it like other people treat words that have been eradicated from their vocabulary. Using the word "divorce" to threaten, manipulate, and cajole a spouse into doing what you want them to do is never healthy for a satisfying, functional partnership. If the threat of divorce is continually bandied about between two people like poker players raising the ante back and forth, eventually someone will call the other's bluff and end the marriage.

THE D-WORD AS A WEAPON

Throwing around the d-word as a casual threat in an argument or disagreement is the equivalent of emotional blackmail. If your desire is to make your partner feel vulnerable and disrespected, then do it. But if that is not your intention, and divorce is not really what you want, but understanding and compassion is, reconsider your tactics and do some work to learn how to communicate effectively.

Yes, divorce is commonplace in our culture today, and I'm not condemning it or endorsing it. Sometimes it's necessary in order to save the mental, physical, or emotional well-being of an individual. Often it's unnecessary and becomes a lazy way out of a stormy season that will only thunder and crash around you louder when you're suddenly alone. Divorce is never easy and neither should contemplating it be easy. So allow me to offer some food for thought for those starving for change in their present relationships. You may still end up divorcing—I'm not necessarily here to talk you out of it, only to help you make the best decision. Read on and you will be much more informed of the cost, before you do.

Hard Hearts

From my personal, familial, and professional experiences regarding marriage, you can see that I never trivialize divorce. As an entrepreneur and a minister who discusses many subjects—economics, relationships, business, leadership—all of my thought processes are influenced by my understanding of Scripture. If my own experiences had not taught me to respect marriage, my understanding of God's word surely would.

" 'I hate divorce,' says the Lord God of Israel" (Malachi 2:16, NIV), making God's perspective on the subject plain and clear. Similarly, Jesus says, "It has been said, 'Anyone who divorces his wife must give her a certificate of divorce.' But I tell you that anyone who divorces his wife, except for marital unfaithfulness, causes her to become an adulteress, and anyone who marries the divorced woman commits adultery" (Matthew 5:31–32, NIV).

It's clear from these scriptures alone that our Creator did not desire us to enter into such a sacred oath and leave the back door open for a convenient exit strategy when the heat got too hot in the marital kitchen. But before we chisel in stone an ironclad, irrevocable commitment, we must also consider Jesus' words in Matthew 19:8: "Moses permitted you to divorce your wives because your hearts were hard. But it was not this way from the beginning." His statement seems to imply that there were exceptions made for circumstances resulting from the hardness of people's hearts. And if ever we were living in a time when people's hearts are hardened, it is now.

But we must keep in mind that just because Jesus says that unfaithfulness provides grounds for divorce doesn't mean that it necessitates divorce. It's similar to being stopped on the interstate for speeding. A police officer has grounds for giving us a ticket since we were going over the speed limit, and he would be just in doing so, but in his mercy he may give us a warning ticket or none at all. Our human nature is to live out of the double standard that we hold: we seek justice when we are wounded but want grace when we inflict the wounds. Where our marriage is concerned, we must not rush to judgment if mercy can heal the relationship.

However, there are situations that point to divorce as a solution. Another biblical justification for divorce is when the partners are unequally yoked. In 1 Corinthians 7, there's some indication that if an unbeliever wants to depart from a believing wife, such a one is not bound by the law. No matter what your theology is on this issue, none of us can deny the fact that some toxic relationships become so lethal for every reason ranging from health issues (contracting diseases) to safety issues (spousal abuse) that they necessitate separation and dissolution of the marriage.

Over the years of my ministry, I have counseled countless people who have found themselves trapped in sexless, loveless, and sometimes violent relationships that were so destructive that I no longer felt comfortable counseling them to stay in the marriage. I have seen the bloodied, beaten bodies of children caught in the crossfire of an abusive parent on one side and a codependent one on the other. One child in particular is seared into my memory, a boy whose father tied him to the back door and beat him with a bicycle chain until the wounds were inverted and white chunks of the child's flesh formed a horrific mosaic.

Such knowledge keeps me from rushing to judgment and telling people to wait for God to deliver them at any cost. I've learned that behind the smiles and professional demeanor of many people lie the terrified hearts of those caught in a snare of abusive control. I've seen individuals caught in such overwhelming abuse that I could no longer in good conscience encourage them to stay in the same house with their abuser, let alone in the marriage, when I knew that personally I would remove myself and my children. Sometimes divorce is the only way to put an end to a season of

pain, suffering, and loneliness that is far worse than the after-
effects of the separation.

OFFENSES THAT WARRANT DIVORCE

The decision to divorce should be taken very seriously. Lives, including yours, will be affected for years to come in ways you probably can't anticipate. Yet, we all have our deal breakers: Those
offenses for which you know that, for you, there will be no going
back. For some, this point is infidelity, for others it's substance, ver-
bal, or physical abuse, or serious dishonesty. You have to decide for
yourself what this point is for your marriage and discuss it with your
potential partner before you get married. Knowing where our loved
ones stand on certain issues up front can go a long way to making us
think twice before taking actions that may result in ruining our relationships.

Fool's Gold

At the heart of considering why you want to divorce your spouse,
you must look at what's absent from your present relationship. Is
it romance? Sex? Intimacy? Connection? Communication? All of
the above? Regardless of what's lacking, it eventually becomes so
tempting to look for what's missing in your marriage in the arms
of another person.

The scent of his cologne. The feel of her silk teddy against your
skin. The touch of his caress. Someone to hold you like your husband once did. Someone to whisper in your ear like your wife once
did. It's so tempting to think that this other person can provide
you with everything that your current spouse has let fall by the
wayside.

Before you have the affair or before you divorce your spouse to be with this person, you must consider what I call the 80/20 rule. We look for someone to marry who has 100 percent to contribute to us and to the marriage, someone who's exactly right for us, who seems to really get us and is into us completely. However, such a perfect person does not exist. At best our spouse, as the flawed, work-in-progress human being that he or she is, has 80 percent to bring to the table. In fact, if he or she can bring 80 percent of what we need to the relationship, we are doing extremely well.

Sometimes this seems like enough, but over time, as the years etch crow's feet along her eyes and protrude love handles around his waist, as the weight of bills and mortgages and ailing parents and struggling kids presses in, you long for the other 20 percent. You miss the romance and the intimate conversations before falling asleep. You miss the surprise gifts and the little notes in your briefcase. We become more and more aware of what we're missing and start looking, subtly or not so subtly. And when we're looking for something we usually find it. Suddenly we encounter someone who seems to have everything we want and need.

Like a shimmering oasis in Death Valley, our perception is an illusion, for the other person does not have 100 percent, either. They simply have the 20 percent that we're not getting from our spouse at home. This is why an affair infuses us with a sense of romance and passion, of idealism and inspiration. We suddenly get something we need that's been missing and think we've discovered a gold mine. But it's only when we truly get to know the other person, when they leave the toothpaste cap off the tube and leave the seat up on the toilet, that we discover that they don't have it all. It's the alchemy of fool's gold in which we spray-paint our vision of a rock with a golden hue in hopes that it can be as valuable as we need it to be.

Tyler Perry heard me speak on the 80/20 rule and was so taken by its truth that he asked to use it in his movie *Why Did I Get Married?*, in which characters struggle with this very misperception. They learn as we all do that there are no perfect people or perfect relationships. The reality of intimacy is that we only grow close to each other when we struggle, fail, forgive, persevere, and press on together. When someone sees you fail them and still loves you and wants to be with you, then you have something that is richer and deeper than even 100 percent could provide us.

INAPPROPRIATE RELATIONSHIPS

If you find yourself relating in an inappropriate way with someone outside your marriage or relationship, it is likely a sign that there is something wrong at home. Sure, after years of marriage or a steady monogamous relationship, the passion and excitement that you once felt for your partner has probably evolved into something less explosive. As we settle into the routine of life, we have the tendency to focus on the day-to-day concerns of living: children, careers, bills, caring for aging parents, etc. But if you find yourself looking outside of your relationship for a reconnection to those feelings of euphoria you once had, it should be a warning signal that your relationships could be in trouble. It may be flattering to get the undivided attention of another person who, unlike your spouse, has only your needs in mind; it is highly unlikely to be the answer to your woes.

Art Lessons

While other chapters in this book are devoted to relational issues that should be considered prior to marriage, the couple who seeks to return from the brink of divorce faces some unique wrinkles that must be smoothed from the garment of their relationship. Facing the harsh blows of life, whether they be circumstantial, such as a layoff or foreclosure, or relational, such as a betrayal or addiction, a couple must learn how to reconnect, rebuild, and revitalize what they once had. In order to accomplish such a feat, each individual must be willing to take some art lessons.

Just as the artist's hand has five fingers that clasp the brush and apply it to the canvas, couples must learn to grasp five key areas if they are to apply hope across their prior portrait of despair. The first and fundamental key is the art of knowing the other person. Individuals often try to figure out the other person, put them in a box, and label them for the rest of their lives. Knowing someone is a progressive art, not a static science with immutable data.

You must view the other person as a mystery that requires ongoing scrutiny and lifelong learning. The Bible tells us that a man and a woman should dwell together according to knowledge (1 Peter 3:7) and, as we've seen, encouraged couples to spend the first year together without other distractions. Couples who wish to save their marriage after giving divorce a long, hard look must be willing to revision their partner. The other person may not be who you thought they were, but neither are you. Allow room for both of you to evolve, revolve, and resolve!

Next, the art of listening must be practiced on a regular basis. The reason many couples consider divorce in the first place is because each gives the other a monologue, a sermon, or a politician's speech without leaving room for a real conversation. Counseling is sometimes so effective simply because it forces each of you to slow down and hear the other person's language. Most couples are so busy trying to get their point in and outscore the other one in the fight that they don't listen for solutions and places of negotiation.

Divorce would not be so common if we would listen with open

hearts instead of closed minds. Remember, God said that he only permitted divorce because the people's hearts were hard. This means that their hearts would not melt to the level of understanding and the place of negotiation. Some couples find it easier to write each other letters expressing their feelings as they move back into learning how to communicate at a new and deeper level.

Many artists pause and wait for the light to hit their subject just right in order to capture it on the canvas. They may sit an entire afternoon waiting for sunset to cast the golden peach illumination across the horizon. Similarly, the art of waiting must not be underestimated in its ability to restore beauty to your relationship. This art combines patience with perseverance and can be excruciating at times as you bend but refuse to break.

When the Bible says that a man must leave his mother and father (including his culture, background, and family language) and take unto him a wife (developing a new culture, background, and family language), they shall cleave and become one. Like the birthing of a new nation of people, bonding takes time and work. While we wait for the new skin of love to graft, we need patience. We know they that wait on the Lord shall have their strength renewed. His timing produces a healing deeper and richer than anything we can force to happen. There can be a time to cut losses and move on in your life, but you both should exhaust yourselves and every option before severing the relationship.

Perhaps the hardest art to master is the art of forgiving. Although it's fodder for tabloids and talk shows, public figures' private scandals are no one's business but those involved. It is not our place to say whether a politician's wife or celebrity's husband should forgive him or her for their transgressions. No one stays married to anyone without some forgiveness involved. God doesn't stay with us without our asking his forgiveness.

We are told to ask him, "Forgive us our debts as we forgive those who trespass against us." Trespassing against us includes infidelity, among other things. If you don't practice forgiveness in the little things, it makes it that much harder to extend and receive grace during the crisis moments. The art of forgiveness requires letting go of perfection and performance and grasping hold of grace and gratitude.

Finally, the art of openness requires us to remain vulnerable, transparent, and willing to trust again. You know how you feel pain when the doctor gives you a shot? Your first reaction is to tighten up. Similarly, our hearts naturally clench and tighten after pain or rejection. It is a reflex mechanism in the soul, a way we protect ourselves subconsciously.

This is a great attribute anywhere else but in marriage. Because if you do not turn off this mechanism, you will close your soul. This is the state where you love the person, you still come home at night but you are braced, no longer present in the moment. You have closed yourself for fear of disappointment or hurt. But marriage is an open covenant consummated by sex which removes all barriers and celebrates the joy of nothing between the two people. It is difficult to attain and maintain such intimacy, both emotionally and physically, after betrayal and disappointment. If you lost the closeness, however, you can get it back if you're willing to relax your soul and open your heart toward the other person.

Earn Your Way Out

If one is governed by the headlines or tutored by the television set, it's easy to come to the conclusion that divorce has no consequences. Despite what *Desperate Housewives* or *People* magazine would have us think, this is not so. Some have suggested that divorce is more traumatic to the divorced person than death would be to the widow or widower. Think for a moment that when your spouse dies, all your intimate secrets, private talks, and personal details go to the grave with them.

With death, you avoid a degree of the anguish invoked in the heart of those separated who lie in the bed at night and wonder if their secrets have become fodder for pillow talk as their former spouse lies in bed with someone else. This violation of privacy alone is enough to suggest that divorce carries unseen ripples of regret and tremors of second thoughts for the rest of your life. Not to mention the orphaned memories that continue to survive in the person who has now been ripped away from the partner that helped them make those memories. There is always the heartache that exists between in-laws as you lose friendships and intimate family connections when they are forced to choose sides.

Then think of all the little daily moments that form the core ingredients of intimacy. Before you divorce, you must ask yourself if you're prepared to come home to an empty apartment where you barely have space for the kids in the second bedroom on your weekends with custody. You must ask yourself who will laugh at your little jokes or smile at you when you talk to yourself. Who will run your hot bath at the end of an exhausting day? Who will sort the bills so you know what is due when? Who will toss out the old lettuce from the fridge or make your favorite cake for your birthday? Who will mark the anniversary of the death of your parents with you? Who will put their cold feet on you beneath the covers?

Marriages build equity over time like a property growing in value year after year. The little things add up. The trials endured, the crises averted, the joys celebrated. The birth of your children. Their first day at school. Their first night out past curfew. That promotion you worked so hard to attain. That season of loss when your mother had Alzheimer's. The anniversary when he surprised you with the romantic getaway. The collage of intimacy that had been artistically assembled by the former life you shared peels away layer by layer until there's nothing left but a smeared canvas of bitter brush strokes. Are you ready to throw away all that equity and start all over in some fixer-upper that will take years to get to the same level that you gave away?

This equity is not only figurative but literal as well. Divorce is expensive. The life you've spent years and tears building together is suddenly, violently ripped asunder with the signing of a document. Insurance policies change—are your kids covered now?—along with bank accounts, property assignments, alimony payments, joint custody calendars, and 401(k)s. Split the assets. Divide the household. Allocate the savings. When love doesn't last, the collateral damage goes beyond anything either of you could have ever expected. We may not go as far as Johnnie Taylor did when he said it's cheaper to keep her, but we all understand what he means.

Before you sign on the dotted line and terminate your legal status as a married individual, you must look at all facets of the relationship along with your motives. I like what my friend Dr. Phil McGraw says about people pursuing a divorce: they must *earn* their way out of the marriage. By this he means you have an obligation to do everything you can possibly do before initiating the suicide of a relationship that was meant to give life to the one you love and the children that you birthed together.

Children deserve special consideration. Certainly, it's better for them to have a stable environment with one parent than an unstable or abusive home with two. Yet every parent knows that raising children requires a certain measure of sacrifice. Sometimes you must be willing to give up the illusion of happiness in exchange for the reality of your children's well being. It has been said that the hand that rocks the cradle rules the world. This usually testifies to the influence of a mother on an individual's life. In reality, however, not one hand but two rock our cradles. Ideally, both mother and father create a safe nesting place for children to experience their first interactions with the world around them.

Many if not most of my associates who have come from single-parent homes are wise enough to realize that there are successful ways to parent children with one parent. However, having a mother and a father present brings balance and complementary dynamics into a child's life. As children mature into adults, their understanding of the opposite sex develops more effectively when they are exposed to the opposite sex in their parental experience. Severing this socialization process without a detrimental influence on the children is difficult but not impossible. When all else fails and it's necessary to end the marriage, your children must not become part of the collateral damage.

And there will be damage. It's tragic to see the ones who come to me thinking they'll get a nice, neat civil divorce. Over the years, there seldom exists a civil divorce. The very act reeks of rejection, abandonment, depression, and turmoil. The process is laced with anger and revenge and a desire to make the other person feel the same level of pain.

DIVORCE AFFECTS MORE THAN THE TWO OF YOU

Divorce doesn't impact just the two parties immediately involved. It also has further-reaching effects. Obviously children are affected, often blaming themselves and feeling stuck between two parents, both of whom they love and adore, and are often worried that they must choose sides. Your parents are affected; they may have grown to consider your loved one a part of the family, even see them as the son or daughter they never had. Friends are impacted, too. It's very hard to be friends with a couple who divorces; being asked to choose sides and offer support to one friend over the other can be difficult and confusing.

Divorce will also affect your future love relationship. While the grass often looks greener in the single lawn in front of the bachelor or bachelorette pad down the street, looks can be deceiving. Many people are wary of dating someone who is once, twice, or many-times divorced. After all, their track record isn't so great where marriage is concerned. There is also the fear, if there are children involved, that there will be issues with the ex-spouse over custody, weekend visits, child support, and finances. There is nothing romantic about any of that. And depending on how many divorces you have experienced, your financial obligations can mount, making you a less than attractive catch for a potential mate who may love you but not your baggage.

The After Life

I was teaching on relationships at an international ministers' summit recently when one of the ministers from another country pointed out that we in America are seeing a rash of divorces even among clergy. He found the fact reprehensible and clearly had no use for clergy and perhaps anyone who was divorced. While I agree that clergy should set an example and lead the way in providing role models of patience, passion, and perseverance, I reminded him that divorce is no respecter of persons and strikes relationships in all cultures. It may not have been as socially acceptable, but it has been around as long as the institution of marriage. He seemed to forget preachers are people, too.

I cautioned this man to reconsider how we perceive those who are divorced. We must not teach in principle that a murderer can be forgiven for murder but a divorced person can't be forgiven for severing a marriage. In God's sight is it better to kill our spouse than to divorce him? No. People are flawed human beings who make wrong choices, both in marrying and in divorcing.

In fact, I see so many couples who never should have married in the first place struggling in their relationship. We must be reminded that just because we hooked up with someone doesn't mean that God put us together. So many decisions to marry are made for the wrong reasons: feeling lonely, being on the rebound, improving living conditions, escaping our past, avoiding fornication, on and on. Many of the couples I've counseled not to marry have later thanked me because they realized that they were forcing a relationship for the wrong reasons.

If we can admit that there are some people who shouldn't marry, then we must rationalize that not all were stopped before their wedding. Many times we as parents try feverishly to discourage our children from marrying someone who in our view is not a good match. Why then would we believe this as a parent and not accept that some adults are suffering from wrong decisions that were not circumvented? Just because you begin a journey going in the wrong direction does not necessitate that you can't change course and find a new map.

I'm grateful to share that there is life after divorce. The afterlife can become a season of starting over and loving yourself and meeting your own needs for the first time. You can rebound from the trauma of a life reconfigured and reposition yourself for the remaining years. You can recover without dragging the baggage of your past into the next relationship. Many clergymen have survived it, along with kings, presidents, princesses, managers, and CEOs. People we respect and admire have endured it and gone on to make sizeable contributions to the world. Getting a divorce is not the eulogy to your life and your capacity to love. But it can be a catalyst for rebounding and repositioning your future.

When two people divorce, they clash with the force of an atomic bomb, leaving them with no choice but to pilfer through the rubbish and rebuild their lives elsewhere. Divorce is not a death sentence, but you must examine your life with honesty, candor, and wisdom . . . before you do.

sixteen
Before You Settle for Less

"Effort only fully releases its reward after a person refuses to quit."

—*Napoleon Hill*

M any men and women reach a certain plateau in their lives where it feels like the best of their lives is behind them. They've chosen a career field and have arrived at a certain measure of success. They've been in a serious relationship, married, had children, and enjoyed the rewarding responsibilities of building a family.

On the surface, their lives seem fulfilling and they often feel guilty for their discomfort. They go to church, take a nice vacation every other year, and drive a dependable, late-model car that gets them where they need to go. They may even have larger measures of success and achieved everything they set their minds to obtaining. But still something's missing.

Their zest for life has been ground down to a fine powder that becomes scattered to the four winds every time one of life's storms blows through. They are burned out by the obligations of the office, tired of the drama with their teenagers, weary of the disconnection with their spouse, and exhausted by the giant treadmill their lives have become. Consequently, they begin to self-destruct, looking to an affair, a career change, a face lift, or a new sports car to escape their boredom, anger, and frustration.

Quitting Time

Many of the people who come to me for counsel have shared their secret fantasy of running away and leaving everything behind, starting over in another country, culture, or relationship. Can you relate? "I want to quit my life," one man told me. "I'm sick and tired of everyone sucking the life out of me without putting in anything in return. I want to disappear and never look back." To this man and others, I usually point out the obvious: you might leave the circumstances behind but you'll never escape yourself. Those who have quit life end up no happier than those who stuck it out. The cast may change but the script usually stays the same.

Before you quit anything—your job, your marriage, or your life—I encourage you to think about why you want to leave and where you want to go next. If the trapeze artist must relinquish her hold on the swinging bar in order to catch the next bar coming her way, then we must have a clear perspective on what we're releasing and what we're moving toward. We're doomed to repeat the past if we don't examine our prior choices.

Too often, we have quit the wrong things at the wrong time.

We have relinquished the dreams that would have sustained us on our journey in favor of the dreams of others. Pleasing our parents, conforming to others' expectations, and taking the most convenient opportunities that came our way will eventually catch up to us and lead us into a season of slow-burning rage and inverted depression.

On the other hand, maybe we have been so afraid of change that we now need to quit something in order to make room for the next season of our lives. You may need to quit your present job, relationship, or church situation in order to make room for the next career, person, or fellowship. For most of us, we often dig our own ruts in life through a stop-start, start-stall style of decision making in which we vacillate between our boredom with what we have and our fear of future uncertainty.

Before you quit anything, you should look within and seek to determine your real motives for such a severance. Are you settling for less than you're worth? Staying in a relationship because you're afraid to be single and alone? Keeping a job that's beneath you because it's too tough to change careers at your age? Resigning yourself to the mediocrity of the present because of the fearful uncertainty of leaping off the cliff of your future?

The only way to know is to examine your dreams. The secret to making powerful decisions throughout your life is often the difference between keeping your dreams alive and settling for a walk-on part in someone else's dream. Before you quit, it's time to revive those unrecognizable longings that have been languishing with freezer burn deep in the bottom of your heart.

The Lazarus Syndrome

You may be familiar with the story of Lazarus, the brother of Mary and Martha, who suffered an illness that claimed his life, even while Jesus was notified of his condition. His sisters buried him in the family tomb and had been grieving four days when Jesus finally arrived to ask after his sick friend. "Where have you laid him?" he asked. This is the powerful scene where we find the simple understatement of "Jesus wept" (John 11:35, KJV).

Then despite the smell of decay emanating from the gravesite and the frustration of the women over why he had not arrived prior to their brother's death, Jesus called for Lazarus to come out. Mary and Martha's brother emerged and Jesus then commanded, "Take off the grave clothes and let him go" (John 11:43–44, NIV). His premature burial could hardly prevent the God of the universe from rekindling the beating of his heart and the flow of lifeblood through his veins. Lazarus was very much alive.

In the same way, we have dreams that we may have buried prematurely that God now wants to resurrect in our lives. These dreams may center on completing your education, starting your own business, pursuing a relationship, or expressing a creative talent that you have had to stifle.

Most of us learn through the process of maturation and enculturation that all of our dreams won't come true. In fact, based on the circumstances of life—just the daily grind of living, working, and supporting a family, not to mention the harsh blows of loss and the gravity of grievances—we learn to be realistic and see the glass half-empty no matter how much it may have contained at one time. However, I found the only way to overcome the midlife doldrums (which can assault you at any age and stage of your life) is to call forth your dreams from the tomb where you buried them. Otherwise, you will end up on a self-destructive path to follow them into the grave, either literally or figuratively.

First, you must make a conscious choice to believe that a resurrection is possible. Such a transformation requires a level of faith that you may have abandoned as well. You must be willing to face your past disappointments and recalibrate your expectations. You must dare to hope and silence the hype of the internal critic that has held the keys to the prison for the artist within you. You must dare to hope and ignore the critical chatter from others in your life who are either incapable of supporting or unwilling to encourage you in your endeavors. You must dare to hope when another client cancels her order or another bill transcends your credit limit.

Then you must be willing to grieve the past choices you've made, which have either directly or indirectly resulted in another layer of dirt being heaped on your buried-alive longings. You likely had good reasons and logical self-justification for choosing what you chose, but if the result placed greater distance between you and your dreams, then you must be willing to forgive yourself as well as others who have discouraged you.

In Lazarus' story, his sisters grieved for four days before Jesus came to restore their brother to life. Jesus himself wept at his friend's tomb. It might be tempting to think that these tears were wasted because Lazarus came back to life. Yet perhaps it took the loss of their brother for Mary and Martha to fully appreciate how much they loved their brother and missed his presence in their lives. Sometimes we must lose our dreams in order to realize just how precious they are to us. Then when they are restored and emerge with new life from the tomb of our regret, we can celebrate their resurrection with true appreciation.

Finally, you must be willing to remove the grave clothes from your dreams and unwrap the tattered rags that have accumulated through the years of dormancy. This process includes facing the facts about how you have changed over the years. If your dream was to become an astronaut on the space shuttle or to be a star forward on an NBA team, then your age, lack of experience, and physical condition may have eliminated those possibilities.

However, your dream can still live if you will allow it to evolve. You have changed over the years since your dream first took root so you must allow that it has changed as well. It may yield different fruit than you first imagined but fruit nonetheless. You may not be able to become an astronaut but you can become a science teacher, passing along your passion for the solar system to seventh graders. You may not have the stamina left to take on Allen Iverson or Dirk Nowitzki on the court, but you can channel your passion into coaching some young men who share your dream and have time on their side.

Consider how your dream can bless others as well as fulfill your own purpose and desire for a meaningful life. If our dreams only involve more money, possessions, and personal achievements, then we'll continue to feel empty because we're not giving back and passing along the passion to fuel someone else's dream. We must allow our dreams to evolve just as our lives have evolved and we must be willing to see them transcend our own happiness.

WE ALL HAVE MOMENTS WE WANT TO QUIT

If you are like most people, as you get older, you think of dreams as a luxury you can no longer afford. Especially if you are married with children, dreams have been replaced by mortgage payments, tuition bills, trips to the orthodontist, and other more serious concerns. After working all day, and cooking, cleaning, and helping with homework all night, the only dreams you have are the ones that come to you in your sleep, after your exhausted head hits the pillow, and usually you are too tired to even remember them.

There are certainly realities and responsibilities of life that prevent us from picking up and quitting our jobs, or going off to travel around the world on a whim. But, often, those realities are really excuses or fears that if we try to do something different, something we dream of doing, we will fail. We convince ourselves it's better to quit while we are ahead, well, maybe not ahead, but at least we are comfortable. When asked why they have quit pursuing a dream you often hear people quote the old saying, "The devil you know is better than the devil you don't."

This kind of pessimistic attitude keeps you stuck in life. Giving up on dreams is like giving up on hope. I've heard it said we are Easter people living in a Good Friday world. Hope, dreams are all we really have. Sure, some dreams are not meant to come true. After all, only a very fortunate few of us can be Olympic athletes or movie stars. Yet, many of the dreams we give up on, with a little love and care, like Jesus, can be resurrected. Sometimes it seems easier to just quit; to just give up and accept your lot in life. Life is not necessarily good, but it is good enough.

But before you quit your dream, consider if nothing changed from this point forward, are you satisfied with your life? If your answer is no, then quitting may be premature. Consider reassessing, readjusting your dream to better suit your circumstances and the person you are now. If you want to start a business, take a trip, or begin a second career, whatever it is, inject some positive energy into your dream by taking a seminar, joining a support group, returning to school, or reading a book on the subject.

Devise a new plan. Surround yourself with like-minded, positive people for support. And then start by taking a risk, a small one at first, some little step toward realizing your goal. Be observant, take notes, consider what you learn, if it works out, great, if it doesn't, adjust and then take another step, maybe a little bigger risk. Do it again and again, until each time the risks you take will get easier to deal with, and soon you'll find yourself stronger, more courageous, and steps down the road toward where you want to be in your life, and closer to making your dreams come true.

As Langston Hughes wrote, "Hold fast to dreams / For if dreams die / Life is a broken-winged bird that cannot fly, / Hold fast to dreams / For when dreams go / Life is a barren field / Frozen with snow."

Fear of Flying

Have you ever had the privilege to witness the flight of the beautiful, majestic bird known as the eagle? I've been blessed to see several of them, both in this country and in Africa, and been fascinated by their prowess. Adult eagles have a wingspan of nine feet, and their eagle-eye vision for which they are so well known can pinpoint movement up to three miles away. As they soar higher and higher, glimpsing the purple peaks of the mountaintop miles away, the eagle embodies an integrity of purpose that we would do well to emulate.

They did not develop their grace, agility, and precision overnight. On the contrary, they were often forced by their parent to leave their home. When the eagle stirs her nest, she shakes things up to make it uncomfortable for her eaglets to stay in their protected environment. She will pick them up and drop them outside the nest. And as the little birds begin falling, they do what's instinctual and begin flapping, breaking their fall and flirting with the breeze in their first attempt at flying.

The mother watches proudly and continues this process for the education of their survival: fall and then flap and then fly. Flailing, falling, flapping, soaring, eagles learn by being pushed to do what they were born to do. Otherwise, they would never learn to exercise their natural gifts and inherent abilities upon which their individual survival and the perpetuation of their species depend.

Everything I ever birthed in my life went through this process. Everything that we endeavor to accomplish, perform, or achieve must go through this back and forth, recursive process of three steps forward and two steps back. We will never reach the eagle heights for which God designed us if we are not willing to flap in the midst of our falls and find the current that can lift us as we spread our wings.

Every successful business has sputtered and fluttered and nearly failed before it breaks through to the next level of its success. People who have achieved great things in life are usually no more gifted, intelligent, or privileged than the rest of us. They simply have learned to lean into their mistakes and persevere through them to the next level of challenge and expectation. How many Olympic gold medal winners didn't make their country's team the first time they applied? How many times has Donald Trump declared bankruptcy for one of his companies? How many times did Dr. King have doors slammed in his face and deaf ears deflect his message before a movement was birthed and people of all colors began heeding his call for change?

Someone told me early in life, "you'll win if you don't quit," and it has proved true time and again. I have never seen a quitter win because there is simply no way possible to win if you quit. But if you don't give up, you can win.

With passion and tenacity, you learn to break the elephant you wish to digest into bite-size pieces. You do the next thing you know to do and take the next step that's in front of you. You fulfill the next order, deliver the next shipment, preach the next sermon, prepare for the next meeting, write the next report, set the next table, or wash the next load of laundry.

You may see no way humanly possible for your dream to be birthed, but that can be a positive because it keeps you humble, willing to seek and accept help from others, and on the lookout for divine intervention. Dreams worth having should not be attainable on your own strength—these are merely goals. Dreams must be worthy of the talent, time, and tears you pour into them so that when your baby is birthed, it is so much larger than you could ever have delivered on your own.

You must know that something that starts out understaffed, underfunded, and underperforming can still learn how to fly. You may have to swoop down and save it several times before it takes flight. Maybe the mother eagle takes the patience to teach her eaglets to fly because of all that she went through. From conceiving in flight to birthing them high above the treetops, the mother goes through so much that she's not willing to let them fail by staying in the safety of the cozy nest. She takes the risk to push her baby out of its comfort zone to let it be all that it was meant to be. She knows it will never learn how to fly in safe places.

I recall how many dreams I have birthed and then had to elevate the risk over and over again. When I birthed a play, I couldn't keep it safe by allowing it to be a nice little church production. So I took it on the road and had to spend $50,000 on radio advertisements on top of the $78,000 a week required to stage and produce the play. I'll never forget that opening night on the road. It didn't sell so well, so we had given away tickets in hopes that word of mouth would spread the news of the quality of our production. Within a week or two, we began playing sold-out shows in every major city in which we performed. Most people don't have the tenacity to withstand the fluttering stage of building your dream. If you believe in it, then you'll fight for it, one battle at a time.

My father is another example of a man with a dream that experienced constant fluttering before the flight. He began work as a janitor for a small business in our town. With one mop and one bucket, he worked tirelessly week after week until the building looked like new. Soon word spread about the quality of his labors and the reliability of his character. He was able to hire a couple of employees and fill in with family and friends. When I was ten years old, he'd toss me in with the rest of the fledgling crew, and my job was to take Brillo pads to the corners and scrub them clean. He started where he was and ended up with a reputable small business that employed a staff of forty-eight.

Before you quit, you must overcome your fear of heights and be willing to risk failing at the next level. Feel the fear and at least try to flutter. You'll never fly if you don't fall, flap hard, and lean into the winds of change. Revive your dreams and refuse to give them up to the tomb of past mistakes and present regrets. "But those who hope in the Lord will renew their strength. They will soar on wings like eagles; they will run and not grow weary, they will walk and not be faint" (Isaiah 40:31, NIV). All of us are tempted to quit at times, to give up the fight and just accept mediocrity. But the next time weariness weighs you down or trials temporarily make you want to give up your dreams, take a deep breath and ask the Lord for your strength to be renewed, before you do!

seventeen
Before You Fight

"The most important of life's battles is the one we fight daily in the silent chambers of the soul."

—*David McKay*

Sometimes the decision that prevents us from settling for less is a decision to fight for what matters most. While most of us don't participate in street fights or boardroom brawls, the decision to fight may not be an option that you're allowing yourself when you should. On the other hand, some of us may have developed a defensive stance that prevents us from accepting what we need. Discerning when to fight and when to let our defenses down is crucial to maturity.

All of us have inherited from our primal ancient ancestors a propensity to defend our turf and club any threatening predator over the head. Our great Creator equipped even the most timid amongst us with the adrenaline needed to kick us into overdrive when the heat is on. This intrinsic flight or fight instinct may be a burden to some, but if managed well, for most of us it can be a tremendous asset.

We might ask ourselves whether our fight instincts have become more refined since prehistoric days. No longer are dinosaurs threatening our existence or are we bound to hunt and gather. However, we still see incredible violence used to extort power with both individuals and entire nations. In ancient civilizations, conflict between cultures was often resolved by the use of primitive destruction. Entire villages were burned, the women raped, the spoils divided, the children enslaved or murdered ruthlessly. In biblical times, this practice prevailed in such dramatic examples as that of the Amalekites invading Ziklag (1 Samuel 20:1–4). We are told that as David and his entourage surveyed the damage, they "lifted up their voice and wept, until they had no more power to weep" (1 Samuel 30:4, KJV).

When we fight, we must be willing to struggle for a solution that's larger than our own agenda. As brutal and blood-crazed as war can be, aggression is not always a bad thing. Our fighting instinct can be put to good use. When we feel passionately enough about something to fight for it, then we are emphasizing its important to ourselves and those around us. Often we can channel our anger, frustration, or feelings of powerlessness into the fight of perseverance, determination, and achievement.

FACING PRESENT INJUSTICE AND RESOLVING CONFLICT

Recently I took a position on the board of the Underground Railroad Freedom Center and its amazing museum in Cincinnati, Ohio, to help draw attention to the often covert atrocity that at least thirty million people remain enslaved around the world. One need not look back too far to find similar inhumanity in the bloody remains sprinkled up and down the streets of rural areas of dry parched regions of Uganda or Rwanda. From South Africa to South America, human blood is hidden just beneath the soil, much of it shed needlessly. Despite the advancements for human civil rights, we still live in a society where slavery abounds globally. I love that the museum uses a look at our past to draw attention to the dirt under the rug of our contemporary society!

Those who say we should not look back are often those who close their eyes to present injustice and live in towers of self-induced deception!

Today terrorist and hate groups aside, most trained national armies and the cultures of our times are moving away from torture and rape to become slightly more civilized in how we conquer conflict and move on. The Geneva Conventions brought some civility to the processes we engage in resolving conflict. Organizations like the United Nations and Amnesty International create platforms for rules of engagement for conflict between nations. Still, Guantánamo Bay has drawn raised eyebrows recently as it is suggested that in spite of our professed civility we may not be living up to the ideals that we so often espouse.

Overall, though, I would like to believe that we are attempting to become more humane, compassionate, and civil in resolving conflict. A great example emerges in the truth commission that was established in South Africa recently. As opposed to the revenge-based bitterness of the past, this movement seeks to facilitate communication and true understanding. Its founding was a choice to move forward by listening to each side's pain. Real truth isn't held in the pain of one side but also understanding the pain of the other.

For example, you cannot stop domestic violence by treating the victim if you are not going to reach out to help the perpetrator. The compassion for one doesn't negate the need of the other. If you do not facilitate healing for both, then while you are building centers for the victim, the ignored pain of the abuser is reproducing itself in the lives of the others. Why fertilize the garden if you are not going to pull the weeds that threaten its survival?

Fight Back

Recently, I was wrestling with some serious back pain. After fighting through tremendous aches for a prolonged period of time, I decided to undergo surgery on my back. Little did I know that the solution would bring as much hurt as the problem! Often the process of getting well releases new, acute soreness, but it is this very process that is necessary to heal the chronic pain.

So there I found myself lying in a hospital bed with my back opened up four inches deep for a complete and intense surgery. I awoke from anesthesia to find that I was going to need to fight the brutal savage throbbing of my resulting muscle spasms. It felt like knives were ripping through my glutes and thighs. It was torture to get up and walk on so many bruised and lacerated muscles. But if I hoped to get well, I had to fight off the temptation to stay in the bed and then fight off the new pain of muscles that were in shock!

Every time I tried to stand up, I wanted to whimper from the shards of pain cutting through my muscles. My nerves would jump around wildly inside of me like hot popcorn! Recovery was as anguishing as my previous denial of the pain had been, but the ends of one was different than the other. I knew that I had to endure one intense bout of pain if I ever hoped to overcome the chronic pain that threatened to debilitate me.

This lesson holds true for all of us as we enter the fight. We must choose where to direct our energies of aggression. If you are going to heal any conflict, you have to give up the need for revenge, retaliation, and being right and fight for the greater good. But I must warn you: this choice brings its own pain and some people choose to repeat the injury rather than initiate the healing of forgiving and understanding each other's pain and fear. Clubbing your enemy in the head may bring a temporary gratification, but in the long run he will get back up again and the war continues when the healing could have been underway!

The Art of Fighting

In infinite wisdom, the good Lord did not create us to be passive and hide like slugs under rocks avoiding conflict. God gave us the gift of anger and the fuel of adrenaline. Without our use of such tools, the many predators of our well-being would pilfer our possessions, ransack our riches, and bludgeon our self-esteem. You have to fight to walk, to improve, to graduate, to love, to live, to survive.

But before you fight, you must think deeply to understand whether the spoils of the war justify the fight. If yes, stand up to the pain, not just your own but the pain of all those involved, the innocent who may be hurt in the fight, and those against you. Because, try all you want, if you truly want to escape the hold your enemies have on you, you must understand their pain. One-upping him is like scoring points in the pain game after the final buzzer rings: you aren't winning, only delaying the healing process.

As you think through which fights to engage and which to avoid, realize that some people are not as interested in results as they are in conflict. Too many times we are led by people who love to fight. They may be warmongers and hate baiters or they may even wear the camouflage of justice, but they don't want to find a solution as much as they want to continue the battle. They don't love winning—they're in love with fighting!

Many people seek justice but their power is diluted by their association with those who only seek drama. These crusaders never give credit to the other side even when good is done because they love the fight more than the facts. Always wanting to be heard is a sign of not listening, and no conflict is resolved without listening to both sides.

The truth of the matter is that some of us have fought so much over the years that we become stuck in fight mode. Eventually as we get older, we become such veterans at the art of fighting that like old war heroes we wake up in the night in defense mode and attack. You and I have both heard of men who pull knives on their wives sleeping soundly next to them in bed because they heard thunder in the night and thought it was gunfire. They don't know in their subconscious minds that Vietnam or the Korean War or whatever war they fought has ended. This tragic condition comes to those who remain shell shocked from real war, locked in a perpetual state of anxious alert.

Big Brother

I see this fighting proclivity demonstrated in the life of my older brother, Ernest. He is a calm, caring man but has always been a fighter instinctively. While he isn't a bully at heart, let's just say that he has had bully tendencies! When he was younger, he would fight a pregnant gorilla or a rabid rattlesnake just to show them who was in charge. To me, he was the original Crocodile Dundee!

Now that we are older he says fighting was an environmentally induced habit and attributes it to his early school days. Ernest went to school with children older than himself. He was blessed and cursed with an intellectual brightness that allowed him to graduate from high school at fifteen. Surrounded by older peers who were threatened by his gift, you can only imagine what he dealt with on a day-to-day basis. Add to this the fact that he was the part of that first group of black children to desegregate public education, and you can see why he thought fighting was a part of getting home from school every day. It didn't take long for his emotional stick shift to get stuck in fight gear! Ernest's environment *had* prewired him to protect himself. Then later, as is the case for many eldest siblings, his fight instinct was reinforced as he sought to protect the rest of his family.

Maybe your battle background was different, but many of us grew up encountering obstacles that conditioned a fight-prone personality. Many of us come from cultures and communities where anger is applauded. Some of us were raised in the 'hood or incubated by brawling neighborhoods.

This wasn't just in the black communities, either. I knew some young white guys in West Virginia who would turn red-faced, break beer bottles over their own heads, and spit healthy wads of snuff out of their mouths prior to getting in the mood for a bone-crushing conflict.

I've seen dignified professors and distinguished CEOs lose their cool and explode like a human grenade during a botched board meeting. My own sweet grandmother trashed the hospital when she thought she was being treated unfairly, and I was told it took several orderlies to get her back in the bed and restore her usual calm, cookie-baking eighty-year-old-grandma demeanor!

Many sisters were raised in environments that applauded quick tongues, sharp attacks, and ice maiden responses! Yes, I grew up around fighting women. It was unwise if not life-threatening, when I was a kid, to assume that my opponent couldn't fight because she was a girl. Most girls fought each other, but a few young ladies could deck a boy with extreme effectiveness, leaving him dazed by the taste of blood and a bruised ego. These Amazons were fighting long before Laila Ali ever put on her first pair of boxing gloves!

One day while moving through the house, I glanced up at a window and to my shock saw an angry man snarling back at me. I thought he must have been an attacker about to break in and destroy all that I had worked to attain. In unrestrained rage, I leapt with clenched fists to release an assault on him like you have never seen. As I struck the glass, I was shocked to hear it shatter and find it was not a window at all but a mirror I had hit. The angry guy who I had seen was only a reflection of myself staring back at me!

Clearly, fighters transcend gender, race, age, and status.

WAR AND PEACE

Nations who rush to war are like people who rush to fight; they soon learn that what they lost is not worth what they gained. As body bags come quietly rolling down the ramps of airplanes, one realizes that the cost of war is far more than the billions of dollars that we expend, which could feed the hungry and clothe the naked. The real cost of war is the children who lost their parents, the parents who lost their children, and the men and women who lost their spouses and siblings. This cost cannot be measured but it can be questioned.

These brave men and women who gave their lives and forfeited their youth to defend their country made the ultimate sacrifice. We never waver from the deep appreciation for the noble gift they selflessly offer in the name of freedom. However, our gratitude becomes infused with rage when we realize that they might have died because some trigger-happy politicians with anger management issues didn't exhaust every possible method of resolution. Too often leaders pay the bill for their authority with the blood shed from those they serve!

Nonetheless, amazing strides are being made among calmer minds and more peaceful hearts. Just think of the recent highly touted event that took place in North Korea. North Korea's hostility toward America is no secret. From the Korean War until now, a lingering fog of anger and antagonism has enveloped our international relationship. This is evidenced in North Korea with slogans such as LET'S TAKE REVENGE A THOUSAND TIMES ON THE U.S. IMPERIALIST WOLVES! on T-shirts and billboards. It's a far cry from GOD BLESS THE U.S.A.!

Most of us wouldn't choose to spend a vacation in such an acrid atmosphere. However, none of this deterred the New York Philharmonic from performing in Pyongyang. In February 2008, the Philharmonic performed its melodious music with passion and professionalism in an atmosphere that many thought would be a nightmare experience. Out of respect, the orchestra included both Korean music and American ballads in its repertoire.

Somewhere in the process of the musical presentation, suspicions waned and hostility melted like a glacier slowly dissolving into the sea of sound. In its stead a warm and amazing sense of kinship prevailed among those who had previously viewed each other with unabashed disdain. No reconciliation referendums were passed in a boardroom. Nor did negotiation derive from some crafty bill promising aid for trade. No, it was the soft sound of violins and an honest respect for each other's culture and humanity that came through the music that night.

It certainly could not have been easy to build a bridge strong enough to engage both the North Koreans and the Americans in a peaceful exchange. Assistant Secretary of State Christopher Hill, considered controversial by many political insiders, demonstrated his commitment to changing the mood in international affairs. Like a deejay who turns down the flashing strobe lights and throbbing tempo of a retro disco set and plays a soft ballad in the caress of shadows, Hill used his trademark diplomacy and persuasion to get the New York orchestra on the Korean stage. As reported in publications such as the *Washington Post,* the concert of reconciliation would not have occurred without Hill's vision for a cultural exchange.

I watched a part of the concert myself and felt deeply touched to see that there are alternate methods to this slash-and-burn way we tend to approach conflict that might change the world! We need more people who keep seeking peace even when there are old wars and old wounds. We need people like Christopher Hill to overcome the barriers and discontentment of those who find it easier to pre-judge than to grow together and seek common ground.

The Sound of Peace

"Blessed are the peacemakers: for they shall be called the children of God" (Matthew 5:8–9, KJV).

Sooner or later most of us realize that we cannot resolve every conflict with our bravado and brass knuckles. We soon learn that real strength isn't caged in our biceps, but in our brains and ability to rationalize what is and is not an appropriate response in any given situation.

Now to be sure, making peace isn't easy. Peacemakers have to work with great skill and diplomatic dexterity since they often experience resistance from both sides. If you decide to seek middle ground, then I must warn you that there is some truth to the old adage, "he who stands in the middle of the road gets hit by both sides!" It's much easier to live in the apprehension and animosity than the threat of change that comes with reconciliation.

In the interest of peace, we must learn to speak and to interact with people who think differently than we do. It doesn't mean that you have to change your views or your message, but if you are hate-filled it does mean you need to change your method. Much can be accomplished when we're willing to engage in real dialogue rather than the sound bites of dogma reported by the press. Many times we have demonized people we don't even know.

I have for a long time thought that our nation would be better served if the church were more open to showing love and not hostility. I am embarrassed by those who rush to divide rather than to unite. If black people would talk to white people (not shout) and white people would talk to black people (as respected equals), a lot of myths would be destroyed. If Democrats and Republicans would just speak to each other, truly exchanging ideas, then there might be more opportunities to work together. It would be a better, more peace-full world if Muslims and Jews, gays and straights would at least talk to each other rather than mark dividing lines. We might learn something from each other that would leave us better off than we are apart.

Crossing lines into territories where we risk rejection isn't easy for anyone. This is why the power of peacemakers (funny that we don't hear the term "war makers") is so crucial to conflict resolution. It is too lofty a goal to expect all differences to homogenize into one *melting pot*, but a realistic goal is a *salad*—a combined mixture of ingredients with each retaining its unique flavor and texture.

RECIPE FOR "PEACE SALAD"

What does making a "peace salad" look like? Often I find that responsible risk and emotional vulnerability are key ingredients. A few months ago, I was scheduled to fly to Venezuela for three speaking engagements. I had never been to this intriguing South American country, and I was looking forward to experiencing its unique and exotic locale, food, culture, and ambiance.

However, my team was having trouble getting the required government permits to land our plane there. The visas had not been approved by the Venezuelan officials for us to enter the country. The American embassy, which we rely on so much for international travel, was squeamish (to say the least) about encouraging our trip. On top of that, the American press was full of the ever-increasing conflict between Venezuela and Colombia! If these two strikes were not enough to deter my plans, then the fact that the White House had reportedly issued a statement that Venezuela was to be added to a list of countries suspected of hiding terrorists would seem to rule it out. Reinforcing the danger, President Chavez seemed less than encouraging in his remarks in response to the allegation.

I provide this information only for context. I do not presume to know what the government of Venezuela should be doing nor what our government's involvement is between the two countries. But these were the factors we were up against as the deadline loomed for our departure.

Three times we toyed with canceling the meetings and not going because I was uncertain of what I was walking into. As is the case with most leaders, you have to consider not only your own safety but, more important, the well being of those who are with you. I had a team of several men who work in various areas of conferences with me, whose wives and children would not appreciate their becoming prisoners of some conflict, which we had been warned to avoid! Yet the threat of danger did not keep me from being drawn to this unique opportunity; in fact, the unknown may have been part of the attraction. While I had never even met the apostle Raúl Ávila who was my host, my curiosity played tug-of-war with my concern.

Still undecided, we finally overcame the visa hurdles two days before our scheduled arrival, and received our required landing permits at the last minute. I decided reluctantly to proceed with the trip. Haunted by the ill feelings that seemed to exist between our countries, and the stern warning from the American embassy (which I had never ignored before in making my travel plans around the world), I decided not to bring along my thirteen-year-old son, who was out on spring break. I had enough to worry about with getting the adults on the crew in and out safely. With so many dynamics swirling around my destination, I knew he would be safer at home.

So you may be wondering, why did I go? And what does this have to do with the putting-together of a "peace salad"? Two reasons: I am a person who really tries to keep his word; and I knew that organizing a meeting with more than fifteen thousand delegates attending is no small feat. I did not want to disappoint anyone. I always hate it when people say they are coming and then do not follow through. While the previously mentioned reasons were legitimate ones that most rational people would ultimately accept, I still don't back down easily. And without trying to overspiritualize my decision, I truly felt the prompting of the Holy Spirit which overrode my caution and said to me, "Go anyway!"

Sometimes you have to listen to that inner voice of wisdom that God provides for those who seek Him. I obeyed, but as we were landing, I was very quiet. I could still hear my coworkers laughing and jesting as we often do on such trips. They were having fun and enjoying the moment. But for me, I found little consolation in frivolity. Frankly I was extremely concerned, "Did I do the right thing?" "I hope I don't live to regret my decision," were just a few of my thoughts as we approached the runway and prepared for our descent. I heard the wheels drop down on the plane and the usual sounds of flight preparations as we were coming in for a landing. I looked out of the window to the distant ridge of mountains surrounding the airport and imagined men hiding up there, living in bushes, armed with M16 guns and sharp knives ready to abduct us to make some political statement about issues, of which I knew nothing. As the plane hit the ground, I wondered if we would end up listed as missing persons or show up on the next *Unsolved Mysteries*!

I had visions of being incarcerated in a Venezuelan prison or being captured by insurgents and spending the next ten months in the fetal position somewhere inside a bamboo cage, in the bush. It was fear pure and simple and that is often what has one people afraid of the other. I was soon to discover, though, that what my imagination conjured about these "foreign" people was far more dangerous than reality. Often what you must realize before you fight is that the battle is more within than without.

After landing in Caracas, I was looking everywhere and almost waiting on something or someone to come out and bite me. And it did in the form of the incredibly gracious enthusiasm of a five-foot-six-inch-tall, portly Argentinean man who I would later learn was Apostle Ávila. He is short of stature, but clearly a big man in the country. The moment I met him and his entourage, I was engulfed in an ocean of love and a sea of tears. My fears and biases dissolved as he explained that it had been his dream for twenty years to meet me and that I had preached many messages (unbeknownst to me) that changed his life. His sincerity and love touched me deeply!

My host introduced me to Alejandro Andrade, a friend who was with him, and explained that he is in charge of the national treasury of Venezuela as well as a Christian. And though I admittedly do not know either of these men well, I really look forward to getting to know them both better. Until then I cannot deny that I was awed by their kindness, and it left my team and me with a feeling of gratitude that God had allowed us to experience what could be a new and abiding relationship. If nothing else, it served as a great life lesson for me. I had never experienced a warmer reception and to have it so lavishly displayed at a moment when I felt so vulnerable and out of my environment was overwhelming. Our fight mode evaporated and our flight plan disintegrated and there on the spot two people from two different worlds found common ground. We all started weeping right there in the airport! I wasn't even sure why I was weeping; it might have been relief that I was not trapped with my team eating rotten bananas in the imagined cage!

But I think I was crying to see what the love of God does to people and why we should always obey Him rather than accept even the most reliable information that makes blanket statements about people. People are not their country, and stereotypical ideas about any people can be quite dangerous! In all fairness, I cannot attest to what your experience would be if you should choose to visit Caracas without the care and support that such a reliable host brings to the experience.

The rest of my days in Venezuela only reinforced this first dramatic encounter. We ate delectable South American cuisine (they like their meat, and it comes hot, hot, hot—caliente!), sang Latino music, and several times I felt like a long-lost family member being celebrated for his return! After Apostle Ávila invited me into his home and we ate together with his family, I was fascinated by their culture. The sense of family was overwhelming and fulfilling.

Similarly, the services that ensued were both powerful and life-changing. The cultural exchange was intense and only reinforced by the revelatory fascination we had with each other. I have never felt so much love nor eaten so much delicious meat, and I have never seen a people hungrier for God's Word than these people are!

As our time there came to a close, the "peace salad" that Apostle Avila served left an incredibly pleasant taste in my mouth. The hospitality and love experienced was a meal in itself! I shared with him, his gracious wife, his staff, and fellow pastors details of my upcoming MegaFest International in South Africa, and how much it would mean to me if they could attend. Without hesitation, they asked for the details and pledged to come! It was a wonderful feeling to know that all of us were going to break past barriers and experience new connections with people whose cultures and ideas may be different from our own. Beneath the fears, the uncertainty, and the unfamiliarity, we were all brothers and sisters in the most profound way. I would see my new friends in only a few short months!

I felt so privileged as I left that country. I look forward to having new experiences and overcoming fears and getting out of the box of preconceived ideas and into the vast space of open-minded, open-hearted willingness to evolve! I went dreading a fight that I would surely lose when the real battle was one of remaining open, fearless, and receptive to the differences confronting me.

Sometimes, our expectations can be shaped not only by misperceptions and stereotypes but factual information and solid data. No one at the state department was trying to create prejudice; they were simply doing their job. And yet, there are times when we must follow the example of Jesus and risk going where God leads us. If we leave our hearts open to the possibility of human connection and not raise barriers out of fear of our differences, then we can literally change the world we live in.

Choosing Your Battles: from Warfare to Worship

In addition to learning from those we often rush to fight, we may also miss an opportunity to experience the very provision for which we've been praying. My favorite example of this phenomenon of shooting first and aiming second occurs in the life of Joshua. Consider the following scene:

> And it came to pass, when Joshua was by Jericho, that he lifted up his eyes and looked, and, behold, there stood a man over against him with his sword drawn in his hand: and Joshua went unto him, and said unto him, Art thou for us, or for our adversaries? And he said, Nay; but as captain of the host of the LORD am I now come. And Joshua fell on his face to the earth, and did worship, and said unto him, What saith my lord unto his servant? And the captain of the LORD'S host said unto Joshua, Loose thy shoe from off thy foot; for the place whereon thou standest is holy. And Joshua did so. (Joshua 5:13–15, KJV)

A fighter all of his life, Joshua has made his living through his skillful combat. Think of him as Moses' secretary of defense. Now that Moses is dead, Joshua has assumed leadership and finds himself confronting someone he doesn't know. Instead of any kind of greeting, his immediate response is to ask, "Are you for us or against us?" Such a question carries an ominous undertone as if he's prepared to fight at the drop of a hat. However, the only problem is that he's about to fight his God-given help.

When we think of peacemakers, let us not confine this truth to public, social, or political issues. Many of us struggle in our personal relationships to recognize friend from foe. Sometimes when you are used to being attacked, if you are not careful you can fight the very one who has come into your life to help you. I cannot begin to tell you how many times I have seen people fight away the very ones who would have been a help to them if they had only let them. Because they lacked the ability to discern when and where it was necessary to engage in conflict and when peaceful solutions were possible, they missed the blessing God had sent their way.

There is a big difference between being a coward and being careful. God often sends us help in unlikely places from unexpected sources, but those who fight quickly often destroy the provision intended to enhance their opportunities. Such people don't often grow beyond normal and average because they lack the ability to draw strength from unusual resources. God fed Elijah through the mouth of ravens. He may send you a friend who is like the Good Samaritan—someone of a different race and background. Sometimes past pain makes it difficult for you to accept current caring.

The struggle God has with Joshua is to get him to move from warfare to worship. God finally gets him to take off his shoes and move into a worship mode. Worship requires openness. Like love, it requires vulnerability, but when you are trained to respond to most issues by fighting, conflict seems less threatening than compassion. Maybe this is a time in your life to put away your sword and open your heart! Could it be possible that you are fighting those who could help you? Do you tend to ask, "Are you for me or against me?", and immediately put those who want to help you on the defensive? I must warn you that sometimes divine help comes in an odd uniform. Your next place of affection, affirmation, and affiliation may not come packaged in the way you expected it.

I am not against fighting. I have already shared that many times fights are a strength and a necessary part of life. But few of us choose our battles wisely. In this world we all have to fight to get through school, to overcome ills and adversity, to get ahead and achieve our dreams. Many are those who are diagnosed with cancer or some other dread disease who fight against the odds of a less-than-glowing prognosis and win the battle for life.

To be sure, life presents challenges that require personal warfare to survive. But in order to channel our energy and resources into the right battles, we must exercise patience, wisdom, and faith in God's goodness. The next time your blood pressure escalates and your temper flares, the next time you dismiss someone's offer of help or assume that finding a solution is a lost cause because of the historical hostility, I hope you will examine your motives before you fight. Sometimes we must fight our own inclinations rather than those around us!

We must look carefully to realize who we're fighting. Maybe we are fighting the wrong enemy.

Maybe the fight you must win is not an external but an inner one that will give you the greater liberty, if you think about the true battle before you do!

eighteen
Before You Take Flight

"May your love soar on the wings of a dove in flight."
—*Debbie Crabtree*

As we saw in the prior chapter, when faced with a crisis, catastrophe, or conflict, our bodies naturally react with the fight or flight instinct in order to keep us alive. Just as there is a time to fight and a time to make peace, there is a time to take flight and a time to commit to staying in the midst of the conflict. Indeed, sometimes we must dig in and fight, although if that is our natural stance and automatic posture, then we will miss some of the gifts God sends our way. Similarly, if we are always running away from problems, then we will never mature into the adult men and women that we're designed to be. And if we keep facing toxic relationships and abusive situations, then we haven't learned to spread our wings and fly to greener pastures.

Maturity necessitates that we know how to discern and decide when to run and when to roll up our sleeves and get down to the business of figuring out how to make something work. In our primary relationships, it can be too easy to run from the other person for innumerable reasons. Some people run when things are going too well: They're terrified to taste intimacy because they have been starving for it for so long that they fear it won't last. They are emotional anorexics who have starved for so long that they cannot bear to indulge in the banquet of love.

Other people don't want to face the hard work of loving someone when the going gets tough. As long as the romance and infatuation lasts, they're fine. But as soon as communication breaks down or trust fractures, then they're out the door. They make flight into an art form, finding more than fifty ways to leave their lover. It seems like a game of conquest and personal power. If they can use their personal gravity to seduce someone into orbit, then they're ready to spin on to the next galaxy, leaving a blazing trail of failed commitments like shooting stars behind them.

Just Not That Into You

It's tempting to assert that men tend to run from commitments in relationships more than women, and perhaps there's some truth to this. Women often come to me and my wife for counseling after their latest serious relationship has ended with the object of her affection going AWOL. Many times these ladies maintain that there were no indicators prior to his abrupt retreat. However, upon discussing the details of how they interacted, it often seems clear that "he just wasn't that into" her.

This catch phrase, long spoken by many of us, emerged from an episode of *Sex and the City* penned by writers Greg Behrendt and Liz Tuccillo. They went on to write a book of the same title in which they describe the male warning signs of ambivalence, immaturity, and an unwillingness to commit. Many times the women they choose are so desperate for romance that they become blind to his reluctance to go the distance. When he's consistently late, breaks dates at the last minute, doesn't call when he tells you he will, or seems unmotivated to spend time in your presence, then he's definitely just not that into you!

Ladies, you're worth more in time and attention than these gentlemen are willing to pay. As soon as you discern that he's not really into you, decide to act—waste no time and fly away! These men can be on-again, off-again types who hover but never land. You should take flight from such men and move on to others who want to engage in a mature adult relationship. As the Bible reminds us, it's better to be hot or cold than to be lukewarm!

Too often these tentative relationships set up expectations without the ability to close the deal. It's like being in an airport waiting to fly off together on a romantic vacation. You fill the time together waiting in the airport lounge, enjoying a drink or a bite to eat, looking at magazines at the newsstand, shopping, and killing time. It's pleasant and enjoyable but not the reason you're both there at the airport. You're there to travel to your ultimate destination of a committed relationship.

I cannot tell you how many women and even some men find themselves investing huge amounts of time in relationships that they later realize go nowhere. In this rapid, fast-paced world in which we live, patience isn't something in high supply. Most of us are unwilling to spend years at the wishing well of life. We go to the airport to travel, and while there are nice places to browse, we ultimately want to get off the ground and go somewhere. When what was meant to be a temporary amusement becomes its own destination, then something is wrong. When people travel to the airport and spend day after day browsing the shops rather than boarding the plane, there is a real problem.

Let's talk about the phobias that keep us in the get-ready mode but will not allow us to go further into commitment and completion. More times than not, I have found that when the plane never gets off the ground, it generally indicates that either there is total disinterest ("He's just not that into you") or avoidance of commitment out of fear of failure. These window shoppers can never seemingly find their way to the checkout line. They are afraid they will have regret, so rather than take a risk they make no commitment at all. These are men and some women who really and sincerely care for the other person, but lack the relationship skills and personal maturity to fully commit. Most of us have neither the time nor the skills to counsel the unwilling partner through the process to a place of commitment. But this is exactly what they need.

Your decision boils down to a few crucial questions: Is he into you or not? If he's not, then waste no more time or emotional energy trying to get water from a dry well. If he is and just finds it difficult to commit, then you must ask him if he's willing to work through his issues. And if he is, then are you willing to wait for him? Your answers to these questions can provide you with a relational GPS if you will let them.

Flight Risk

Some relationships require you to take a stand and fight for its improvement. If you are well past the game-playing stage, and you know that there is love between you, then you will need to dig in and work through the conflict.

In the '60s many young people wore T-shirts declaring, I'M A

LOVER NOT A FIGHTER. At the time it made great sense, but today I realize that lovers must also be fighters. You have to fight to love.

You have to fight not to lose your ability to love. Many people must fight through the grief of a terminal love experience to open their bruised heart again. They get so hurt that they automatically run at the first sign of another serious relationship. They have to learn to cancel their tendency toward flight.

I remember vividly as I was rehabbing from back surgery that the pain of healing was incredibly intense. I am a fighter by nature and I wanted to see improvement. I had to learn to fight with more than stubborn tenacity but also understand that rest and sleep were part of my fight. I had to learn that avoiding the pain and staying in the bed might feel better but wouldn't further my goal of attaining the thrill of ambulatory motion—standing, walking, running, skipping, dancing.

Real lovers must fight off bombs of depression and the ever-looming propensity to become cynical and bitter. If they succumb to the pain of a broken heart, they become a walking casualty, enslaved to a wretched disdain for life, love, and longing. A person who gives up on love becomes no more than a body waiting to be buried.

Yet I see all around me a growing cynicism and indifference. People today seem ready to throw in the towel on life, on love, and on each other. If our relationship doesn't happen quickly and conveniently, then we are off to the next flight, changing our planes without understanding that people who make love work, work at love. Like fugitives from love, these flight-risk people consciously or unconsciously slip into a perpetual state of avoidance and seek the convenience rather than the complexities of working through the issues and seeing the relationship through.

The death of personal romanticism is a great loss. And the war to destroy all optimism drags on for many of us who face the dismal frontier of disappointment and the bleak statistics that remind us of the low success rates of ongoing passion and contentment. Those who try again must defeat the fears of emotional abandonment and sustain the lifeblood of passion in their clogged arteries. Those who do not try again seek the comfort of avoidance and only become comfortable by easing the pain. They will not risk being hurt again and their fear of pain causes them to lose the mobility and sensitivity that comes from opening your heart, clearing out the debris, and hobbling with a wounded soul.

I remember one morning sitting on the side of my bed slumped over on my walker with tears in my eyes and thinking, "It hurts too much to get well. I am tired of fighting and I want to quit." But then I thought how foolish it would be to allow the pain to win so I pulled my aching body up and finally stood up and forced myself to walk. Sometimes you have to walk with the pain of life until you can walk away from it!

JUST LIKE YOU

Where did we get this pathology of avoidance? To me it is quite clear that the decompression of air on a plane will only allow the outside winds to blow in. In fact, if that happens it will endanger the flight because the outside is getting in. Likewise, what is happening in our private world is now leaking into our interpersonal activities. We may not get more adept personally until we find a way to connect more effectively publicly. Consider with me the sociological environment that spawned such indifference as we have today.

The security of avoidance has taken a horrible toll on more than our interpersonal relationships. In our culture today, it has become too easy to take flight from the individuals in our lives who challenge us with their differences. Because we feel threatened or intimidated by those who are not just like us, we run away instead of trying to learn and grow from each other. How many times do we see it happen at a social event that the men cluster in one section, talking sports and telling jokes while the women gather in another to discuss children and fashion? I realize in more progressive areas new inclusive cultures exist and more diverse social skills are adopted. Yet in far too many cases we are still sociological segregationists.

Recently I attended a top-tier magazine's gala in New York. Filled with bright, successful, and charismatic people, the black-tie event featured icons from both the business and entertainment worlds. My table was abuzz with conversation, and all was well until they found out I was a minister.

Now I was the only black person at the table, but being black was a non-issue here. But when they found out I was clergy, it seemed that I had immediately grown a tail! You would have thought I was a terrorist with a bomb in my tuxedo! I had to fight off an outright confrontation just because I differed from my new agnostic and atheistic friends who sat around the table with me. In short, I was different!

And it's not just one group, such as liberals or conservatives, who shun those who are different. We're all prone to such exclusionary cliques. I view myself more as a moderate than a conservative or liberal, but all groups struggle to get out of the box of similar ideas and seek to understand others. My point is that we live in a world that doesn't teach us to respect differences or learn each other's perspective. We live in a world that avoids diversity by tribally migrating into comfort zones and surrounding ourselves with people who fit.

I most frequently see this played out politically. Every comment, every sound bite, each and every action or inaction becomes fodder for a racial, gender, or sexual preference tug-of-war. We have come dangerously close to the edge of losing our ability to dialogue, to listen, and to remain open-minded. It is no accident that our personal lives show the erosion of negotiation. It is my way or the highway personally because our society has given up on understanding differences and seeking common ground.

My friends, the United States of America has trouble uniting like never before. Too often we cannot disagree without being disagreeable. We have gotten to the point that we write blogs and articles, spread myths and half-truths without any remorse. If you want to know how people really feel watch what they write when they can remain anonymous!

It may be one nation, but we have many differences that we have to manage, and history shows that we have changing trends on how we accomplish this feat. The overarching problem is that we don't spend enough time with people who are different from us. Often what we find out is that our views may be different, but people aren't really that different from each other at all. When you only interact with people who look like you and think like you, you have no checks and balances to avoid extremes and to provide balanced wisdom. If you only have friends who vote like you or worship like you, you have no sense of the world, only your world. After all, my friends, heresy is often truth that lost its balance!

If we are going to raise respect from the dead we must go to the graveyard and admit where we lost it. Jesus when he was about to raise Lazarus from the dead asked Mary to show him where she laid him down. Maybe one of the places we laid it down was when we started living in homogeneous clubs again and left the town square for the soft suburbia of clannish neighborhoods. There was a time when we met more frequently with those who were different from us—in schools, on jobs, and in our churches. We were forced to look for points of unity rather than to sink into the all-too-easy state of divisiveness. It is easy to see how we are different, but you have to be a real lover of people to look deeper for what unites us.

The Potter's House is trying hard to draw inclusive circles and bring people together rather than to paint lines that divide us into our sides and perspectives. For example, our church is building a community called Cappella Park featuring an estimated one thousand two hundred homes upon completion. These are not low-income houses but mixed income, because it is a fact that when different types of people live together they do better and learn from each other. Low-income neighborhoods, though well intended, often end up becoming slums because cross-pollinating is critical to development and advancement.

This is a far bigger principle than just an economic one. We are losing economically and spiritually and politically simply by polarization. Self-segregation threatens our development today. You might have seen the surprising commercial about global warming that featured Reverend Pat Robertson and Reverend Al Sharpton. In it, the two amicably converse about the dangers of global warming and assert that we must find common ground to overcome it. How amazing is that? Apparently, they know that saving the planet is more important than saving face or being "right." Maybe they know that what unites us should be more important than what divides us.

Beyond the Fight or Flight

Our romantic relationships, as well, require that we overcome our differences. The art of relationships requires that a man who is very different from his woman find common ground with her and vice versa. I don't mean the obvious biological differences alone.

No, it isn't that simple. The differences run much deeper than externals. We tend to become attracted to people who are different from us. The extrovert often marries an introvert. The spontaneous person is attracted to the always-scheduled person. Have you noticed how often the quiet demure person marries the outspoken opinionated individual? The spender marries the saver, the flamboyant person ends up married to the quiet individual?

However, herein lies the rub. Often what attracted us to the person in the first place later disgusts us. Why does she want to stay in all the time when I want to go out? Why is he talking all the time when I need peace and quiet? I believe that we were meant to balance each other by attracting people whose strengths may be our weaknesses. Together, as a result of our differences and unique distinction, we complement each other.

But in order to enjoy that beautiful union of diverse tendencies and ideals, we must learn to stand up to the pain of readjustment and avoid our innate tendency to fly away from the hard work of making things work. The next time you think it is easier to fly away from the person you are involved with, remember that understanding only comes when you stand under a real desire to know, to love, and to comprehend them, embracing the uniqueness of who they are.

When to Fight for Your Relationship

Even the best relationship requires negotiation, deliberation, and a lot of work to get it off the ground. The resolution, centered around this idea, is simple: We need to know when to fight and when to take flight and move on. While there is no magic formula that can apply to everyone every time, some applications come to mind. As I close this chapter I want to give you some tips that will help you understand when to fight for a relationship, when to take flight from it, and when to just get off the plane and take the bus!

When it's about money

Money can stir up a whole bunch of other issues. But generally, how to manage money and how to manage it within a marriage relationship, depends on the set of skills you've developed and the amount of discipline exercised. One of you may be more financially minded than the other. One of you may be prone to spend frequently without considering the consequences.

Without going into a whole financial seminar here, my best advice is to work within the boundaries of your reality together. In other words, consider how much debt you have, how much income, and how much you want or need to save. Work together to make joint decisions that affect both of you. Allow some discretionary income, even if it's only a few dollars a month, that you each get to spend however you wish. Find a way to exercise fiscal responsibility as well as financial freedom.

When it's about time

If you're not spending enough time together, then one of you is missing the other. Ideally, you both want to spend more time together, but if one of you holds this complaint, then take it as a compliment that they still enjoy your company. If your relational conflicts revolve around time, then schedule some items on each other's calendar that will be strictly your time alone together—no kids, no jobs, no BlackBerry, no cell—no intrusions, period. The old saying about the quality of time being more important than the quantity holds true, but if you're not spending enough hours together, then it will impair the quality.

When it's about jealousy

Obviously, there's a limit to what is sane and rational, and I am not talking about possessive psychopaths who won't allow you to glance at the waiter without accusing you of cheating. But generally, when there's jealousy in a relationship, it's an indication of insecurity and power. You may need to have a frank discussion about your commitment to each other. Talk through those little habits and mannerisms that your spouse interprets as flirtatious. Communicate and do not allow the jealousy to grow into bitterness, distrust, and disgust.

WHEN TO TAKE FLIGHT FROM YOUR RELATIONSHIP

Again, I am not saying you should stay when he isn't into you. I am not suggesting that you fall in love alone. I'm most certainly not saying that you stay in a relationship where you are abused, disrespected, or mistreated. Here are some considerations for deciding when not to fight for a relationship.

WHEN IT'S ABOUT SAFETY

Anytime that you do not feel safe—physically or emotionally—in a relationship, then you should take flight. Domestic abuse cuts across all demographics—rich and poor, black and white, Baptist and Buddhist—and should never be tolerated. In most cases there will be warning signs, either the threat of physical violence (which produces its own emotional bruises) or physical interactions bordering on abuse—pushing, shoving, grabbing. You must realize that no relationship should cost you your safety. The essence of love is about giving to each other, providing a secure place where the two of you can grow together, and committing to serve each other. It's not about injury of any kind.

WHEN IT'S ABOUT SANITY

Now this one gets tricky because we each have different thresholds of what we think of as crazy. One man's crazy is another man's true love! However, you should take flight from a relationship where there are constant psychological game-playing, manipulation, and control issues. Consider the little things that only annoyed you slightly when you first started seeing each other because over time they will grow larger and larger. The occasional critical comment often snowballs into an avalanche of unsolicited critical feedback on every aspect of your life. Think about what you can live with and what is compatible with your personality. It's okay to come from completely different vantage points—you can be direct opposites—as long as you communicate constructively. When the exchange of feelings and ideas becomes a stagnant pool, then you need an airlift out of the water!

WHEN IT'S ABOUT SURVIVAL

Some personal issues, particularly addiction, are so large that it feels like the relationship never had a chance to get off the ground. I'm not saying that just because someone's addicted or has a terminal disease that you should take flight. But you must consider what you are willing to tolerate for the sake of the relationship. Be honest with yourself—you are not a martyr. If you know that you cannot tolerate his alcoholism because you grew up with it in your household, then you may need to leave if he's not committed to getting help. If your spouse is a chronic liar, then it may be difficult for you to ever trust her. If your spouse is not willing to share the parenting and providing, then you must think twice before thinking that you alone can create a relationship.

These are just a few general pieces of advice based on my experiences. Please do not assume that they can be dispensed in a one-size-fits-all methodology. Only you can know what you must do to have a healthy relationship. The tragedy for me is that so many know what they should do but fear the uncertainty of being alone or, on the other extreme, risking their heart again. If you are to be the person you want to be, the one your Creator intended, then you must know when to fight, when to take flight, and when to pause, before you do.

nineteen
Before You Gamble

"It is never too late to be who you might have been."
—*George Eliot*

As we face new horizons and ventures, we can only be effective if we discern whether what we do is an investment in the future or a gamble in the moment. If you know anything about me, you know that I live by faith and support faith as the integral part of a person's life. Living by faith requires responsibility and not its absence.

However, some people use the word "faith" as a religious license to gamble. They say, "I believe everything will be all right despite evidence to the contrary because I have faith." I've seen people write checks on faith, knowing that the funds were not in their account but hoping that they would somehow miraculously appear before the check gets processed. I have seen people marry on faith hoping and believing that the other person would change later. I have seen people accept positions that they knew they were not qualified for because they had faith that they could learn it later.

Is this faith? No, it's no better than gambling. As Shakespeare so aptly put it, "a rose by any other name would smell as sweet." Just because you want something doesn't mean that you should claim faith and overextend yourself to go after it. You may use faith as an excuse, but the reality is you gambled away precious moments in your life and it is time to get back what you lost!

Recently, I flew into Las Vegas for a business meeting. Walking through the luxurious hotel casino, I was immediately distracted by the clanging sounds of slot machines, lounge music, and enthusiastic tourists. Gamblers from all over the world had come to Vegas specifically to take the risk of losing money. It struck me that the entire hotel establishment was gambling on its clientele taking this risk. With five-star accommodations, celebrity-treatment spa service, and gourmet cuisine, more and more hoteliers there count on their guests taking the risk of gambling.

Like so many other aspects of our culture, gambling has evolved into an acceptable pastime in our society. A few decades ago, our fathers played penny poker on the front porch, laughing as they caught up over a cold drink. Then gambling became synonymous with Las Vegas and the Rat Pack, with casinos and gaming houses run by shady characters in dark suits and mirrored sunglasses. Then from this sexy, glamorous image it evolved into something more mainstream and family friendly with child care, theme parks, and kid-friendly restaurants.

You may not think of yourself as someone with a gambling problem. But if you are taking risks in important areas of your life, repeating the same mistakes—in relationships, at work, with your kids—over and over again, then you might as well be betting on a lame horse in its last race.

You cannot avoid taking risks in this life. Most of daily life involves taking a risk. Every time we sit down, we risk the chair breaking. When we drive in our cars on the highway, we risk our car breaking down, or the possibility of an encounter with a drunk driver. Flying is the same way. We all risk every day simply by the choices we make. It's not about avoiding risks; it's knowing which risks to take.

A Leap of Faith

My life has been filled with taking risks. Thirteen years ago when I loaded up the truck and moved from West Virginia to Dallas, the risk involved with this move dominated my thinking. Certainly I could have stayed where I was, doing what I was doing, and enjoyed a secure, stable life. But God's calling was leading me to Texas, and numerous other tangible pieces of data reinforced its desirability as the center of my ministry and business endeavors.

Like any leap of faith, my move and the risk of it produced fear and uncertainty. However, it was not a blind leap off a cliff into an unknown sea below. I had a job, a ministry, a way of supporting myself. I had fifty families committed to going with me and starting The Potter's House. We were going to something, not just leaving something behind. I realized that I had to live with the consequences of my move whether conditions improved or deteriorated from what we had known.

But before I moved, I had reflected, discerned, accepted responsibility and I had done my due diligence—my research and development. I had sought the counsel of so many wise individuals who knew me and my calling, and studied the demographic and spiritual needs in the area that became my new home. I had faith, but I also had done the hard work of gathering data and listening to others. The move was not a gamble. Faith without works is dead just as works without faith limits you to your own abilities. Faith plus works produce the investment in our purpose that all of us are required to fulfill.

Both gambling and investing require a financial commitment as well as the courage to take a chance. However, one is built entirely on chance while the other creates a chance to put legs under your dreams.

When you stroll down Las Vegas Boulevard—"The Strip" as it's called—you should not be expecting to double your money to finance your new business. You should be expecting to enjoy a relaxing time, and if you enjoy paying money to play games, then you've come to the right town for recreation.

When you stroll down Wall Street, you need to make educated decisions about which corporations' stocks you want in your portfolio. You have to consider both long- and short-term goals for yourself and your finances. You have to study the market and look at past performance and future projections. Investing requires the resources at your disposal, including your own intelligence and the counsel of others, applied to opportunities for enhancement.

Life will always require us to take risks, but we must discern which risks are worth taking and which will short-circuit our long-term goals for short-term payoffs. The Bible asks us, "For which of you, intending to build a tower, does not sit down first and counteth the cost?" (Luke 14:28, KJV). If we only think about what feels right in the moment, then our weaknesses will undermine us every time. We must keep our eyes on the prize of our larger goals and greater calling if we are to make the right decisions at the right times.

Count Your Losses

My concerns about gambling transcend the economic impact and fiscal consequences. When a gambler makes a buy-in to play poker, he trades his hard-earned cash for different-colored chips that represent various dollar amounts. Casino owners use this buy-in as a psychological advantage so that people think of losing as part of the game, not as watching hundreds of dollars go up in smoke. Similar to using a credit card, one can spend massive amounts of money unaware of the true value of what has been charged.

My fear is that too many of us don't realize the value of the chips of life. In our life, such markers may not seem valuable initially, but eventually you find that you have lost precious commodities—your time, your influence, your name, and your opportunities. When we waste time in dead-end relationships, then we have lost priceless moments that can never be recovered. When we remain in a career that numbs us and stunts our growth, then we lose a part of our true identity.

From all the people who come to me for counseling, perhaps the most common refrain I hear involves regret. Out of fear of rejection, they didn't speak up. Out of fear of failure, they didn't step out. Out of fear of being alone, they didn't tell the truth. They've invested quantities of their time on this earth in endeavors that offered no return on quality.

If you want to make the most of your decisions, then you must never lose sight of this fact: *Time is our most limited resource and can never be recovered once it is spent.* You can go bankrupt and recoup your money. You can endure a scandal and rebuild your reputation. But your time passes and is gone *forever*. Think for a moment how much younger you would be if you had back the time you wasted.

Some people look back at time invested in dating someone who didn't have what they were looking for. Others have given their name in marriage to someone, and even after divorce they are still paying for the collateral damage of a bad decision. You have many valuables to lose, and people wouldn't be pursuing you if you didn't have something to give. Don't let the chips fool you. Every investment you make in people, in business, in life is an important risk that can lead to an irredeemable loss! Gambling away your life's chips sacrifices more than the certainty of losing time in lost causes. When you take risks on short-term goals for the wrong reasons, it consumes your energy and becomes an expenditure of the capital of your reputation.

Time will always be one of your most precious commodities. Before you invest it in someone or something, define what the return should look like on your investment. If you have invested amply and see little coming back, then it is now time to reposition your investment in endeavors that will give you the biggest return. After all, you and I are running out of time and sometimes we must cut our losses.

WHAT CAN NEVER BE REPLACED

The late Archie Dennis, one of the most gifted musical artists of his generation, frequently told the story of his boyhood music teacher who taught him this most valuable lesson. Archie showed up a half hour late for his lesson and tried to downplay it as kids often do. However, his teacher slammed shut the piano, and said, "Young man, you have taken from me thirty minutes that I can never replace." When we do not invest our time deliberately and wisely, we squander one of the only commodities that is uniquely ours. A moment becomes an hour, a day, a week that we will never see again.

I have given my preaching platform to someone or written a fore-word for someone's book who then didn't value or manage such in-fluence well. In such situations, I lost something that the accountant cannot add up—credibility. It took me a long time to realize that when I associate with someone I invest my name in who they are. And I've become increasingly more careful where I put my name because you don't have to be sitting at the blackjack table to gamble away the integrity of your identity.

Several years ago a friend of mine who pastored a very prominent AME church in California inadvertently gave his pulpit to a pastor who used my name to get the engagement. The members of this very prestigious, intellectual church were shocked when the speaker opened his mouth. Their pastor realized too late that I never would have attached my name to a person of this caliber. When I found out, I was horrified and warned my friend that the next time some-one claimed to be coming in my name, he should call me to verify before giving him the opportunity to speak.

My experience reminds me of the situation with Oprah and author James Frey. I haven't spoken with her about this directly, but I gath-ered from watching the interviews that she was angry because his behavior—fictionalizing details he presented as facts—jeopardized her name and the value of her endorsement. It was more than just an eye-opening revelation about a selection for her book club. It was potentially a statement on her judgment and familiarity with the se-lection made. Why did she go to war? She knew the value of her chips. Many times people do not defend what they lost because they do not know the value of the investments they have made. I am ask-ing you to count the chips and know the extent of your investment. If the return doesn't warrant the commitment, you are not investing, you are simply gambling away some precious commodity that you may never regain again.

Names are vitally important in the Scriptures. Jesus said that if we receive the disciples that come in his name, then we have received him. He also said, "Whatever you ask the Father in my name he will give you" (John 16:23, NKJV). God told Abraham that his name would be great. The power of your name is better than an impressive title or an inherited fortune. When your name is great enough, you don't even have to have money—you can purchase a house or car on the value of your name, the inherent integrity of your character.

Before You Leap: Faith vs. Foolishness

In Scripture, there's a world of difference between gambling away opportunities and stewarding the resources with which we're entrusted. Jesus told a parable about what it means to risk appropriately. He explains that a man went away and gave each of his three servants a certain amount of money to oversee while he was away. When he returned, the first two servants had doubled his money by investing wisely. The third servant buried his money because he was so afraid of losing what the master had assigned to him.

> "His master replied, 'You wicked, lazy servant! So you knew that I harvest where I have not sown and gather where I have not scattered seed? Well then, you should have put my money on deposit with the bankers, so that when I returned I would have received it back with interest'" (Matthew 25:26–27, NIV).

At the very least, God expects us to return the investment created in us by utilizing the resources at our disposal. In the parable, each man is given a chance to be more and have more, and most important, to discern the difference between a gamble and a wise investment.

When God gives us an opportunity, we should make something happen with it. Don't hide the chance and lose it out of fear or spend it foolishly. Many people would love to get the shot you are missing. They feel that all they need is a chance and you have it and won't maximize what you have been given.

Let's look at this issue of risking by faith in another light. Yes, God requires us to risk, to have faith, and to be good stewards. But before you take a leap of faith, you must draw a line of delineation between faith and foolishness.

The defining factor emerges from what we place our faith in. Jesus taught us to have faith in God. Secular humanism and all its cousins and extended relations of thought teach us to have faith in . . . faith. There is an incredible degree of difference between faith in the One who orders our steps and has a design-logic that's so certain we can rest in it, and faith in believing what we want to happen will transpire if we squint our eyes and imagine it enough times in our heads.

Visualization can be a powerful motivator and performance enhancer; however, you must have your higher priorities as the lens through which you see your achievements.

Or consider this metaphor: Faith is to the believer what gas is to a car. No one tries to ride home on the gas. Fuel is only powerful when used to run the car's engine. You can't sit on a barrel of oil or a can of gas and expect it to take you anywhere. Similarly, faith is only powerful when placed in God. Many people are disappointed because they only have faith in their own faith, not in God. They then erroneously distance themselves further from God because their own faith was not powerful enough to actualize their desires.

Starting with faith in God, you still cannot win big if you do not cultivate some simple inner characteristics. First, you have to know the value of your own chips. Do not think that your intangibles aren't valuable—they are the priceless part of everything. Get away from luck-living or gambling for the things you want and need. Real results require study, research, action, and yes, again, faith. Understand that real progress is not made by closing your eyes and wishing.

Once you have done the research and invested your chips wisely, I encourage you to live without fear. The Vegas style of living is over for you. Those who remain affixed to such antics almost always end up in regret! Sooner or later, luck changes and all that they have built collapses in a vortex of disappointment.

The only other tip I want to tell you is simple. You will still win some and you will still lose some but proceed without fear. It is true that even the investments that seem wisest don't always yield a return, but they are far more likely to do so than wild gambling. I have lost in the stock market, both figuratively and literally. But I have also won big. Take the bitter with the sweet. An occasional loss isn't a sign you are living a Vegas life.

Move into your destiny valuing yourself and your time, your opportunities and your influence. Live your life without fear or regret. You have minimized your risk by understanding what you have and by not allowing your investment to continue to depreciate.

Today is the day that the Lord has made. God has given it to you. What you do with it is your gift back to your Creator. The Almighty has given you the talents and the time that you have. You are highly favored. As you live wisely, God gets a return on creation—God's investment in you. Make it a big win for yourself and God, and, before you do, know the difference between faith and a gamble!

Conclusion:
Now You've Done It

"If one advances confidently in the direction of one's dreams, and endeavors to live the life which he has imagined, he will meet with a success unexpected in common hours."

—*Henry David Thoreau*

Decorated with bouquets of roses and lilies tied with Tiffany blue ribbons, the sanctuary of The Potter's House hums with whispered conversations beneath the lilting notes of beautiful music. Among the hundreds of people gathered to celebrate this most memorable occasion, I see so many family members and loved ones. Tyler Perry and Dr. Phil are here, along with Cathy Hughes, Deion Sanders, Michael Irvin, preachers of every stripe,

Martin L. King III, Bernice King, and other dear friends. Soon the familiar song cues me to walk her down the aisle. Everyone stands and turns toward us.

Tears pool in the corners of my eyes as this beautiful, ivory-gowned woman takes my arm and we glide down the carpet. The moment has come for me to hand her off to the young man awaiting her at the altar, the bridegroom with tears streaming down his face from the joy of seeing his beloved. My baby girl is about to leap from being my daughter into a brand new family—the one she has been called to make with her new husband.

The time for preparation and planning has passed. The hundreds of details, from dresses to diamonds, cakes to candelabras, have all converged into these next few minutes when this couple's love will be articulated and celebrated. So much work, time, and, yes, money (after all, I am the father of the bride!) have now come together to frame the action of the ceremony. It's finally time to say, "I do!"

On Your Mark

My daughter's wedding is not the only event where such planning and preparation determines its success. My years in the theater have given me an insider's peek at what goes on behind the scenes. The curtain is only minutes away from parting and ushering in the opening-night performance. The excitement, adrenaline, and nervous energy can barely be contained within each participant. Months of read-throughs, preproduction meetings, set design, lighting and sound checks, and grueling rehearsals have led to the moment now before them. Each member of the cast is poised to contribute all they can and more to ensure that a seamless production scintillates and entertains the awaiting audience.

My many good friends who are professional athletes assure me that the experience is the same for them in their own unique performance on the playing field. The crowd is only moments away from cheering their favorite team to victory in what is sure to be a championship match-up. Inside the locker room, the team suits up with an air of nervous anticipation. The coach goes over plays one last time. Muscles flex and shift beneath the uniforms that brand them as a united team. Months of recruiting, off-season training, summer training camp, strategy meetings, film reviews of the competition, and two-a-day practices have led to the moment now before them. Each player awaits the opportunity of a lifetime to show their athletic prowess and team unity before the multitudinous fans.

Perhaps you have never participated in a Broadway production or a professional ballgame, but I know that you have undoubtedly experienced the preparation needed to begin an extraordinary performance of your own.

If you have read through these pages and reached this point in our journey, then I can guarantee that you are readier than you've ever been to face the crucial decisions that will determine your destiny. Like a performer who has rehearsed her lines for her big moment in the spotlight or an athlete who has practiced his game to peak performance, you are now ready to shine like never before.

Before You Do, Visualize

Toward the goal of launching you into the next level of success in your life, I encourage you to consider one last exercise. Just as a vocalist must warm up his chords before belting out the first note of the performance or just as an athlete must stretch and warm up his body before the big game, you need to warm up your entrance into a new area of growth, productivity, and fulfillment. In fact, this exercise that I'm going to recommend to you is one that successful individuals in many different fields utilize.

What is this technique that tends to elevate their game? Successful people often envision themselves going through the intricate motions of their most exceptional performance. From beginning to end, they mentally visualize each detail that must be included, each step or stride, each note or line that they will include in the execution of their role. Like watching a movie of themselves in an Olympic-medal, Oscar-winning performance, they perform a mental dress rehearsal to prepare for the actuality of their success.

You must now do the same, you must envision yourself doing what you have decided to do.

Many people know all of the information that I have presented here and still struggle to pull the trigger and make regret-proof decisions. They seem shocked to realize that their future requires action now. They've done the due diligence of research and development, of seeking counsel from their confidants, and of preparing those around them for change. Yet they often experience stage fright and find themselves glued to the floor backstage while the show goes on without them.

The missing ingredient is often their ability to see themselves succeeding, regardless of past mistakes and future challenges. The key is often being willing to trust your gut, take the necessary risk, and to seize opportunities when they come to you. It can be tempting to paralyze yourself because of the possibilities. But as we have seen, deferring your decision until other people or circumstances decide for you *is a decision*. Living passively is a choice even if you aren't willing to acknowledge that you've chosen it!

After all preparations have been made, all excuses laid aside, then you must not be afraid to act. Talent applied to skill produces unequaled success. Talent is your God-given gift; skill is the hard work, practice, and preparation you yourself do. But you must recognize opportunities when they present themselves. Make your business plan so when you unexpectedly find yourself at the entrepreneur's luncheon seated next to a venture capitalist looking for an investment you can tell her about your dream. Start your screenplay so that you can explain it to the producer at the writers' conference. Write out a mission statement for your ministry so that you can present it before the deacon board. Take the steps, one after another after the next, to bring your best life to living color.

Just Do It

When I was a little boy in West Virginia, my siblings and I would sometimes get into trouble by getting into Mama's cookie jar or tracking muddy shoe prints all over her clean carpets. When my brother or sister or I misbehaved, one of us would look at the other and say, "Well, now you've done it!"

I suspect that for most of us, this phrase emphasizes a mistake we have made or an accident we were not able to prevent. However, I would like you to realize that its meaning captures your present state of preparation, motivation, and actualization.

Our decisions have the unequaled power to shape our lives one day at a time. We can continue to drift through life, bouncing like a loose leaf on the breeze, at the mercy of where it takes us. Or, we can anchor our roots in the fertile soil of intelligent preparation. If we make sound decisions, we may be like a tree planted beside living waters, as the Psalmist calls those seeking God's righteousness (Psalm 1). We must water our tree with self-forgiveness and nourish it with good relationships. With the sunlight of God's grace shining down on us, we can then reach for the sky, and grow beyond our wildest dreams.

My goal for you is that moments after you finish this last page and close this book, you will take a small step toward giant success. My prayer for you is that you will look within, unleash the wellspring God has placed within you, and allow your Creator to flood your life with the joy of the Almighty's blessings. My hope for you is that you will become all that God has created you to be and that you will advance confidently in the direction of your dreams by practicing the power of positive decision making on a daily basis.

Make decisions without regrets, knowing that, yes indeed, now you've done it!

Acknowledgments

Before I do something as challenging as writing a book like this, I count on the contributions of so many others to enhance this collaborative endeavor. My decision was predicated on the incredible support, encouragement, research, and resources of so many talented individuals. Thank you to my staff and team members for freeing up numerous hours in my schedule, allowing me the time to reflect, recollect, write, and revise. I pray their decisions to commit to my ministry and my mission will never be ones they regret in any way.

No publishing partnership can function at maximum capacity without the dedication of key leaders and contributors. With this in mind, I find my gratitude for my family at Atria Books only continues to grow. Thank you to Judith Curr, Carolyn Reidy, Gary Urda, and Christine Saunders for catching my vision for this book and breathing it into life with a fervent passion for excellence. My appreciation for the efforts of Michael Selleck and Larry Norton on behalf of this book continues to grow. Sue Fleming's participation in the process of producing this project greatly enhanced its quality.

A special note of gratitude to Malaika Adero for her editorial expertise, flexibility, and grace under pressure. I'm also grateful to Dudley Delffs for his feedback and input on this book.

Jan Miller and Shannon Marven at Dupree Miller & Associates continue to amaze me with their passion for my work and their relentless commitment to the very best solutions. I cherish their wisdom, friendship, and shared vision for where my message can go. To Dr. Phil McGraw: thank you for your support, guidance, counsel, and camaraderie as I stretch and grow into new possibilities.

Finally, to my wife Serita, a wordless thank-you of eternal gratitude for your decision more than two decades ago to join me on this joyful adventure. Your love, patience, support, and encouragement enrich every area of my life and our life together. To our children, I offer a father's loving appreciation for the ways you continue to grow into maturity and responsibility that comes with making adult decisions.